P9-DDM-799

BIBLE 101

SIX SESSIONS FOR SMALL GROUPS

COVER TO COVER

Getting the Bible's big picture

ĢERRY MATHISEN

BILL DONAHUE, SERIES EDITOR

InterVarsity Press
Downers Grove, Illinois
Leicester, England

InterVarsity Press
P.O. Box 1400, Downers Grove, IL 60515
World Wide Web: www.ivpress.com
E-mail: mail@ivpress.com

Inter-Varsity Press, England
38 De Montfort Street, Leicester LE1 7GP, England

©2000 by the Willow Creek Association

All rights reserved. No part of this book may be reproduced, stored in a retrieval system or transmitted in
any form or by any means, electronic, mechanical, photocopying, recording or otherwise, without the prior
written permission of InterVarsity Press.

InterVarsity Press® U.S.A., is the book-publishing division of InterVarsity Christian Fellowship/USA®, a
student movement active on campus at hundreds of universities, colleges and schools of nursing in the
United States of America, and a member movement of the International Fellowship of Evangelical Students.
For information about local and regional activities, write Public Relations Dept., InterVarsity Christian
Fellowship/USA, 6400 Schroeder Rd., P.O. Box 7895, Madison, WI 53707-7895.

Inter-Varsity Press, England, is the book-publishing division of the Universities and Colleges Christian
Fellowship (formerly the Inter-Varsity Fellowship), a student movement linking Christian Unions in
universities and colleges throughout the United Kingdom and the Republic of Ireland, and a member
movement of the International Fellowship of Evangelical Students. For information about local and
national activities write to UCCF, 38 De Montfort Street, Leicester LE1 7GP.

All Scripture quotations, unless otherwise indicated, are taken from the Holy Bible, New International
Version®. NIV®. Copyright ©1973, 1978, 1984 by International Bible Society. Used by permission of
Zondervan Publishing House. All rights reserved. Distributed in the U.K. by permission of Hodder and
Stoughton Ltd. All rights reserved. "NIV" is a registered trademark of International Bible Society. UK
trademark number 1448790.

Cover design: Grey Matter Group

Photo image: Photodisc

Chapter icons: Roberta Polfus

USA ISBN 0-8308-2063-9

UK ISBN 0-85111-526-8

Printed in the United States of America ∞

15	14	13	12	11	10	9	8	7	6	5	4	3	2

10	09	08	07	06	05	04	03	02

Contents

Introduction

Some time ago, Russ Robinson (director of small group ministries at Willow Creek Community Church and concept editor on these guides) and I were talking about how to help groups get a firm grip on the Word of God. Both of us had studied and taught courses on the Bible, but what about small groups? What if we could put something together that could be studied as a group and yet have much of the information people would normally find in a class or course? Well, hats off to Russ, who came up with the idea for Bible 101 and cast the vision for what it could look like. Soon we were outlining the books, and the result is what you have before you. So welcome to the Bible 101 adventure, a place where truth meets life!

Traditionally the subject matter in this series has been reserved for classroom teaching or personal study. Both are places where this curriculum could be used. But this work is primarily targeted at small groups, places where men and women, old and young, rich and poor gather together in community to engage fully with the truth of God's Word. These little communities can be transforming in ways that classrooms and personal study cannot.

Few things in life are more fulfilling than drawing out the deep truths of Scripture and then seeing them at work to change a life into the image of Christ. Getting a firm grip on the Bible and its teachings is paramount to a mature and intelligent walk with God. We are to worship him with all our heart, soul, mind and strength. And the Word of God is central to accomplishing God's desire that we be fully devoted to him.

The team from Willow Creek—staff and volunteers alike—has labored diligently to provide you with a group-friendly process for understanding the Bible. Kathy Dice, Gerry Mathisen, Judson Poling, Michael Redding and I have worked to provide something that merges content and process, learning and application. Now it is up to you to work together to discover the riches that lie ahead for those willing to do some work and take a few risks. But we know you are more than ready for that challenge!

To make these studies more productive, here are a few suggestions and guidelines to help you along the way. Read carefully so that you get the most out of this series.

Purpose

This series is designed to ground a Christ-follower in the study and understanding of Scripture. It is not designed for someone who became a Christian last week, though sections of it would certainly be good. And it is not as rigorous as a Bible college class or seminary course might be. Bible 101 means *foundational,* but not easy or light. So be prepared for some challenge and some stretching. This may be the first time you are exposed to certain theological concepts or terms, or to some more in-depth methods of Bible study. Celebrate the challenge and strive to do your best. Peter tells us to "make every effort" to add knowledge to our faith. It will take some effort, but I can guarantee it will be well worth it!

Prayer

When approaching the Word of God you will need to keep a submissive and teachable attitude. The Holy Spirit is eager to teach you, but you must be willing to receive knowledge, encouragement, correction and challenge. One educator has taught that all learning is the result of failed expectations. We hope that in some ways you are ambushed by the truth and stumble upon new and unfamiliar territory that startles you into new ways of thinking about God and relating to him through Christ.

Practice

Each session has the same format, except (in some cases) the last session. For five meetings you will learn skills, discuss material and readings, work together as a team, and discover God's truths in fresh and meaningful ways. The sixth session will be an opportunity to put all you have learned into practice. Studies are designed as follows.

Establishing Base Camp (5-10 minutes). A question or icebreaker to focus the meeting.

 Mapping the Trail (5-10 minutes). An overview of where we are headed.

 Beginning the Ascent (30 minutes). The main portion of the discussion time.

Gaining a Foothold (3 minutes). Information to read that identifies core issues and ideas to keep you on track with the journey.

 Trailmarkers (10 minutes). Important Scriptures for memorization or reflection.

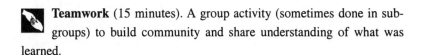 **Teamwork** (15 minutes). A group activity (sometimes done in subgroups) to build community and share understanding of what was learned.

 Reaching the Summit (5 minutes). A chance to summarize and look back at what has been learned or accomplished.

Close in Prayer (as long as you want!). An opportunity to pray for one another and ask God to deepen the truths of Scripture in you.

You can take some shortcuts or take longer as the group decides, but strive to stay on schedule for a 75- to 90-minute meeting, including prayer time. You will also want to save time to attend to personal needs. This will vary by group and can also be accomplished in personal relationships you develop between meetings.

Preparation

Preparation? There is none! Well, almost none. For some sessions reading ahead will be suggested to provide an overview. But the sessions are designed to be worked through together. We find this builds a sense of team and community, and is also more fun! And there is something about "discovery in the moment" rather than merely discussing what everyone has already discovered outside the meeting that provides a sense of adventure.

We wish you the best as you draw truth from the Word of God for personal transformation, group growth and kingdom impact!

Bill Donahue, Series Editor
Vice President, Small Group Ministries
Willow Creek Association

Session 1

The Law

Meeting God as he has revealed himself through the creation story and the law and covenants.

 ### Establishing Base Camp

Recently I was asked this question: If I had two or three days to use in whatever way I wanted, what would I do? My answer came quickly. I would get into my car and drive about six hours to our family cottage in northern Wisconsin. Even though our spot in the woods can be described as semi-primitive—no electricity and no indoor plumbing—our cottage on one of Wisconsin's many Bass Lakes has been our family retreat and vacation spot for the last twenty years. Whether I am sitting on the front porch, walking in the woods, relaxing in our paddleboat on the lake in the quietness of morning, or standing on the dock on a clear, starry evening, Bass Lake represents to me some of the best of God's creative work.

But as obvious as the beauty of Bass Lake is, something else is clear: the effects of humanity's intrusion into this wonderful place, and the subsequent limits that have been placed on the people who come here. Fishermen have to be licensed and their boats registered. Now cottages must be built farther from the lake and contain septic systems to replace outhouses like the one that still graces our property. People must be regulated in order to preserve and maintain God's creation.

✔ What evidence of God's creative work can you see around you?

✓ What evidence of our intrusion into creation do you observe?

Mapping the Trail

Consider the importance of laws by discussing these questions:

✓ Why are laws necessary in our society? (For example, what would driving a car be like if we did not have laws to govern our roads?)

Beginning the Ascent

The purpose of the first five books of the Old Testament, also known as the Pentateuch or the Law, is to provide the story of God's creation of the world and to describe how God chose to govern his creation through human leaders and through the laws and covenants he instituted. The historical period covered in the Pentateuch consists of three eras:

Creation. Adam is created by God, but he sins and destroys God's original plan for humankind (Genesis 1—11).

Patriarchs. Abraham is chosen by God to "father" a people to represent God in the world (Genesis 12—50). His son Isaac and grandson Jacob became the leaders through whom the nation of Israel would rise.

Exodus. Moses delivers the Hebrew people from Egyptian slavery and then delivers God's laws (Exodus—Deuteronomy).

Overview Chart of the Creation, Patriarchs & Exodus Eras

Era	Key Location	Biblical References	Key People	Key Events
Creation	Eden	Genesis 1:1-11 (3:14-16; 6:5-8)	Adam, Noah	Creation, the Fall, the flood, Tower of Babel. (confusion of languages)
Patriarchs	Canaan	Genesis 12—50 (12:1-3)	Abraham, Isaac, Jacob, Joseph	Covenant with Abraham; Jacob fathers 12 sons (fathers of the 12 tribes of Israel); Joseph in Egypt; enslavement in Egypt following Joseph's death
Exodus	Egypt	Exodus through Deuteronomy (Exodus 20:1-26; Deuteronomy 6:1-19)	Moses	Deliverance from slavery, giving of God's law (Ten Commandments), Kadesh Barnea rebellion, wilderness wandering (40 yrs.)

✓ As you read the summaries of the three eras and the overview chart, what picture of God emerges in your thinking?

✓ What words would you use to describe the God who reveals himself during these earliest periods of history?

In Genesis 12, 15 and 17 God makes a covenant promise to Abraham. In this covenant (laid out in chapter 12, ratified in 15 and explained fully in 17), God promises Abraham he will

- make him a great nation
- bless him
- make his name great
- make him a blessing to others
- give his descendants the land of Canaan
- bless those who bless him
- curse those that curse him
- make him the father of many nations
- bless all the nations of the earth through him.

This covenant required Abraham and his descendants to obey in order to receive the blessings of the covenant (17:9). The covenant was sealed by God as he passed between the slaughtered animals in Genesis 15:17. The sign of the covenant was the rite of circumcision, to be performed on each newborn male on the eighth day after his birth.

Covenants are built on love and commitment, on faithfulness and kindness. God reached out to us in love and asked us to respond in love (shown through obedience and trust) to him. Jesus also has reached out in love and instituted the new covenant with us through his shed blood on the cross.

✓ Why do we find it so difficult to respond faithfully to God, who desired to initiate such life-giving relationships with us?

The purpose of the laws given by God to humankind is not only to provide a means of governing men and women. These laws do not comprise a legal code that when obeyed to the letter enable individuals to find favor with God. They actually are designed to have the opposite effect. Because disobedience of God's commands was inevitable, God provided his law in order to lead individuals to realize their need for God's grace.

✓ Describe how most people normally interpret the meaning or significance of God's commandments. Do they understand those laws as a means of leading them to faith?

> "The Ten Commandments are the perfect tool to help us understand our spiritual condition. They show us what we cannot do ... so that we come to God for what he can do—forgive us through the power of Jesus Christ." *(The Journey Bible)*

The most familiar set of laws in the Bible is the Ten Commandments. They are recorded in Exodus 20:1-17.

The Ten Commandments
1. You shall have no other gods before me.
2. You shall not make or worship any other gods.
3. You shall not misuse God's name.
4. Remember the sabbath day by keeping it holy.
5. Honor your father and mother.
6. You shall not murder.
7. You shall not commit adultery.
8. You shall not steal.
9. You shall not give false testimony against your neighbor.
10. You shall not covet that which belongs to your neighbor.

✓ What do these commandments reveal to us about God?

✓ Why do you believe there is such a negative tone to many of the commandments?

✓ The Ten Commandments primarily refer to two basic relationships: one's relationship with God and one's relationship with his or her neighbor. Why in your estimation is this an emphasis of the commandments?

Gaining a Foothold

God's grace is rooted in his awareness that our failure, our disobedience of him, is inevitable. As you study the law of God, remember two important themes. First, our inability to keep God's law reveals our need of him. Second, the law reflects God's perfect character. Therefore, our failure to obey God perfectly does not have to be fatal. Rather, our trust in the God of the Bible leads us to life through faith in his Son.

Trailmarkers

Read Romans 1:18-20, Romans 4:1-5 and Galatians 3:23-25.

✓ What does Paul say about the significance of the events described in the Law?

✓ Of what spiritual significance are they to us today?

Memorize Galatians 3:24.

Teamwork

Pair off and discuss the following scenario.

Picture yourself having a conversation with a family member, neighbor, coworker or friend who does not profess to be a Christian. As the conversation gradually moves to spiritual matters, this person responds to your witness by saying, "I don't think I need to talk about this religious stuff. I think I'm a pretty good person. After all, I try to keep the Ten Commandments. Besides, I don't really believe God would send anyone to hell."

✓ Based on what we read of God in the Law and what Paul says in the passages in the "Trailmarkers" section, how would you lovingly respond to this person?

Reaching the Summit

Briefly review the three eras described in the Law. Then also briefly review the purpose God had in giving his Law to us and the importance of his covenant with Abraham. What role did the Law play in leading you to Christ?

Next Session

The section of the Bible studied in this session sets the tone for the sections to follow. We will explore why we have such a hard time trusting God and remaining faithful to him even though he is faithful. In preparation for next week, make a list of the most common reasons for your unwillingness to always be faithful to God.

Close in Prayer

This section of the Bible reminds us of the blessing of God's creation and our need to be faithful stewards of it. Thank God for what he has made and ask God to enable us to be wise in our use of what he has provided. Then pray that we would be able to be faithful to God in every area of our lives.

Session 2

History & Poetry

Telling the story in word and song.

Establishing Base Camp

Have you ever noticed how often conversations are built around personal stories? Young children learn early to understand ideas and feelings based on how they experience them and therefore learn to define them through anecdotes and stories. The practice of communicating ideas through stories is typically maintained into adulthood. As we get older we learn to communicate our thoughts in other ways. For example, while we may come to understand love experientially, how many of us have taken that same love and turned it into a song or poem written about a special person. While stories commonly communicate ideas and feelings, poetic expression has a special way of touching the heart.

✔ Think of a special experience you have had with someone you love. It might be a special event, a date, a meal, a trip you took together, a party. What is it about that experience that is particularly representative of the love you feel for them?

✔ If you were to write about the experience, how would you express your feelings? What kind of words would you use?

Mapping the Trail

✓ What inspires you more, a moving story of courage or the heart-rending words of a great poem? An inspiring biography or a rousing rendition of a patriotic song? Take a few minutes to cite specific examples that represent your preferences.

In a similar fashion, God chose to communicate with us in varying written forms because he realized that spiritual truths could be communicated in many ways.

Beginning the Ascent

Because God is the master communicator, it should not surprise us that he chose to employ a variety of literary styles when revealing himself to us in the Bible. In this session we will explore how God communicated in the Old Testament through two common, distinctive, yet often-interrelated methods—the use of story, and poetry. Specifically, we will survey the twelve historical books (following the Law) that pick up the story of Israel, and the five books of poetry, most of which probably were written during the period described in the historical books.

In the previous session, three of the eight eras encompassed within the Old Testament were outlined. These were the eras of creation, the patriarchs and the exodus. Four of the five remaining eras are described in the historical books. The five eras are

Conquest: Joshua leads the conquest of the Promised Land.

Judges: Judges were chosen to govern Israel for four hundred rebellious years.

Kingdom: David, likely the greatest king of Israel, is followed by a series of ungodly kings so that God eventually judges Israel by sending her into exile.

Exile: Daniel gives leadership among the exiles for seventy years. (This era is described in the prophetic books of Ezekiel and Daniel, which are parts of the next section of the Old Testament.)

Return: Ezra leads the people back from exile to rebuild Jerusalem and reestablish the religious life of the people.

The historical and poetic books can be summarized as follows:

Conquest: Joshua

Judges: Judges and Ruth (major judges were Deborah, Gideon, Samson and Samuel)

Kingdom: 1 & 2 Samuel, 1 & 2 Kings and 1 & 2 Chronicles (key leaders were Saul, David and Solomon)

Exile: Ezekiel and Daniel

Return: Ezra, Nehemiah and Esther

There are five poetic books: Job, Psalms, Proverbs, Ecclesiastes and Song of Songs. Job likely was written as far back as the time of Genesis. The other four were written during the kingdom era.

God uses both types of literature to teach his truths. In fact there are common themes such as the need for repentance and faith that weave their way through this entire section. Any study of the stories and poems should focus on the discovery of those themes.

While the historical books primarily are composed of stories, and the poetic literature consists of songs, don't be surprised to discover a mixing of these types of literature throughout this section of the Bible. For example, there are some beautiful songs in the historical books, such as Hannah's song of thanksgiving for the life of Samuel in 1 Samuel 2. On the other hand, the book of Job combines the account of Job's testing with the poetic dialogue between Job and his friends.

Let's take a look at how these two kinds of literature can be used together to communicate truth about God and his work in the world. *Read 1 Samuel 1:1—2:11.*

✔ What is the historical context of Hannah's poetic prayer?

✔ What do we learn about God in 1:5-6, 19?

✓ Describe the feelings she expresses in the prayer.

✓ Why does she feel that way?

✓ What does Hannah affirm and believe about God?

The writers of the poetic literature also connected their themes to the stories of the historical books. David's prayer for forgiveness in Psalm 51 is in response to his sins of adultery and murder described in 2 Samuel 11— 12. Solomon, who was gifted with great wisdom in 1 Kings 4, wrote about that wisdom in the first five chapters of the book of Proverbs.

Gaining a Foothold

There are many reasons people might give to explain why they do not read or study the Bible more than they do. We often hear statements like "The language is archaic." It contains contradictions. "I don't know where to start." But the most common excuse given might be that the Bible, written thousands of years ago in cultures that seem to be light years away, is simply irrelevant to the modern person. But can a person who reads the Bible carefully say that honestly? The messages communicated in the stories and poems of the Old Testament exemplify that old axiom "the more things change, the more they stay the same." God's faithfulness, humanity's sin, the seeming futility of life, the need for wisdom— the core issues of life are no different today than they ever were. The message God communicates to us in his Word are timeless!

 ## Trailmarkers

Read Psalm 23.
✓ How would the experience of being a shepherd have influenced David in writing what is probably

the best-known and most-beloved psalm?

Many have memorized this psalm. It is easier than most passages because we have heard it recited often. Beginning now and continuing this week, see if you can commit these beautiful words to memory. To begin, try to memorize Psalm 23:1-3.

Teamwork

A respected seminary professor once said that what we think about when we wake up in the middle of the night is the issue that most concerns us at the time. I do not know to what extent that is true, but I have noticed how often I find myself awake thinking about a negative experience the day before. Sometimes my mind focuses on a difficult task I have to face the next day, or on concerns about finances or health or fears related to someone I love. I also realize through these situations how easily a person can become overwhelmed with the negatives of life.

In the book of Ecclesiastes, Solomon addresses the futility of life. *Read Ecclesiastes 2:17-26.*

✔ Discuss with someone in the group, or as a group, the contemporary relevance of these verses. In what ways might Solomon be writing about today?

✔ Do you sometimes view life as being futile? If so, how do you deal with these feelings?

> "This refreshing picture of a caring shepherd in Psalm 23 is an unforgettable image of God. Compared to the angry, unforgiving figure many of us have imagined him to be, wouldn't you rather live in this God's house forever?" *(The Journey Bible)*

Reaching the Summit

Briefly review the structure of the historical books, relating them to the eras in Israel's history. Discuss the relationship of the poetic books to the historical books.

✓ Why, in your estimation, did God choose to reveal himself through story and song?

Next Session

Thus far in our study we have seen God reveal himself to us through creation, laws and covenants, stories and songs. But nothing about God's ways of communication with us appears to fascinate us more than his use of prophetic messages. This should not surprise us. Human beings seem to be almost obsessed with a desire to discern the future. For next time, make a list of ways in which this fascination with the prophetic manifests itself in our culture.

Close in Prayer

Thank God for the relevant way he communicates with us by providing literature that deals with the common problems and frustrations of life we can relate to and understand.

Session 3

The Prophets & Revelation

Understanding biblical messages from God.

Establishing Base Camp

Once a friend and I shared a meal at our favorite Chinese restaurant. The good food and quiet, intimate environment combined to provide a pleasant evening of dining and conversation. Our time at the restaurant concluded in the usual manner: paying the bill, having the leftover food boxed up to take home and, of course, cracking open the traditional fortune cookies. I noticed again how eagerly we opened them, read the messages inside and laughed about the prospect of having these optimistic fortunes fulfilled. What is it about fortune cookies that makes us so eager to discover a message which always is so positive and yet so unlikely to be realized? Maybe that is just it: we have a curiosity about the future and live in the hope it will be good. From psychic phone counselors to horoscopes to tarot card readers, people seek insights that will give them a peak at the future.

✔ Have you ever been in a situation where you desperately wanted to know the future? What steps did you take, or were you tempted to take, in order to discover what that future might hold for you?

Mapping the Trail

The subject of Bible-orientated prophecy is a media favorite. *Newsweek* magazine recently did a cover story on the subject. The bestselling Left Behind series of prophetic fiction is setting all kinds of Christian publishing records.

The last book will be given an unprecedented two-million-copy printing to launch it! *The Omega Code*, a millennial film produced by Christians, is being shown to relatively large audiences in local movie theaters.

✓ Why is the subject of prophecy so fascinating, to the extent that it crosses religious boundaries?

✓ What does this interest in prophecy tell us about our culture?

✓ Why is it of particular interest to Christians?

Beginning the Ascent

Discuss the following observations regarding biblical prophecy.

1. The nature of prophecy. Contrary to popular assumptions, biblical prophecy is not devoted exclusively to predictions about events yet to come. Even the New Testament book of Revelation has a scope wider than "end times" prophecy.

Biblical prophets from Jeremiah to the apostle John typically served a dual function. These two purposes commonly are referred to as "forthtelling" and "foretelling." That is, biblical prophets not only foretold coming events, they also devoted much of their prophetic writings to divinely-inspired commentary on current events. They condemned existing sin and corruption and warned of impending judgment.

✓ Why do you think both of these prophetic functions were

important to God?

2. Prophecy in biblical context. All but one of the eighteen prophetic books are contained in the Old Testament. Most of the Old Testament books, like most of the poetic books, were written during the eras described in the historical literature. The Old Testament prophets are divided into two groups. The first four, Isaiah, Jeremiah, Ezekiel and Daniel, are considered the major prophets because of the length and scope of their messages. Lamentations likely was written by Jeremiah. The final twelve writers are considered the minor prophets.

✓ Are any of the prophets' names recognizable to you? What do you associate with them?

3. Categories of biblical prophecy. The writings of the biblical prophets can be placed into three main categories of prophecy.

General: All of the prophets addressed situations that were current at the time they wrote. Familiar examples of general prophecy include the story of Jonah, some of the events in Daniel (the handwriting on the wall, the fiery furnace and the lion's den) and the letters to seven churches in Revelation 2—3.

Messianic: Messianic prophecies foretold the coming of Christ as the Messiah. Old Testament prophets such as Isaiah and Micah wrote of the coming Messiah in prophecies obviously fulfilled by Christ.

End times: End times prophecies also were common among the biblical prophets. The writings of the prophet Daniel and apostle John in Revelation are the most familiar examples of this category.

Prophetic writings often fit into more than one of these categories. Popular interest in prophecy appears to be weighted in favor of the "end times" foretelling function.

✔ Read Malachi 1 and note the character of this prophecy. It is not a predictive, future-oriented prophecy. What is the focus? How is this prophet being used in the life of God's people?

Gaining a Foothold

The interest in biblical prophecy may reflect how easy it is for people to become fascinated with the mysterious, the futuristic or the supernatural. Sadly, this curiosity about the future may not have any positive effect on people's lives. But if we look at biblical prophecy from a proper perspective and observe how consistently God has fulfilled what was predicted, then our familiarity with biblical prophecy can have a significant positive impact on our lives. The God who keeps his promises is a God we can trust and who is worthy of our service.

Trailmarkers

Read Isaiah 9:1-7.

✔ What evidence do you see in these verses that this passage is a prophecy regarding the life of Jesus? Make a list of each of the specific references to Christ that you can find in this text.

✔ Why did God feel it was important to prophesy regarding the coming of Christ as the Messiah?

"Now, it takes no more than a mustard seed-sized grain of faith to be sure of unfulfilled things in the future. It takes no great faith to be aware of unseen divine realities all around us. If you are aware of realities you can't see, and if you're certain there are many more realities yet to be fulfilled, you are halfway to solving the mystery!" (Joni Eareckson Tada, *Heaven: Your Real Home*)

Memorize Isaiah 9:6.

Teamwork

Consider this hypothetical situation: Suppose your group has been meeting apart from any existing church for several months and you decide to explore the idea of starting your own little congregation. Let's call it "Our Small Group Community Church." You are concerned that your new church gets off on the right foot with an appropriate mission and set of values. Revelation 2—3 contains messages sent through John to seven churches. Assign one of these churches to each member of the group and have each person spend a brief time drawing up a list of dos and don'ts based on his or her assigned church. Then, as a group, develop a list of priorities for your new congregation.

Reaching the Summit

Briefly review this lesson on biblical prophecy by answering the following questions.

✓ What were the primary roles of a biblical prophet?

✓ Where do the biblical prophets fit into Old Testament history?

✓ What are the three main categories of biblical prophecy?

Next Session

Biblical prophets looked ahead to the coming of the Messiah. But would the Jewish people recognize him when he came? Begin to consider why you think people then and now reject him.

Close in Prayer

Remember to thank God that he is faithful to his Word and that he can be trusted completely. Pray that we will be faithful to him in return, especially in sharing with others our belief in Christ.

Session 4

The Gospels

Discovering the picture of Christ's life portrayed in the four Gospels.

Establishing Base Camp

I spend much of my time in college classrooms instructing students about the art of public speaking. In the course of my work I listen to students give presentations on a variety of subjects. One of my students delivered a speech in which he attempted to persuade us that alien beings might exist. I became particularly interested in what he was saying when he suggested that the Bible contained evidence that such beings may exist. For example, he contended that the bright star that appeared in the sky when Jesus was born may have been the result of alien activity. It was easy for me to discount what he was saying. Then I realized that that simple contention by the student represented a larger phenomenon: the biblical account of Christ's birth and the unusual events that accompanied it are dismissed easily by people not willing or able to accept the truth about the coming of God's Son.

✓ Think of an event that you heard, read about or even observed yourself that was or might have been described as a miracle. How do you account for such an event?

Mapping the Trail

Jesus is the most unique person in history. His birth, teaching, claims, lifestyle, death and resurrection all represent profound departures from normal life. Even people like Alexander the Great, Caesar, Pharaoh and Nebuchadnezzar pale in significance when you consider all that Jesus did and said. Compared to world leaders of the last millennium he still has an impact far exceeding theirs.

✓ If you were to ask people what they think about Jesus Christ, what responses would you expect to receive? (For example, would there be an emphasis on his humanness? Would you expect people to be able to explain what it means that he was and is the Son of God?)

✓ Why do you think people would answer in the ways they do?

Beginning the Ascent

The story of Jesus is recorded in the four Gospel accounts known as Matthew, Mark, Luke and John. In this section we will consider the significance of the complete life of Christ as it is described in these books and then consider the value of having four separate accounts of Christ's story.

1. Christ's purpose. If the primary purpose of Christ's coming was to give his life for us, then we might ask why God decided to record Christ's entire life story. Why not simply record his death? There are several reasons.

A. As discussed in the previous lesson, the detailed record of Christ's life helps establish his authenticity as Israel's Messiah.

B. Christ's life provides an example for us to follow (see Philippians 2:1-11).

C. From beginning to end, Christ's life demonstrated for us that he could be and was the perfect sacrifice for our sin. Hebrews 10:1-10 explains this aspect of Christ's life.

D. Finally, Christ's death and resurrection became the means by which our sins are paid for and our eternal life is made possible.

✓ Which of these reasons for the Gospel accounts do you find to be particularly significant?

2. *The four writers.* The human authors God employed to record his Word wrote, through the process of divine inspiration, in their individual styles. Thus just as no two histories of your family would be identical, we should not be surprised to learn that those who wrote the four accounts of Christ's life provided perspectives that are marked by both similarities and differences. The chart below provides an overview of some of the features of each Gospel.

	Matthew	**Mark**	**Luke**	**John**
Role of author	Apostle	Disciple of Peter	Traveled with Paul	Apostle
Occupation	Tax collector	Missionary	Physician	Fisherman
Date of writing	Before A.D. 70	Before A.D. 64	Before A.D. 64 but after Mark	Late first century
Representative text	21:5	10:45	19:10	20:31
Prominent role of Christ	Preacher	Miracle worker	Teller of parables	Teacher
Audience	Jews	Romans	Greeks	Everyone
Prominent nature of book	Fulfillment of prophecy	Fast-paced action	Detailed history	Theological themes (7 "I ams")

Read the four passages listed in the chart above as representative texts: Matthew 21:9; Mark 10:45; Luke 19:10; and John 20:31.

✓ What is the composite picture of Christ as portrayed in these passages?

✓ What is the significance of each author's perspective of Christ in these representative texts?

✓ After considering the various features of these four accounts of Christ's life, why do you think God chose to tell Christ's story in this unique manner?

✓ In what ways does this method contribute to your understanding and appreciation of who Jesus is?

3. The life of Christ. Christ's life was described in the Bible with emphasis upon three major periods—birth, public ministry, and death and resurrection.

✓ What is significant about the birth of Jesus?

✓ How does this affect our faith?

✓ In his public ministry, how would you define Jesus' teaching and miracles?

✓ By his death and resurrection, Jesus accomplished something no other person in history will ever do. What is the significance of this?

Gaining a Foothold

A common criticism of the Bible is that it contains internal contradictions that result in an unreliable text. It is important to realize that there are no specific places in the Bible where the writings of the various authors contradict each other in ways that detract from the significance of what God inspired to be written. The four accounts of Christ's life provide vivid representation of this fact. God inspired four men to tell the story of Christ in accounts that are in complete harmony with each other. Therefore, when these four books are studied side-by-side in a thorough, honest manner, the result should be a greater understanding and appreciation of the person of Christ and the manner in which God communicated his Word.

Trailmarkers

Read John 3:16.

✓ John 3:16 is a cardinal statement of Christ's mission. In light of our study to this point, pair off and explain this passage to each other in your own words. Discuss the significance and meaning of this key verse. What do you think Jesus might have meant by the phrase "gave his one and only Son"?

Memorize John 3:16 if you have not yet done so.

Teamwork

✓ Go back to the beginning of this session to the account of the student who speculated that the star that guided

"Inevitably though, a search for Jesus turns out to be one's own search. No one who meets Jesus ever stays the same. I have found that the doubts that afflict me from many sources—from science, from comparative religion, from an innate defect of skepticism, from aversion to the church—take on a new light when I bring those doubts to the man named Jesus." (Philip Yancey, *The Jesus I Never Knew*)

the wisemen might indicate alien influence. If you were this student's instructor and could respond to him with total freedom, what would you write on your evaluation of his speech? Write out your response below, and then verbally share your response with another member of your group as though that person was the student in question.

Reaching the Summit

Briefly review the Gospels' picture of Christ. Review the unique features of Christ's story as revealed in the three main periods of his life: birth, public ministry, and death and resurrection.

✓ Why is it important for us to have a narrative of Christ's life?

Next Session

It is one thing to look back at Christ's life almost two thousand years later and contemplate its significance. But being a follower of Christ in the last half of the first century provided challenges unique to that time. What do you think it would have been like to be a first-century believer?

Close in Prayer

As you pray, focus on thanking God for the wonderful gift of his Son, and ask God for opportunities to speak with unbelievers about that same gift.

Session 5

Acts & Epistles

Exploring the early life and teaching of the church.

Establishing Base Camp

My mother died at eighty-five in the summer of 1998 after a lengthy struggle with leukemia. My family and I carried out our responsibility of disposing of my mother's remaining possessions. She was a saver. Though she maintained a small apartment until she passed away, she had saved a lot of family memorabilia. For example, I found and kept a stack of cards that my parents had received when I was born almost fifty years earlier.

Recently, I went through those cards again and took particular note of a letter my aunt had enclosed with a card she sent. She congratulated my parents on my birth, and while acknowledging that my mom might have wanted a daughter after already having two sons, she admitted that another male was always a welcome addition to a farm family. With that note of congratulations for my birth still in mind, I soon found myself going through another group of cards—the sympathy mail I had received when my mom died. An emotional note from a cousin in California helped me to see how a simple letter can be a powerful tool used to convey messages from the joy of new birth to the sorrow of death.

✓ Can you think of an occasion when you had to write a difficult letter to someone? a situation when you wrote a letter that conveyed good news? occasions when you were on the receiving end of such letters? Compare and contrast your feelings in sending or receiving positive and negative messages.

Mapping the Trail

Using your own experience in the church as a starting point, consider the following questions:

✓ Has your experience in the church been generally positive or negative? What factors have contributed to those feelings?

✓ In general, what do churches have to do or become in order to be more effective in reading today's culture?

Beginning the Ascent

The book of Acts begins after Jesus has been resurrected. He is preparing his disciples and other followers for life in the kingdom when he ascends to heaven. Specifically, he has announced to them the coming of the Holy Spirit that will coincide with the birth of the church. The book of Acts and the letters that follow contain transforming and corrective teaching to the early church. This new community needed all the help it could get!

Acts reveals how believers empowered by the Holy Spirit began to carry the message of Christ to the world. (Acts 1:8 provides an outline of this activity.)

Key Facts About Acts

The church began in Jerusalem on the day of Pentecost; Acts 1—7 describe the early days of the church in Jerusalem. Key events to note are the coming of the Spirit, Peter's powerful sermon, the baptism of thousands, the emergence of the new community and initial persecution leading to the martyrdom of Stephen.

Read Acts 2:42-47 and 4:32-35.

✓ Describe the early life of this new community.

✓ What clues does this passage provide to account for the early, rapid growth of the church?

✓ In your view, how did the events leading up to this time inspire the rapid growth of the church?

✓ How does this compare to churches today?

The persecution in Jerusalem scattered believers, and they took their message next to Judea and Samaria (see Acts 8—12). Key events in this section include the witness of Philip, the conversion of Saul of Tarsus (Paul) and the vision that appeared to Peter exhorting him to take the gospel to the Gentiles.

✓ Read Acts 10:34-48. Briefly list the factors that now make it clear that the gospel is moving from primarily a Jewish audience (Jerusalem) to the world beyond.

Paul led the effort to take the message of Christ to the remainder of the known world and to plant churches in cities where he had preached. Chapters 13-28 contain the narrative of this activity that focuses primarily on Paul's three missionary journeys. Key events are the council at Jerusalem (chapter 15), Paul's imprisonment in Philippi (16), his sermon in Athens (17), his visit to Ephesus (19) and Paul's imprisonment and trials in Jerusalem and Caesarea (22-26).

> "Believers in the first-century church, when challenged or told to cease proclaiming the Good News by the authorities of the day, burst out, 'We cannot stop telling about what we have seen and heard.' In the same way, modern-day evangelizing must exuberantly flow from our character as a worshiping, godly community." (Charles Colson, *The Body*)

The New Testament Letters

God inspired some of the early church leaders to write letters of encouragement and instruction to various individuals, churches and other groups of believers. Twenty-one such letters are in the New Testament. The letters are divided into three sections.

1. Paul's letters to churches (Romans through Thessalonians).

2. Paul's letters to other leaders (Timothy, Titus and Philemon).

3. General epistles written by several authors to other groups (Hebrews through Jude).

Almost all of these letters were written during the time spanned by the events in the book of Acts. James was written first. Paul wrote during and after his missionary journeys. The general epistles were authored in late A.D. 60 around the end of the book of Acts.

The instruction contained in these letters covers a variety of issues. But much of the teaching focuses on providing greater clarity about the person of Christ and his relationship to believers and the church. Specific emphases include

1. *The person of Christ* (Colossians 1:13-29 and Hebrews 1—3)

2. *Living like Christ* (Philippians 3:7-16 and 1 Peter 3:8-22)

3. *Being the body of Christ* (Ephesians 4:7-16 and 1 Corinthians 3)

✔ In your opinion, why did the writers of these letters emphasize the centrality of Christ to their readers?

Paul wrote that Scripture was profitable for three purposes (2 Timothy 3:16-17). These purposes, with representative texts from Paul's letters, are

1. The teaching of doctrine: Romans 3
2. Rebuking and correcting error: Galatians 1
3. Instructing in godly living: Ephesians 5

✓ Why were these purposes important for first-century Christians?

✓ Why are they important for us today?

Gaining a Foothold

God's desire is for the church to reflect the character of Christ and to be committed to being a witness for Christ. However, the same issues that were present in the first century often hinder the church today. We are embattled with internal conflict, adherence to unnecessary or harmful traditions, persecution and a lack of mission or vision. It is easy for us to become self-absorbed and fail to notice the needs around us. Additionally, sometimes Christians rely on other organizations or even the government to achieve our goals. It is important for us to realize that God still desires that the church take the lead in accomplishing his program.

Trailmarkers

Read Philippians 2:1-7.

✓ Discuss these verses in light of the primary emphases of the New Testament letters. How should the church model the attitude of Christ?

Memorize Philippians 2:4-5.

Teamwork

Option 1: Divide into groups of three or four. You have just been commissioned by your church to design the strategy for reaching a segment of the community around you with the gospel. Your goal is to reach each person with a clear presentation of the message. What are some ways you might do this? What will be the focus of your message?

Option 2: Write a letter to a present-day church using the format found in Revelation 2—3 for the churches there. This would include a greeting, affirmation, description of who Jesus is, acknowledgment of what they are doing well and exhortation of what needs correction or attention. Close the letter with a promise that brings the church hope.

Reaching the Summit

Pair off with another individual in the group and try to answer the following questions.

✔ What are the three primary stages of church growth described in the book of Acts?

✔ What are the three main divisions of New Testament letters? Give an example or two of each.

✔ With regard to Christ, what are three primary emphases of the letters?

Next Session

Review your notes from this session and the previous four in preparation
for our final session. What are the primary features of the five main sections
of the Bible studied in this series?

Close in Prayer

Take time to thank God for the church and for Christ who is at its center.
Pray for your church, and ask God to make it and the individuals who
attend it more like Christ.

Session 6

Putting It All Together

Finding strength and guidance in God's Word for the journey that is your life.

Establishing Base Camp

Years ago in a seminary theology class, the course instructor asked, "Which one of the attributes or basic characteristics of God do you think is the most important? Is it his holiness or his love? His wisdom or the fact that he is all-knowing or all-powerful?" One of the students gave an intriguing answer. He said he believed that the most significant characteristic of God is that God is immutable, a theological term that means God never changes. The student explained his response by saying that because God does not change, all of the ways in which God is described in the Bible are just as true of him today as they were when the Bible was written.

What a wonderful thought! God never changes. His Word never changes. We can rely completely on him and on what he has said. Our study of the Bible and of its truths is valuable only as far as we can trust in an unchanging God, in a world of seemingly endless change.

✓ What recent changes in your world have been positive?

✓ Have you seen any changes lately that you wish had not occurred?

✓ Do you ever wish for more stability in your world? Explain.

Mapping the Trail

✓ As you have participated with the group in the study of the structure of the Bible, what common themes have you observed threading their way through the various sections?

✓ What truths seem to be most obvious because of their frequent appearance in God's revelation of himself?

Beginning the Ascent

This is your chance to lead the discussion. Each person should read at least one of the following passages to the group: Genesis 49:24; 1 Kings 22:17; Psalm 80:1-3; Isaiah 40:10-11; Ezekiel 34:20-24; John 10:14-17; 1 Peter 2:21-25; Revelation 7:14-17. Then discuss the following questions.

✓ What imagery of God and his Son are common in these texts drawn from every part of the Bible?

✓ What do you believe is the significance of this consistent portrait of God as our shepherd?

✓ What personal meaning does this imagery of an unchanging shepherd have for you?

Gaining a Foothold

The church is pictured as Christ's body, a place where each individual plays a role in the body's growth. God wants each of us to contribute in an appropriate, Christ-like manner to a group such as this. We all have positive contributions we can make to each other's growth, and we all can learn from each other. You have been gifted by God to contribute to the growth of the body, and we are anxious to hear what God has been teaching you.

Trailmarkers

Read Hebrews 13:8. What an appropriate verse to use as our final trailmarker! This passage reminds us that Jesus never changes in his character and nature. Throughout the Bible everything is eventually summed up in Christ. He fulfills God's design and is the exact representation of the Father. All Scripture indeed points to him.

Memorize Hebrews 13:8.

Teamwork

As you share your faith in Christ with other people who may not have trusted in him, you probably will confront a lot of confusion and wrong ideas about the means by which a person becomes a Christian, pleases God, goes to heaven—or any other words one might use to refer to the process of faith. There may be particular questions regarding the Old Testament where the law is portrayed as God's standard of behavior for humankind.

Below is another list of verses drawn from every section of the Bible, including the Law, history, poetry, prophecy, the Gospels, Acts and the Epistles: Genesis 15:6; 2 Chronicles 20:20; Psalm 26:1; Isaiah 26:3; Habakkuk 2:4; John 3:16; Acts 15:8-9; Ephesians 2:8-9; Hebrews 11:1. *Read these verses with your group or in pairs.*

✓ What do you conclude from reading these verses?

✓ How might you use the conclusions drawn from these texts in communicating your faith to a nonbeliever?

✓ List all the components of faith and belief that you see. Then use them to create a definition of faith that you can present to the others in the group. Consider these questions in the definition: What is the basis of faith? How does it work? What is the result of placing faith in God? How consistent is the Bible in describing this faith?

Reaching the Summit

Use the remaining few minutes to share with your group the blessings you have gained from these sessions. What have you learned about God? the Bible? yourself? life? How do you hope to use the insights you have gained from this study?

Close in Prayer

You may have many things to thank God for as you complete this particular study. Thank God for the positive impact these sessions have had on your group, for your increased potential in Bible study and for using this study to grow closer to other members of the group. Pray that God will use the things you have learned from this study to help you grow as a Christian.

Leader's Notes

Few ventures are more defining than leading a group that produces changed lives and sharper minds for the cause of Christ. At Willow Creek we have seen small groups transform our church, offer deeper levels of biblical community and provide an environment where truth can be understood and discussed with enthusiasm. So we have focused on a group-based study rather than a classroom-lecture format or individual study (though these studies can profitably be used in both settings with minor adaptations).

Each method of learning has its strengths; each has its weaknesses. In personal study one can spend as little or as much time as desired on an issue and can focus specifically on personal needs and goals. The downside: there is no accountability to others, no one to challenge thoughts or assumptions, no one to provide support when life comes tumbling down around you. The classroom is ideal for proclaiming truth to many at one time and for having questions answered by those with expertise or knowledge in a subject area. But the pace of the class depends largely on the teacher, and there is limited time to engage in the discussion of personal issues. The small group is optimal for life-on-life encouragement, prayer and challenge. And it provides a place where learning is enhanced through the disciplines of biblical community. But small groups are usually not taught by content experts and cannot focus solely on one person's needs.

Our hope is that you will be able to use this curriculum in a way that draws from the best of all three methods. Using the small group as a central gathering place, personal preparation and study will allow you to focus on your own learning and growth goals. The small group activity will provide you with an engaging environment for refining your understanding and gaining perspective into the lives and needs of others. And perhaps by inviting a knowledgeable outsider to the group (or a cluster of small groups at a Saturday seminar, for example) you could gain the benefits of solid teaching in a given subject area. In any case your devotion to

Christ, your commitment to your local church and your obedience to the Word of God are of utmost importance to us. Our desire is to see you "grow in the grace and knowledge of the Lord Jesus Christ."

Leadership Tips

Here are some basic guidelines for leaders. For more extensive leadership support and training we recommend that you consult *The Willow Creek Guide to Leading Lifechanging Small Groups,* where you will find many suggestions for leading creative groups.

Using the leader's notes. The questions in the study will not be repeated in the leader's notes. Instead, we have provided comments, clarifications, additional information, leadership tips or group exercises. These will help you guide the discussion and keep the meeting on track.

Shared leadership. When leading a small group remember that your role is to guide the discussion and help draw people into the group process. Don't try to be the expert for everything. Seek to involve others in the leadership process and activities of group life (hosting meetings, leading prayer, serving one another, leading parts of the discussion and so forth).

Preparation. Your work between meetings will determine group effectiveness during meetings. Faithful preparation does not mean that you will control the meeting or that it will move exactly as you planned. Rather, it provides you with a guiding sense of the desired outcomes of the time together so that you can gauge the pace of the meeting and make adjustments along the way. Above all, make sure you are clear about the overall goal of the meeting. Then, even if you get appropriately sidetracked dealing with a personal concern or a discussion of related issues, you can graciously help the group refocus on the goal of the meeting. Also, preparation will allow you to observe how others are engaging with the material. *You should complete the study* before coming to the meeting. You can participate in the group activities at the meeting, but take time to become personally acquainted with the material in case you need to alter the schedule or amount of time on each section.

Purpose. The series is designed to help people understand the Word and be confident in their ability to read, study and live its lifechanging truths. Bible 101 is not designed for a group whose primary goal is caregiving or support. That does not mean you will avoid caring for each other, praying for needs or supporting one another through personal crises. It simply means that the *entire* focus of the group is not for these purposes. At the same time, the content should never take precedence over the process of transformation. There will be appropriate times to set the curriculum aside and pray. Or you may want to spend an evening having fun together. Remember, Jesus did not say, "Go therefore into all the world and complete the curriculum." Our focus is to make disciples. The curriculum is a tool, not a master. Use it consistently and with discernment, and your group will be well-served. But be clear about the primary focus of the group as you gather, and remind people every few weeks about the core purpose so that the group does not drift. So even though this is designed for six meetings per study guide, you might take longer if you have a meeting that focuses entirely on prayer or service.

Length of Meeting. We assume that you have about seventy to ninety minutes for this meeting, including prayer and some social time. If you have more or less time, adjust accordingly, especially if you have a task-based group. In that case, since you must complete the task (working on a ministry team or serving your church in some way), you will have to be selective in what you cover unless you can devote at least one hour to the meeting. In the format described below, feel free to play with the time allowed for "Beginning the Ascent," "Trailmarkers" and "Teamwork." We have given general guidelines for time to spend on each section. But depending on the size of group (we recommend about eight members), familiarity with the Bible and other group dynamics, you will have to make adjustments. After a few meetings you should have a good idea of what it will take to accomplish your goals.

Format. We have provided you with a general format. But feel free to provide some creativity or a fresh approach. You can begin with prayer, for example, or skip the "Establishing Base Camp" group opener and dive right into the study. We recommend that you follow the format closely early in the group process. As your group and your leadership skills mature and progress, you should feel increasing freedom to bring your creativity and experience to the meeting format. Here is the framework for the format in each of the guides in this series.

 Establishing Base Camp

This orients people to the theme of the meeting and usually involves a group opener or icebreaker. Though not always directly related to the content, it will move people toward the direction for the session. A base camp is the starting point for any mountain journey.

 Mapping the Trail

In this component we get clear about where we will go during the meeting. It provides an overview without giving away too much and removing curiosity.

 Beginning the Ascent

This is the main portion of the meeting: the climb toward the goal. It is the teaching and discussion portion of the meeting. Here you will find questions and explanatory notes. You will usually find the following two components included.

Pullouts. These provide additional detail, clarification or insight into content or questions that may arise in the participants' minds during the session.

Charts/Maps. Visual learners need more than words on a page. Charts, maps and other visuals combined with the content provide a brief, concise summary of the information and how it relates.

Gaining a Foothold

Along the trail people can drift off course or slip up in their understanding. These footholds are provided for bringing them into focus on core issues and content.

 Trailmarkers

These are key biblical passages or concepts that guide our journey. Participants will be encouraged to memorize or reflect on them for personal growth and for the central biblical basis behind the teaching.

 Teamwork

This is a group project, task or activity that builds a sense of community and shared understanding. It will be different for each study guide and for each lesson, depending on the author's design and the purpose of the content covered.

 Reaching the Summit

This is the end of the content discussion, allowing members to look back on what they have learned and capture it in a brief statement or idea. This "view from the top" will help them once again focus on the big picture after spending some time on the details.

Balancing caregiving and study/discussion. One of the most difficult things to do in a group, as I alluded to above, is balancing the tension between providing pastoral and mutual care to members and getting through the material. I have been in small groups where needs were ignored to get the work done, and I have been in groups where personal needs were the driving force of the group to the degree that the truth of the Word was rarely discussed. These guides are unique because they are designed to train and teach processes that must take place in order to achieve its purpose. But the group would fail miserably if someone came to a meeting and said, "I was laid off today from my job," and the group said a two-minute prayer and then opened their curriculum. So what do you do? Here are some guidelines.

1. People are the most important component of the group. They have real needs. Communicate your love and concern for people, even if they don't always get all the work done or get sidetracked.

2. When people disclose hurts or problems, address each disclosure with empathy and prayer. If you think more time should be devoted to someone, set aside time at the end of the meeting, inviting members to stay for additional prayer or to console the person. Cut the meeting short by ten minutes to accomplish this. Or deal with it right away for ten to fifteen minutes, take a short break, then head into the study.

3. Follow up with people. Even if you can't devote large portions of the meeting time to caregiving, you and others from the group can provide this between meetings over the phone or in other settings. Also learn to leverage your time. For example, if your meeting begins at 7:00 p.m., ask the member in need and perhaps one or two others from the group to come at 6:30 p.m. for sharing and prayer. A person will feel loved, your group will share in the caregiving, and it is not another evening out for people.

4. Assign prayer partners or groups of three to be little communities within the group. Over the phone or on occasional meetings outside the group (before church and so on) they could connect and check in on how life is going.

5. For serious situations solicit help from others, including pastors or other staff at church. Do not go it alone. Set boundaries for people with serious care needs, letting them know that the group can devote some but not substantial meeting time to support them. "We all know that Dave is burdened by his son's recent illness, so I'd like to spend the first ten minutes tonight to lift him up in prayer and commit to support Dave through this season. Then, after our meeting I'd like us to discuss any specific needs you (Dave) might have over the next two to three weeks (such as meals, help with house chores, etc.) and do what we can to help you meet those needs." Something to that effect can keep the group on track but still provide a place to express compassion.

Take time to look at the entire series if you have chosen only one of the guides. Though each can be used as a stand-alone study, there is much to benefit from in the other guides because each covers material essential for a complete overview of how to study and understand the Bible. We designed the guides in series form so that you can complete them in about a year if you meet weekly, even if you take a week off after finishing each guide.

A Word About Leadership

One of your key functions as a small group leader is to be a cheerleader—someone who seeks out signs of spiritual progress in others and makes some noise about it. What have you seen God doing in your group members' lives as a result of this study? Don't assume they've seen that progress—and definitely don't assume they are beyond needing simple words of encouragement. Find ways to point out to people the growth you've seen. Let them know it's happening, and that it's noticeable to you and others.

There aren't a whole lot of places in this world where people's spiritual progress is going to be recognized and celebrated. After all, wouldn't you like to hear someone say somthing like that to you? Your group members feel the same way. You have the power to make a profound impact through a sincere, insightful remark.

Be aware also that some groups get sidetracked by a difficult member or situation that hasn't been confronted. And some individuals could be making significant progress, but they just need a nudge. "Encouragement" is not about just saying "nice" things; it's about offering *words that urge*. It's about giving courage (en-*courage*-ment) to those who lack it.

So leaders, take a risk. Say what needs to be said to encourage your members as they grow in their knowledge of the Bible. Help them not just amass more information, but move toward the goal of becoming fully devoted followers of Jesus Christ. Go ahead; make their day!

Session 1. The Law.

General Note. As your group begins this new study, you have a wonderful opportunity to help the members of your group develop a greater appreciation and love for God's Word. This study will provide the means to enable your group to see clearly that the Bible is not a big, mysterious book that can only intimidate the person who is unfamiliar with its content. The Bible is a wonderful book inspired by a loving God!

Since this study guide moves directly into the first main section of the Bible, you may want to use a few minutes at the beginning of this first lesson to provide an overview of the entire study. Remind your members that the Bible is a book with two main divisions, the Old and New Testaments. The sixty-six individual books (thirty-nine in the Old Testament and twenty-seven in the New Testament) are divided into a number of sections based on content and literary style. For our purposes, we have divided the Bible into five general sections.

Notice that when uppercased, "Law" refers to the Pentateuch, the first five books of the Bible. When lowercased, "law" refers to specific laws in the Pentateuch.

Introduce the Session (1 min.) Go over the purpose and goal.

Purpose: To explain how God revealed himself in Scripture through the narrative of creation and through the laws and covenants God instituted in governing humanity's role within that creation.

Goal: To be able to explain the primary features of the first five books of the Bible and how God revealed himself in them.

Establishing Base Camp (10 min.) Life from the beginning has involved the responses of sinful human beings to a perfect, powerful, loving God. The pattern is simple. God creates, we rebel, God provides the means of redemption and a restored relationship with him, and then we choose to accept or reject his provisions for us. Sadly, many choose to reject his loving gift. The pattern of our behavior, which is explored in this opening question, reminds us of life as it has been since the beginning. The question is designed to help your group begin to see the connection between then and now.

Mapping the Trail (10 min.) Help your group begin to relate this study to our lives and current ways of thinking. Our culture's view of these earliest biblical events typically is marked by unbelief. God wants us to see immediately that believing in the God of the Bible is not always a popular thing.

Beginning the Ascent (30 min.) Our study of this weighty section of the Bible can be simplified by dividing the events of the Law into three eras. Help your group gain a basic understanding of this crucial part of the Bible by walking them through the three eras, focusing on the sentence summaries and the details contained in the overview chart. Seeing how God and humankind relate to one another and are revealed through the books of the Law will help your group.

Encourage group members to talk about their awareness of the key people and events in each era. Even if they are biblical novices, they probably have impressions of such people as Adam, Joseph and Moses. But your group may find it helpful to reserve time to discuss the significance of the passages listed in parentheses in the "Biblical References" column of the overview chart.

When discussing God's covenant with Abraham, focus on the outlandish gifts that God promised Abraham. Remind them that under the new covenant in Christ we too have been given outrageous gifts that we do not deserve. We receive them by faith and believe God (as Abraham did, and it was credited to him as righteousness). Abraham received God's word by faith, which we are called to do as well.

It is important that the people in your group also focus on the significance of the law and its relationship to their lives. Encourage discussion about the Ten Commandments. Even biblical novices often have impressions they have developed about the commandments and the importance of obeying them. Try to help everyone in your group to be clear in their thinking regarding the purpose of the law as a guide to help bring us to God and to faith in Christ. The pullout quote may be helpful here.

Gaining a Foothold (5 min.) Read this key material to your group.

Trailmarkers (10 min.) The purpose of this exercise, which involves discussing passages Paul wrote in reference to texts contained in the section we are studying, is to help your group see the spiritual significance of some of the key parts of the Law. Even the revelation of God in the earliest sections of the Bible provides concepts that directly relate to humanity's relationship to God.

Encourage your group to memorize the verse from Galatians 3. Memory work often is difficult for people, so you will want this part of the lesson to be voluntary.

But stress the importance of the verse to your group. You might break into teams to jump-start the process of memorizing this verse.

Teamwork (15 min.) This group exercise builds on the trailmarkers section. This section of the Bible involves subject matter about which there is great misunderstanding. Rather than God's law providing the means by which we can be saved if we keep it, the law reveals our sin to us because our failure to obey it completely reflects our imperfection. Correcting this misunderstanding may actually lead to opportunities for us to communicate the gospel to others.

Reaching the Summit (5 min.) Depending on the availability of time at this point, this exercise can be completed either as a group or in pairs. Group members should always be encouraged to try to master the basic content of the lessons reviewed in this section. Encouragement is a key aspect of shepherding a group!

Next Session (5 min.) This section of the Bible sets a tone for the rest of Scripture, a tone that extends to today. Men and women have always struggled to be true to the God of creation. Next week's study can help provide hope for all of us who continue this struggle.

Close in Prayer (10 min.) Always provide an opportunity for group members to pray as they want. Take the lead by example, but allow the prayer time to be as spontaneous as possible. Take time to thank God for the Law, which shows us that we needed as Savior.

Session 2. History & Poetry.

General Note. The primary challenges of this session are the volume and nature of the biblical literature to be discussed. The history and poetry section comprises seventeen books, including Psalms, the longest book in the Bible, as well as some lengthy historical books. The biblical material in this section is both significant and interesting, so you again will want to achieve a balance between walking your group through the section and allowing for contributions from the group.

Introduce the Session (1 min.) In reviewing the purpose and goal statements, provide a brief transition from the last lesson, which ended with the people of Israel wandering in the wilderness, to this new lesson, which begins with the commissioning of Joshua to lead Israel to the Promised Land.

Purpose: To explain how God revealed himself to the nation of Israel at a critical time in its history and how this revelation occurred through two of the most familiar forms of communication: stories and poetic songs. This study will confirm the character and creative ability of a God who always is at work in human history and who delights in communicating with us in a variety of written forms.

Goal: To be able to summarize the flow of God's work and communication in Old Testament history and the vital role that the five books of poetry served in enabling the authors to communicate their feelings about God and life.

Establishing Base Camp (10 min.) This opening question is designed to encourage group members to think about the means by which we communicate our thoughts in verbal form. God again displays himself as a skilled communicator by choosing to emphasize his truth in meaningful styles. Storytelling is the most common style of human communication, while poetry is perhaps the most personal. God chose to communicate with us in a manner we can relate to.

Mapping the Trail (10 min.) These questions are designed to set a tone for the discussion before actually getting into the biblical material.

Beginning the Ascent (30 min.) The challenge you face is to walk your group through the highlights of this section of the Bible in the time available to you. The eras encompassed within the historical books of the Old Testament should be discussed briefly, with emphasis given to the transition from the eras studied in the first lesson. Encourage your group members to participate by asking them to identify familiar names and events at any point during the discussion. A simple word-association game is one way in which this might be accomplished.

As a way of demonstrating how biblical narrative communicates truth, briefly relate a story from the historical books and ask group members to try to identify the lessons taught by these stories. If you can't think of one, you might use the story of King Asa who, after relying on God for strength, later turned to human kings for help and did not seek God. It is a sad story. Use 2 Chronicles 15:1-2 and 2 Chronicles 16:1-14. Just read through these as a story and stay focused on the decisions Asa made and their consequences.

Hannah's song is a great combination of history and poetry expressed in song. Try to highlight what is revealed about the nature of God and the character of Hannah's response to him. Others might see God as cruel for "closing her womb," but Hannah simply recognizes God's sovereign rule and choice in her life.

Gaining a Foothold (3 min.) Read this section to your group to help remind them that the Bible should never be discounted because of a seeming lack of relevance.

Trailmarkers (10 min.) A brief discussion of Psalm 23, because it already may be familiar to at least some members of the group, will encourage the group to see another connection between history and poetry as types of biblical literature. Also encourage the memorization of at least some verses of the psalm.

Teamwork (15 min.) The book of Ecclesiastes provides another insightful exploration of life as many people experience it. Encourage your group to reflect on the relevance of the passage suggested for reading. Why is commitment to God, cited by Solomon, the solution to the feeling of futility that many of life's experiences seem to produce. How does this commitment overcome feelings of futility?

Reaching the Summit (5 min.) One of the best teaching methods is having people discuss the material you want them to learn. Encourage group members to discuss with each other the basic structure of this section.

Next Session (5 min.) Challenge group members to make a list of examples of our culture's fascination with the future and the subject of prophecy.

Close in Prayer (10 min.) Take some of the prayer time to worship God as Hannah and others did after learning about his character and mighty acts of grace. Continue to pray for group needs.

Session 3. The Prophets & Revelation.
Introduce the Session (1 min.) You have the opportunity to capitalize on whatever interest in and knowledge of the prophetic writings your group already has. But you also may have to defuse misunderstandings about prophecy, especially the notion that biblical prophecy primarily involves predictions regarding the return of Christ and the end of the world.

Purpose: To explain how God revealed himself through prophetic messages, and to discuss the three primary purposes of biblical prophecy. This study should encourage us in our belief in a faithful God and in the hope of an eternal tomorrow.

Goal: To be able to explain the nature of biblical prophecy, see where the prophetic books fit in the Scripture and understand the purposes for which prophecy was given.

Establishing Base Camp (10 min.) Any interest your group has in the subject of prophecy may derive from a combination of the subject itself and our more general interest and curiosity about what the future holds for us. This interest in the future may manifest itself in a variety of ways—from reading horoscopes to a fascination with science-fiction movies to reading books by so-called futurists. You may want to use a few minutes to discuss with the group its degree of interest in the future and prophecy.

Mapping the Trail (10 min.) Non-Christians may have their own reasons for being interested in prophecy. Discussion of the subject with friends may provide the group member with a ready opportunity to share his or her faith. By gaining a clearer understanding of biblical prophecy, we may be able to better understand and communicate with the culture, especially with individuals gripped by fear because of uncertainty regarding the future. Encourage your group to grow in their knowledge of the subject. (For more on how to study prophecy, refer to *Parables & Prophecy* in the Bible 101 series.)

Beginning the Ascent (25 min.) This section is divided into three parts: the nature of prophecy, its place in biblical context,and the categories of biblical prophecy.

1. The key point in part one is that biblical prophets not only foresaw future events but also addressed contemporary issues. In fact the latter probably was their primary role. Your group may need to be reminded that any study of prophecy must involve an effort to balance these dual emphases.

2. Because the book of Revelation stands by itself in the organization of the New Testament, it has been included with the Old Testament prophets with whom Revelation shares common subject matter. Encourage your group members to study the Old Testament prophets with a view to the context provided by the historical books discussed in session two.

Point out to the group that most of the Old Testament prophetic books were written during the same period of time as the historical and poetic books. Most were written during the kingdom era. Ezekiel and Daniel were written during the time of Israel's exile in Babylon—605-535 B.C. Ezra, Nehemiah and Esther were authored during and following the return from exile. Placing these books in their proper historical setting helps the reader better understand the tone of much of the prophecy.

3. Your discussion of part three can be highlighted by referring to some of the examples of the three types of prophecy provided in the lesson itself. Emphasize the importance of keeping a balanced perspective on these three types. It is also important to reflect on the significance of the messianic prophecies and their fulfillment as they provide vital validation of our belief in Christ as the Messiah.

As you read Malachi 1, ask the group to observe the tone of the prophet's message. They should easily identify it as one of judgment. God is displaying his anger because Israel has turned from him to a complacent, minimum-effort religion. They treat God with contempt and worship him out of habit instead of heart. This prophecy is not predictive. It is a forthtelling of the terrible state of Israel's devotion to God. (There is some predictive prophecy at the end of chapter four, but most of the book is a ringing judgment against the people and a call to repent.

Gaining a Foothold (3 min.) Read this section as a way of emphasizing the practical value of a knowledge of biblical prophecy.

Trailmarkers (10 min.) The passage from Isaiah included in this exercise is remarkably vivid in its prophetic description of the coming Messiah. The fact that Christ's coming was a fulfillment of Old Testament prophecy is a significant help in enabling a person to accept the validity of Christ's identity as Messiah. This exercise may be valuable to the faith of the group member for that reason. Encourage your members to interact with the questions in this exercise on their own if time becomes a limitation for you when your group meets.

Teamwork (25 min.) This exercise is designed to be another practical means of understanding the relevance of the prophets. Churches today can learn much from what God said to New Testament churches, including this section in Revelation. Participate actively with your group as you consider the positives and negatives of these early churches. Watch time here. Each member should spend five minutes gaining the major insights. Then each can share with the group.

Reaching the Summit (5 min.) This simple closing exercise may help reinforce the entire discussion of this lesson. If you have time, pause a moment to allow for group reflection on how this study has been helpful.

Next Session (3 min.) With this study of prophecy, including messianic prophecy, the transition to the next session should be a smooth one. Encourage group members, as always, to work on the session beforehand if possible and also to reflect on their own impressions of Christ.

Close in Prayer (10 min.) Encourage heart-felt prayer about the group's appreciation for God's clear self-revelation in the Old Testament Scriptures, which often are perceived as being so difficult to comprehend.

Session 4. The Gospels.
Introduce the Session (3 min.) This session provides a wonderful opportunity for you to help the members of your group gain greater clarity about Jesus Christ as revealed while he was on earth. The community environment of the group is a good place to allow the members of your group share their understanding of Jesus Christ with others. The group also should provide a safe environment in which individuals

can ask their own unanswered questions of Jesus.

Purpose: To explain the process by which God revealed himself through the birth, life, death and resurrection of his Son, Jesus Christ, and through the writings of four different individuals who wrote what are referred to as the *Gospels.*

Goal: As a result of this session the participant will be able to explain how God revealed himself through his Son and how each Gospel author uniquely contributed to that story.

Establishing Base Camp (10 min.) Faith in Christ as God's Son is the most important factor in a person becoming a member of God's family. The events in the Gospels were designed to help confirm the true identity of Jesus as the Messiah. But many people in the first century and today have failed to accept these events as sufficient evidence of Jesus' divine origin and therefore never place their faith in him. The question is designed to stimulate thinking and discussion about the causes of miracles and possible miracles that are difficult for us to explain.

Mapping the Trail (10 min.) Clarity about the true nature of Jesus Christ is important to us for two primary reasons: First, such clarity is vital to retaining a strong faith in Christ. Second, as we share our faith with others, we can anticipate resistance from people who doubt the reality of Jesus' divine nature. This lesson can help contribute to our faith as we review the events of Christ's life as recorded in the writings of four divinely inspired authors.

Beginning the Ascent (30 min.) A study of Christ's life as described in the four Gospel accounts could become a seemingly overwhelming task for any small group. Since this session is relatively brief, keep the discussion focused to the general theme of the organization of the Bible and the manner in which God revealed himself in his Word. Stay with two primary questions: (1) Why did God provide the life story of his Son, Jesus Christ? (2) How did each of the four authors contribute to that revelation?

In considering the first question, be prepared to discuss with your group the reasons listed for the record the life of Christ. Don't feel that you need to get involved in deep theological questions. The texts provided, in the context of the previous lesson on prophecy, will help create an effective picture of the significance of not only Christ's death, but also of his life.

By answering the second question individuals can, with the help of the chart, get an overview of the four accounts of Jesus' life. The group should also be encouraged to see that God used four different people to relate the story of Christ's life. This adds to the legitimacy of the events contained in the Gospels and to the credibility of Jesus' claim to be the Son of God. Group members themselves may have experienced doubts about the accuracy of the Bible, particularly in the face of claims targeted at supposed contradictions in Scripture. They also may expect resistance from people they talk to about Christ for the same reason. God inspired four people to write the story of Jesus so that our faith in Christ might be strengthened rather than made weak.

You can help your group by walking them through the overview chart of the four Gospels. Christ is portrayed as the Son of God, totally human and fully divine, the suffering servant sent to die for sins. Each author has a window into the life of Christ. Their unique perspectives are influenced by their audience, what they saw and heard about Christ, and what the Spirit chose to say through their unique personalities.

By telling the story in this manner God makes his message clear and credible. Joseph Smith, founder of Mormonism, claims to have seen an angel who revealed new truth to him on special tablets. But who was there to see this? Where are the eyewitnesses? Jesus acted in full view of his disciples and hundreds of others. The four accounts corroborate the evidence and add perspective to the story. Jesus is revealed to us in many episodes of teaching and ministry.

The three major periods of Christ's life (birth, public ministry, death and resurrection) each contain unique elements.

Birth: Christ was born of a virgin, fulfilling Isaiah 7:14. This birth, brought about by the Holy Spirit, makes Jesus unique; in fact, it makes him God!

Public ministry: His teaching came with authority (Luke 4:31-32). His miracles proved he was God (John 20:30-31).

Death and resurrection: His death and resurrection accomplished our redemption, making eternal life and forgiveness of sin possible. We can be reconciled to God and escape judgment. We have a new and abundant life!

Trailmarkers (10 min.) What did Jesus mean by the expression "gave his only Son" (John 3:16)? As you discuss this question with your group, feel free to refer back to the representative texts of each Gospel discussed earlier in the lesson. John 20:31 is a verse that is particularly helpful at this point.

Teamwork (15 min.) One significant result of this lesson is that the members of your group, by developing a clearer understanding of who Christ was and is, can have greater confidence as they share their witness with people who do not believe. Encourage the group as they participate in this exercise and gain experience in putting their faith into words. Focus on the nature of who Jesus is and the events surrounding his life.

 Reaching the Summit (5 min.) This is another place where group members may have an opportunity to verbalize the message of the Gospels in light of the events of Christ's life. Listen to their thoughts and then summarize the lesson and its implications for their faith.

Next Session (5 min.) Since the church is the focus of the next session, encourage members to reflect on their own positive and negative experiences and impressions of the church.

Close in Prayer (10 min.) Thank God for Christ, his work and his life. Ask the group to consider their present relationship with him. Pray also for group needs and concerns. Consider praying a blessing on each others' lives, affirming one another for who we are in Christ.

Session 5. Acts & Epistles.
General Note. This study may be a challenge. First, there is, as always, a large portion of Scripture covered in the session. Second, the session focuses on the church, and your group may have numerous ideas and opinions to offer as they reflect on their own church experience. Part of your responsibility will be to discern how much time to devote to the biblical materials and how much time to allow for discussion.
Introduce the Session (1 min.) Go over the purpose and goal.
Purpose: This session is designed to explain how God revealed himself through the birth of the church, which he referred to as the body of Christ, and how God provided instruction to the church through divinely inspired authors.
Goal: To be able to describe the birth and growth of the early church and how divinely inspired instruction to the early church could help produce growth both in the early Christians and in ourselves.

 Establishing Base Camp (10 min.) Throughout this study of the organization of the Bible, we have observed the various ways in which God has communicated with people. There are two such primary methods involved in this lesson: historical narrative, which also makes up a large portion of the Old Testament, and letters of instruction and encouragement.

Just as the letters we send and receive serve a variety of purposes and can evoke a variety of responses, the New Testament authors penned epistles that were designed to instruct the readers on many subjects and express numerous feelings. By encouraging your group members to reflect on their own letter-writing (and receiving) experiences, you may make an easy transition into the lesson by listing various reasons for the writing of these letters, many of which were to individuals and groups first mentioned in Acts.

Mapping the Trail (10 min.) Help your group understand that just as their ideas and experiences regarding the church may vary, so the church has taken numerous forms and served many functions. What we need is not new ideas but a clear understanding of God's vision for the church as communicated through texts that relate its earliest history and teaching.

Beginning the Ascent (30 min.) Lead your group through an overview of the early history of the church as recorded in Acts and then through a survey of the divisions of the New Testament letters. Read and discuss individual texts as time allows.

There are three main divisions of Acts as outlined in 1:8. The first part, on the birth of the church in Jerusalem, includes so much interesting material that it will be easy to get behind in your study. Try to focus on what the early church was like—as told in the final verses of chapter 2.

As the church expands into Judea and Samaria, the narrative includes fewer events. But the issues—Philip's evangelistic zeal, Paul's changed life and Peter's vision of a gospel meant for all humanity—are significant. Be sure to emphasize each, even if your comments must be brief. And allow the members of the group to express their observations first. Unfortunately, the design of this study provides little time for discussion of Paul's missionary journeys in the final half of Acts. Since we have not included maps of the journeys in this study guide, you may want to locate maps through your church library or by talking with a staff person at your church. Many versions of the Bible detail the journeys in a map section.

Discussion of the Christ-centered themes of the Epistles is one way to provide your members with a general overview of their content. But it also provides you with an opportunity to discuss with the group the radical changes brought by the coming of the Holy Spirit and the birth of the church. Even though the believers to whom the epistles were written had professed faith in Christ, the message of Christ was relatively new. Believers needed to be sure of their faith, wary of false teachers and able to endure persecution. Thus they needed all the encouragement, instruction and warning provided by these writings.

The section on 2 Timothy 3:16-17 may help your group see that Paul emphasized the importance of character through an effective balance of (1) what his readers believed, (2) who they were, and (3) how they lived. Stress the importance of maintaining this balance.

Gaining a Foothold (5 min.) Read this to your group.

Trailmarkers (10 min.) Philippians 2:1-7 was chosen for this segment because it draws together into one passage the primary emphasis of the Epistles on the centrality of Christ in both their individual lives and their community. This would be an appropriate time for a gentle reminder to your group that this should be a goal for your small community as well.

Teamwork (15 min.) Complete this in subgroups. Encourage your members in their discussion by helping them see that God has designed the church to be a vibrant, growing, Holy Spirit-empowered body functioning to produce life change in its attenders, to witness to a lost world and to impact the needy in the community.

Reaching the Summit (5 min.) As each member responds to the three questions, he or she will have the basic content of this section of the Bible reinforced in their thinking. Remind the group that as they do this, they are taking another step in developing a greater appreciation for God's Word. Hopefully, they will be encouraged to move on in their study of the Bible.

Next Session (5 min.) Encourage group members to review the five sessions studied to this point. The final session will involve exercises that help the group to draw together the main features of the various sections of the Bible around some central themes.

Session 6. Putting It All Together.
Introduce the Session (1 min.) The basic purpose of this lesson is to give your group an opportunity to review and reflect. Your primary role will be to facilitate a balanced discussion by encouraging each member in whatever contributions made, and through effective clock management.

Go over the purpose and goal.

Purpose: To review the material studied to this point, and to relate the sections of the Bible to each other by discussing common biblical themes.

Goal: To be able to explain the organizational structure of the Bible and briefly describe each of its five primary sections.

Establishing Base Camp (10 min.) One point you want your group members to see clearly is that God's Word is a book of unchanging truth. The separation caused by time and cultural differences does not negate the relevance of God's Word. The basic issues addressed in Scripture are the same issues that confront us today. Encourage your group through the discussion of the questions in this section to see that the Bible—a guidebook for life—provides stability in a world of rapid technological, moral and ethical change that can be frightening.

 Mapping the Trail (10 min.) The questions in this section are designed to encourage the group to begin the session by reflecting on some of their dominant impressions from this study guide. Since the next section of this lesson allows each individual to lead the discussion for several minutes, the conversation at this point should be a helpful "warm-up" time in getting everyone talking.

Beginning the Ascent (15 min.) Notice we have shortened this portion of the meeting to fifteen minutes so that more attention can be given to teamwork in this final session. In contrast to the previous sessions, you will function much more as a facilitator and encourager than as a teacher in this section. In assigning individuals to be responsible for reviewing the material in each lesson, you should be sensitive to each member's comfort level with this type of exercise. Group size and time will dictate the extent to which each person participates. Any misstatements by individuals should be handled sensitively and always balanced by encouragement. If your group has developed a positive, caring and supportive environment for discussion, this section should proceed smoothly.

The exercise in which group members discuss passages related to the theme of God as our shepherd is designed to help the group see the unity of the Bible by observing how the various sections address a common theme. In other words, this exercise may have both a spiritual and practical value. The message of the Bible is united around common themes, and one of those themes is that we can rely on God as our spiritual shepherd.

Gaining a Foothold (3 min.) This reading is meant to be an additional source of encouragement to your group, particularly to those individuals who may be concerned or frustrated by their relative unfamiliarity with the Bible.

Trailmarkers (10 min.) Hebrews 13:8 reminds that the Bible reveals a Christ who is unchanging. He is Creator, Redeemer, Messiah and Lord. Whether described prophetically or in the Gospels or in a New Testament letter, he is Jesus Christ, the unchanging Lord.

Teamwork (30 min.) We have added some time here in this session to help the group work together. Because God is our faithful shepherd, we can place our faith in him completely, beginning with a faith in Christ that makes us his children. One practical application of this principle occurs in our witness to nonbelievers.

Faith is one of the most important themes of the Bible, and each section of the Bible addresses the subject. There is great unity concerning the subject. Those who have a right relationship to God live by faith. Christ's work is the basis for our faith, and faith requires belief in Jesus and what he has accomplished. Our own works accomplish nothing. We trust that Jesus will actually do what he has promised—forgive us and give us eternal life. We have never met him physically. We have never seen heaven. We have never met the writers of Scripture. Nonetheless, we trust in the truth that has been revealed. Our lives are different. The Holy Spirit confirms that we are God's, and we are set apart as holy because of what Jesus did.

Each definition in this exercise will be a little different but should include many of the comments listed in the paragraph above. Help members see the essential nature of faith and how it is consistently portrayed throughout the Word of God.

▲ **Reaching the Summit (5 min.)** In past sessions the objective of this part was to review the content of the lesson, but here we recognize that the ultimate goal of Bible study is personal application and life change. Asking these questions is an appropriate way to conclude our study.

Close in Prayer (10 min.) Encourage group members to take as much time as appropriate to thank God for this study and for the group and to pray for continued application of the lessons learned. Also pray for any other specific needs presented by group members.

WITHDRAWN

Into the Fire

Meredith Wild

Mount Laurel Library
100 Walt Whitman Avenue
Mount Laurel, NJ 08054-9539
856-234-7319
www.mtlaurel.lib.nj.us

WATERHOUSE
PRESS

WITHDRAWN

Into the Fire

This book is an original publication of Meredith Wild.

This is a work of fiction. Names, characters, places, and incidents either are the product of the author's imagination or are used fictitiously, and any resemblance to actual persons, living or dead, business establishments, events, or locales is entirely coincidental. The publisher does not assume any responsibility for third-party websites or their content.

Copyright © 2016 Waterhouse Press, LLC
Cover Design by Meredith Wild.
Cover images: Dreamstime & Shutterstock

All Rights Reserved.
No part of this book may be reproduced, scanned, or distributed in any printed or electronic format without permission. Please do not participate in or encourage piracy of copyrighted materials in violation of the author's rights. Purchase only authorized editions.

PRINTED IN THE UNITED STATES OF AMERICA

ISBN: 978-1-943893-08-9

For Misti

"We cross our bridges when we come to them and burn them behind us, with nothing to show for our progress except a memory of the smell of smoke, and a presumption that once our eyes watered."
—Tom Stoppard

CHAPTER ONE

DARREN

"Get the hell off me!"

Pauly's eyes had shot open seconds earlier, thanks to the Narcan and the bag of oxygen he'd shoved away. A slew of curses and violent thrashing was our reward for bringing him back to consciousness too abruptly. We'd fucked up his high, and he wasn't pleased.

"Bridge, hold him down."

Before I could, Pauly whacked Ian in the face with his angry flailing. Ian shoved him down on the sidewalk harder than he needed to. We were on the twenty-third hour of a double shift, and my patience was growing thin too. Pauly was a frequent flier, and as long as he was conscious and in a decent mood, the medics would usually crate him off to the hospital where they'd monitor his vitals until he came out of it. Today, we weren't that lucky.

"Try that again, Pauly, and next time you're getting the Narcan no matter how good you're feeling," Ian ground out.

It was an empty threat, but one that no doubt felt very real to Pauly under the current circumstances. Narrowing his eyes, he shifted his bleary gaze to me.

I shook my head, keeping my hold firm on his arms, which were unexpectedly strong considering how thin he'd recently become. "Don't look at me for sympathy, man. You can't hit us when we're trying to help you. You going to calm down now?"

Pauly was a junkie, one of thousands in the city. We were two of a few dozen guys on the fire department who periodically made sure he was breathing after someone found him unresponsive on the streets, again.

We seemed to care more about Pauly staying alive than he did sometimes.

The harrowing truth of it would eat away at someone else. I couldn't let his story or the hundreds of others I'd seen play out over the years get under my skin though. Not in this line of work. I just wanted to get back to the station. We'd been toned out all night long. Back to sleep just long enough to get jolted awake again. Nothing meant more to me right now than the promise of a few hours of uninterrupted rest. The sooner Pauly and I saw eye to eye, the sooner I could get my relief and go home.

After a moment, he seemed to relent, his muscles going lax.

"Good man." I let out a sigh, equal parts relief and exhaustion. I nodded toward the medics who'd just arrived with a stretcher. "These guys are going to take care of you now. You going to be nice to them?"

"Yeah." He closed his eyes with a grimace.

Until next time, Pauly.

A couple of hours later, I was walking through the glass doors of Bridge Fitness. The gym that my brother owned and I helped manage had become a second home for me. Cameron had been working his ass off for weeks in anticipation of taking time off for his wedding. I came in every shift I could to help lighten the load, but I was grateful today wasn't one of them.

I needed to burn off just enough energy to crash back at my apartment.

I entered the main gym room, and Cameron's fiancée, Maya Jacobs, was on the treadmill, earbuds in, oblivious to my presence. The pretty blonde had had my brother twisted up for years, and as much as I'd hated to see him go through it, he seemed happier than I'd ever seen him now that they were together again. I gave her a wave when I passed and headed toward the office in the back where I'd likely find Cameron.

As expected, he was at his desk. But he wasn't alone. Raina, our resident yoga instructor, leaned her hip against the side of the desk. She flickered her lascivious gaze from his uneasy expression down his body and edged closer. Damn, the woman was an inch away from climbing into his lap. When she licked her lips suggestively, Cameron looked away.

"Hey, guys," I said loudly.

Raina straightened and moved off the desk. "Hey, Darren."

"What's up?"

She shrugged, pushing her chest out a fraction as she passed by. "Not much. I was just leaving."

"See ya," I said, taking in an eyeful of her swaying ass on her way out.

Cameron frowned and turned back to the paperwork in front of him. I leaned against the doorjamb and tried to gauge his mood.

"What's up with Raina? She didn't get the hint when you proposed to Maya?"

He scratched his pen along his jaw. "I think that's just how she is. I'm trying not to read too much into it."

I laughed. "Picking up on those signals and using them to my advantage is like my second job. She's hitting on you, old man. Maya's going to catch her making moves one of these days, and I'm guessing it won't be pretty. Better for you to shut her down before Maya does."

He sighed and leaned back in the office chair that squeaked with every recline. He pushed a handful of dark hair off his forehead. "Yeah, I guess you're right. Like I don't have enough shit to deal with right now. We're leaving for Grand Cayman in a couple of days, and I'm up to my eyeballs in this proposal for the investors."

I nodded, sizing up the paperwork that always seemed to make its way to his desktop, more so now that he was trying to expand the empire by opening a new gym. "How about I talk to her?"

Cam shot me a wary look. I could read him like a book. I was the oldest, but for some reason Cameron always wanted to shoulder the burdens of life alone.

"Seriously, it'll be less awkward if I do it," I said. "I'll keep it light but make sure she gets the message."

A few seconds passed before the worried wrinkle in his forehead faded. "Fine. Just don't piss her off. I need her here while we're gone. I can't be short-staffed right now."

"I get it." I moved to the locker where I stashed my bag and jacket. I'd gotten my third or fourth wave of energy on the way home from work. Sleep wasn't going to be happening for a few more hours. At least I didn't have to deal with more guys like Pauly or run into any burning buildings for a while.

Leaving Cameron to his work, I headed toward the yoga studio farther down the hall. I expected to find Raina there. She didn't have class until midmorning.

The large studio was cool and empty. Raina was straightening out a stack of rolled-up mats a few feet away.

When the door latched behind me, she looked up.

I flashed her a smile. "How's it going?"

"Good. How about yourself?"

"Wiped from work. Long shift. I came in to unwind for a few before I crash."

She smirked, looking down at her mats again. "Private yoga lesson?"

The smile I wore wasn't forced this time. When our gazes met again, her eyelids were a little lower.

I let out a soft chuckle. "Hmm, sounds relaxing. If I hit the floor though, I may never get back up."

She shrugged, going about her business, letting the invitation linger in the air between us. Cameron didn't know, but she'd given me a "private yoga lesson" after work a few weeks ago. I'd had a weak moment.

The guy in me who rarely said no to a proposition let the possibilities tumble around in my tired head for a bit. No, I was here for a reason, and that was not it.

I cleared my throat and prepared to dive in. "So what's up with you and Cam?"

Raina stilled, her expression more alert now. "What do you mean?"

"I mean...you've got a thing for him, right?"

She stopped what she was doing, the lines of her body becoming hard and tense. Defensiveness quickly took over her pleasant countenance. "What are you implying?"

"Listen, I saw you in his office earlier. Your body language... I mean, call me crazy, but it seems like you're attracted to him too."

Her mouth opened but no words came. She was flustered. Taking slow strides toward her, I looked her up and down.

No doubt, she had a nice body. Fit and lean, not an inch of fat on her. Plain to see when she wore only a sports bra and tight-fitting yoga pants. As hard as I worked on my own body, she just wasn't my type. I wanted the girls who came to the gym to firm up but left a little meat on their bones.

I stopped when I was a couple of feet away from her. "Are you trying to tell me that you wouldn't sleep with Cameron the first chance you got? Tell me the truth."

"I am not *one bit* attracted to your brother," she said forcefully.

"Yeah?" I cocked my head, challenging her. I took in all the subtle cues of her body—the shallow breath, the flush of pink across her chest—that told me I could win this round.

"Yeah." She released the word with a sigh. The anger in her voice had faded.

When she swayed toward me, my tired brain worked to catch up with where this was going.

"Prove it." My voice was low, laced with challenge. I took a step closer, bringing us a breath apart.

She flashed her eyes to the door and then back to me. I knew that look. She had to make a decision. Didn't matter because whatever she decided I could change her mind. Cameron was a good guy. That's why she wanted him. I wasn't, and that's why, at this particular moment, she wanted me.

She proved it when she curved her hand around the back of my neck and rose on her toes, bringing our lips together. She wasn't hesitant or shy. She dove right in, and I kissed her back. Not because I cared about how she tasted, but because I knew that was what she wanted. I was never much for the act.

She pushed forward, pressing her whole body along mine, and my cock stirred to life. Yeah. Fucking was definitely in the cards.

Breaking the kiss I didn't want, I turned her around and pushed her against the wall. She was naked beneath her yoga pants, which I'd shoved down her thighs, giving me just enough access to get what I did want.

Don't do this. I slid my palms along her hips, contemplating what I was about to do. "Are you sure you want to do this?" As if her answer made it any more right.

"Yes," she moaned, tilting her ass back to me, taunting my cock even more.

Every time she made a sound, I envisioned Cam walking in on this atrocity that was happening in our shared workplace. Goddamn, this was stupid. And wrong. The mirrors on three sides of us reminded me every time I dared open my eyes. Screwing around the first time had been a mistake. If I kept going with her this way, I could have a real problem on my hands.

I palmed my growing erection, my partner in crime and the thought leader when it came to who and when to fuck.

Then I froze. "I don't have a condom on me."

An awkward silence fell on the room.

"It's okay," she said quietly.

No, it sure as hell wasn't okay. I never fucked without one, and the way Raina made eyes at half the guys in the gym wasn't exactly confidence inspiring.

I yanked her yoga pants back up and turned her around.

"Not here. Not like this." Maybe not ever.

Her chest moved under her panting breaths. She was wound up, and I could have had her in an instant. That wasn't why I was here, though.

"Raina. You need to back off Cameron. We can fuck

around, but he's about to marry Maya."

I couldn't rein the words back in, regretting the matter-of-fact way they'd flown out of my mouth. Her soft flush noticeably cooled.

"Sure thing, Darren. You never struck me as the jealous type."

I ground my teeth. I wasn't jealous, but if that thought was enough to get her to back off, I'd let it go.

I hesitated a moment longer, looking her over one last time. At least she'd leave Cam alone now. I came close and kissed her once more. Mechanically, like it was my job, deriving no pleasure from it.

"I'll catch you later, Raina."

VANESSA

I hummed along to the pop tune that played through the speakers in the ceiling, singing along just low enough not to be heard in the busy coffee shop.

"Veronica!" the barista shouted across the café.

I jolted back into reality. I edged my way toward the front and took the tray from him. "Vanessa," I corrected.

He didn't linger long enough to acknowledge his mistake, disappearing as my phone rang in my pocket. I fished it out and recognized my mom's number.

"Mom, hey." I pressed the phone to my ear and juggled the tray of coffees as I left the cafe.

"How are you doing, honey? Is everything all right?" The sweetness of her light Southern accent tightened a bit with worry.

We'd started so many conversations this way, as if she'd

caught me in the middle of a disaster every time I picked up the phone. I rolled my eyes and released an annoyed sigh.

"Everything is *fine*."

Everything was always fine. Even when it wasn't. Even when life felt a little disastrous, I didn't want to give her any reason to believe this move had been all the terrible things she'd imagined and worried about. A gust of wind tunneled up the street as I passed through crowds and people's loud conversations.

"Where are you?" Her voice seemed small and unimportant in the nonstop buzz and noise of my surroundings.

"New York City, Mom. It's loud here."

She was silent a moment, and I could imagine the look on her face as she shook her head. She'd never understand why I lived here. How it was the extreme opposite of where I'd come from and that's precisely why I loved it. She'd kept me cloistered in my hometown long enough, but my future wasn't in Callaway.

In that little Florida town, I was someone different—the smart girl with big freckles, secondhand clothes, and a single mom. Mom had held her place in the community for years, serving everyone and their cousin coffee and greasy breakfast at the local diner. I had no secrets in Callaway and no way to escape the story that other people threw around like social currency, whitewashing their own secrets.

According to the whispers back home, I'd moved to the big city to work on Wall Street. That was all I wanted anyone to know. And here, I was anonymous. I could reinvent myself a thousand times and only a handful of people would ever know I had. And God knew I was in good company in a city this vast.

"Are you ready for your trip?" my mom asked.

I kept a steady pace up the street. The exhaust from the crawl of cabs up the street tainted the air. If I missed anything about home, it was the fresh air. Fresh ocean air that I was so close to enjoying again.

"So ready."

She sighed again. "I don't like the idea of you traveling by yourself."

I rolled my eyes again, grateful she couldn't see me. Her relentless fretting came from her heart. "I'm *not* traveling by myself. Eli and the rest of the wedding party will be together the whole way there."

"Maya too?" Her voice softened when she said my best friend's name. She loved Maya.

"She and Cam took a separate flight this morning so they could get a head start on preparations." I smiled at the thought of them already on the island, enjoying the break and alone time they deserved after a stressful winter.

"Wish you all were coming here to visit instead."

"Maya invited you to the wedding, Mom. You should have come. Would be like the vacation we never took."

"Vanessa."

The quiet way she said my name wasn't reproachful. I sensed her sadness, the disappointment that no amount of forgiving would lift.

"It's fine, Mom. But you'd think after half a lifetime on the road, you wouldn't get so stressed about traveling."

Seemed like the second she decided to step off my father's tour bus, weeks away from giving birth to me, she'd never wanted to go too far again. Her few trips to the city came only after a lot of prodding and planning.

"Phil can't get that much time off work. And when he can,

he doesn't want to be running all over creation."

She'd married my stepfather when I was in high school. By then I already had one foot out the door, so I'd never bonded much with my new "dad." She said Phil was the love of her life, but she didn't light up like she did the rare times I got her to talk about my father. Phil had the personality of a lima bean, but they seemed happy enough. He was loyal, reliable, and seemingly equally as committed to living life in one spot as she was.

"Oh!" Her voice went up an octave. "You'll never guess who I saw at the town hall. Phil and I were paying the tax bill, and we ran into Michael Browning. Did you know he's running for mayor? He'd be our youngest mayor. They say he's got a real chance at winning too."

"Good for him. Listen, I've got to run."

"You do not," she admonished. "He asked about you. Wanted to know how you were doing. He's just as handsome as he was when you were together. I'll never understand why you two couldn't make it work."

While my mother was busy making meals and keeping house for her new husband, I'd somehow gotten on the radar of Callaway's reigning prom king, to the disappointment of the many girls who'd been waiting in line for a chance at him.

Michael Browning was the kind of guy all the girls wanted and all the other guys wanted to be around. Funny, good family, promising future, and a soft spot for girls from the wrong side of town. Just the kind of boy my mom wanted for me. Someone who couldn't be more different from the rolling stone who'd neither had the time nor the inclination to raise me.

"We couldn't make it work for a lot of reasons, not the least of which was because I wasn't going to spend the rest of my life in Callaway where he was clearly destined to be."

"You talk about it like it's the worst place on earth. Why you'd rather live in that dirty city with all those people, I'll never understand. You had a life here."

"That's your life, and I'm happy for you, really. But right now, I'm standing in front of David's apartment. I need to go in now. He's waiting for me." I was still a block away from my boss's Soho loft, but I had to get the hell off the phone before this conversation took a real turn for the worse. "I'll text you when I land," I added.

"Thank you. You know I'll worry the whole time."

"I know you will, but there's nothing to worry about."

She paused a moment. "Love you, sweetheart," she said, soft and sweet again, like the sound of a mother putting her baby girl to bed, with the promise that everything was right in the world.

My irritation melted, and for a second she was my mother again, not a woman who'd given up all her dreams and didn't understand why I couldn't give up on mine.

"Love you too, Mom."

I slowed in front of my destination, replaying the conversation I was too quick to end. I looked up to where the architecture met the edge of blue-and-gray sky, delaying my entrance while the cool spring air whipped around me. I shook my head, annoyed with my train of thought and the unwanted emotion that kept bubbling to the surface.

Melody Hawkins and I didn't always see eye to eye, but she was the only mother I'd ever have. She was a part of me, no matter how far away I ran. I'd long ago stopped trying to catalogue all the reasons why I couldn't live the life she wanted for me because I couldn't do it without insulting the life she lived too.

I didn't want to do that to her, because as much as we disagreed, judging her for making the most with what she'd been given wasn't fair. She'd grown up poor in a big family that never had enough time for her. She fell in love with the wrong man and followed him down a path that led to having me, but she'd done the best she could for both of us.

Still, I'd come a long way from Callaway and didn't want to look back. I didn't want to think about the little town she'd raised me in or Michael Browning rising among its ranks. My life moved too fast to go backward. None of that mattered now.

I breathed in the city air, exhaled with a tired sigh, and went inside. When I approached the reception desk, a young man in a poorly tailored gray suit lifted his gaze to mine.

"I'm Vanessa Hawkins, here to see David Reilly," I said with a polite smile.

"One moment." He brought the phone to his ear. "A young woman is here to see you, Mr. Reilly. Vanessa Hawkins. Shall I send her up?"

My stomach tightened as Reilly's muffled voice came through the receiver. Instinct, maybe. Or my body's habitual reaction to his tone, even from this distance.

The young man hung up and nodded toward the elevators. "He's waiting for you. You can go right up."

A few seconds later, I was on my way up. I leaned against the cool metal wall of the elevator and let my mind play ping-pong between the plans I was hoping to keep tonight and the much-needed vacation I was going to be enjoying in less than twenty-four hours.

Despite it being Saturday, Reilly had called in a favor, and I begrudgingly obliged. His dry cleaning was going to be delivered to his townhouse on the Upper East Side. Instead of having me ensure they had his new address, he insisted I pick it up and deliver it myself so he had it for meetings this week.

David Reilly had challenged the limits of my patience for the last two years in his employ. Some days were better than others, but just when I thought I'd taken enough of his shit, I harnessed the will to endure a little more. Something amazing was on the other side of this, I promised myself daily.

The elevator opened and I stepped out, the doors silently closing behind me. Suddenly I felt incredibly small and out of place. I muzzled my internal tirade as I catalogued the enviable features of the loft I'd entered. Between the slick dark wood floors, clean modern furnishings, and the few glass walls separating some of the rooms, the space felt positively expansive by New York City standards. Never mind the floating staircase leading to the second floor with more square footage than I wanted to think about. I had no idea how much a place like this would cost, but knowing Reilly and his financial prowess at our firm, it was well within his budget.

Reilly shuffled down the stairs quickly and approached me where I stood, a few feet beyond the elevator entrance. He was dressed in a dark brown sweater and blue jeans. Soft brown loafers covered his bare feet. His casualness alarmed me. I'd rarely seen him outside of his designer suits. He seemed more relatable maybe, though I couldn't name a single thing we had in common outside of our humanity.

He wasn't bad looking, with sharp features and shrewd gray eyes. He was maybe five feet nine but toned and had enough presence that despite my many frustrations working with him, I wouldn't dream of crossing him. Few men or women in the world of Wall Street would.

He reached for the dry cleaning hangers that had been hooked over my sore pinky. "Good," he said, tossing the plastic encased garments over a nearby chair. Black-and-white prints, a stark modern look that matched the rest of the room.

I blinked, breaking myself out of my sensory overload, between the loft and this different Reilly in front of me.

"Place looks great. Once you unpack, of course, it's going to be really nice."

He almost smiled. "You should have seen the townhouse at Sutton Place."

If the place he'd shared with his ex was half this luxurious, I wouldn't have minded standing around and gawking the way I was now. "I'm sure it was beautiful."

His stare turned stony in a way that had my stomach tightening up again. Had I said something wrong? He made a nondescript sound, his jaw hardening. "Well, the bitch can have it," he muttered.

I nibbled nervously on the inside of my lip. The ink was still drying on his divorce papers, and this was the final stage, it seemed, of his permanent separation from Cheryl. He rarely spoke of her now. For as long as I'd been his personal assistant, their social lives, at least the parts that I'd been exposed to, rarely intersected. She traveled a lot, a common excuse for why she couldn't attend company events. Another reason too why it was so important that I did perhaps.

"I brought coffee." I twisted his cup out of the tray I held and handed it over. Half caff, nonfat, triple grande mocha. He hadn't asked for it, but I figured I would bring it just in case.

He accepted it, never making eye contact. "Little late for coffee."

So much for thank you, I retorted silently. Something I did a little too often around him. Maybe he'd treat me with more respect if I demanded it. But the chances were higher that he'd just fire me.

He took a sip before turning to walk away. "But I guess I have a lot of unpacking to do," he said as he began ripping the tape off one of the boxes stacked in the middle of the room.

He cast me a sidelong glance that rang clear as day in my head with, *Aren't you going to help?*

That's what he wanted. And on any other day, I would have offered without hesitation. If we were at work and something was pressing down on him, I was programmed to do whatever I could to lighten the load. But this was Saturday, goddamnit, and the work week ached in my bones—an ache I had every intention of relieving with a couple martinis and some time with my friends.

"I guess I'd better leave you to it. I haven't even packed for the trip yet," I lied. I was a hundred percent packed, all the way down to funneling my hair products into tiny plastic bottles. The clock couldn't wind down to my departure hour fast enough. Yet as decadent thoughts of fruity drinks and sunshine crossed my mind, I couldn't ignore how my anticipation was slowly morphing into guilt and anxiety.

"Going to be tough without you next week." Reilly's clipped tone left no doubt of that. "Will your phone be on?"

"I'm not sure about phone service there, actually," I mumbled.

Another nondescript noise that meant *Figure it out, Vanessa* sounded between us. I wasn't sure if my ability to give voice to all the things he never said made me a stellar assistant or bordered on crazy. Either way, I had a feeling I was in for a long night.

"Do you need any help?" I finally said, hating the words and hating the response I knew was coming even more.

He jerked his head toward the kitchen and the tall windows that were partially obscured by a few towers of boxes.

"You can start with those boxes over there."

CHAPTER TWO

VANESSA

"Ladies get in free." The guy manning the door of The Bearded Lady nodded toward Eli. "Ten bucks."

Eli did little to hide his irritation, rolling his eyes as he shoved a ten at the man who then stamped our hands, gaining us entrance into the already crowded Brooklyn bar.

"I can't believe he made me pay to get in here," Eli said.

"Just because you're gay doesn't mean you don't have to pay."

I pushed past a few clusters of people. Four hours and a fully organized kitchen later, I'd managed to escape Reilly's clutches. The extended workweek fatigue was even more real now, and I was determined to make the most of these last few hours of downtime before takeoff tomorrow.

One of the few rituals I maintained was keeping plans on a Saturday night. While they weren't quite as wild as they'd once been since my friend Maya had retired as my "work hard, play hard" partner in crime months ago, they were still plans that kept me sane. Almost two years at the firm felt more like twelve, and I couldn't remember a time when I hadn't worked long hours, bending my schedule around Reilly's whims and wants.

"Just because you dragged me into this meat market

doesn't mean I'm not going to bitch about it, Vanessa." Eli slid his slender fingers through his jet-black hair, something he habitually did since it was always overgrown. The tips of his bangs were dyed an electric blue, perfectly matching the bright blue band logo on his T-shirt.

I wedged myself into a place at the bar, hoping to secure enough real estate to flag down a drink. "First round is on me, and we'll call it even."

I tried in vain to get the bartender's attention. I wasn't in my usual barhopping attire, so I didn't have any cleavage to bare to help my cause.

Beside me, Eli scanned the room. "Have to say, this place has some decent scenery. Ladies night brings the man candy, doesn't it?"

I smiled. How quickly the tides had turned. "I thought you hated the meat market."

He cocked his head with a sigh. "Depends on the meat." A mischievous little smirk tilted his lips. "Oh, I see a familiar slice right over there."

I followed his gaze across the bar, expecting to see one of Eli's old flings.

Decent scenery indeed. Not ten feet away stood Darren Bridge. I shouldn't have been that excited about seeing a man I barely knew, but my heart began to beat double time. Something about him called to me...

I wished I could have been blind to what that *something* was, but the bad boy alarms went off like crazy in my head every time I was around him. I needed a bad boy in my life like I needed a second job. Still, no harm in getting an eyeful.

He wore a white Henley that did little to obscure the impressive body beneath. The man was a beast in the gym.

Every hard curve of his muscled body was enhanced by the fact that he was gorgeous as hell. His face was mostly obscured to me now, so I consoled myself with the rest of the view. His dark hair was trimmed neatly on the sides, but he kept it messy and longer on top. Made a girl want to run her hands right through it. Enviable olive skin wrapped around the corded muscles of his neck and forearms. He turned slightly, baring straight teeth and a dazzling smile as he laughed.

Was the object of his attention a woman? I wouldn't have been surprised, but he was talking to another guy, no less ripped or good-looking. As if Darren attracting unnaturally good-looking guys to his circle was as effortless as attracting the women who were eye-fucking him all over the damn bar. Myself included.

Eli elbowed my rib and shot me a knowing smile.

"Shut up," I preempted.

He laughed. "I didn't say anything. Your face, though..."

"He's bad news, and you know it. He breaks hearts for a living."

"Right after he breaks your bed. I bet he fucks like a demon."

The mere suggestion had my skin heating uncomfortably. Wouldn't I like to know...

I resisted the urge to tell Eli to shut up again before he could continue painting a fantasy of Darren Bridge that I'd already stitched together since meeting him months ago. Maya had warned me then that Darren was a manwhore and to keep my distance if I was smart. Easy enough. Drinks and clubbing could always lead to bad decisions, but even though he'd stuck by my side all night, he'd barely given me a peck on the cheek by the time the night was over.

Either the rumors were wrong and he was actually a gentleman, or more likely, I wasn't his type and he was simply being polite by keeping me company that night.

I turned and leaned against the bar, giving up on getting the attention of the bartender. I needed to stare at something other than Darren's toned back.

"Guys like Darren always look great on first glance. It's a mirage. No one is ever that hot *and* good in bed."

Eli lifted an eyebrow. "What kind of bullshit theory is that?"

I shrugged. Sometimes I made up rules to make myself feel better about my personal reality. Deep down I knew my theory was bullshit too. Cameron was equally gorgeous, and Maya didn't have any complaints. Then again, they'd been in love for years. I hadn't known the pleasure of sleeping with someone I loved for far too long, and if what Maya said about Darren's reputation was true, he probably hadn't stopped the whore tour long enough to fall in love with anyone.

"Miss?"

I turned to find two dirty martinis placed in front of me, as if by magic.

"I didn't order these."

"Do you want them? The guy down there put them on his tab." The once-elusive bartender jerked his thumb in the direction behind him.

I narrowed my eyes. "What guy?"

"I think this one, V." Eli nudged me again, gentler this time.

Then a warm hand was at my hip, grazing softly across my back as I turned. My breath caught at the sight of Darren. Somehow his presence seemed to suck up all the oxygen around me.

"Not dirty enough?" He smiled.

And my heart went flying again.

"What?" My confused reply got lost in the din of the bar.

He leaned closer, the cool scent of his cologne wafting over me, his warm breath tickling my ear. "Grey Goose martini, extra dirty. Did you think I forgot?"

Oh. I registered the slightest disappointment that he wasn't taunting me with some overly sexual comment. He had remembered my drink of choice, though.

"Thank you. I mean, you didn't have to do that." I wasn't sure if that was the right thing to say, but for some reason, his presence had my thoughts in a total jumble. Probably because the heat of his body was only inches away. Probably because the sexy curve of his smile and the glimmer in his eye had some sort of paralyzing effect on me, the way it probably did on most women.

Eli offered a little wave, pulling Darren's attentions away from me. "I'm Eli, in case you forgot."

"Good to see you again." Darren's touch fell away when he held out his hand, shaking Eli's. "You guys psyched for this trip or what?"

"Grand Cayman or bust!" Eli lifted his martini glass with a flourish, clinking it with Darren's brown beer bottle.

Eli took a drink and then frowned. A second later, he fished his phone out of his pocket, silenced its ringing, and pressed it to his ear. "Taylor, hang on," he shouted into the phone. He lifted a finger, letting me know he'd be back.

Darren moved into the space that Eli had occupied, resting his arm along the bar so it curved behind me. "Do you come here often?"

I almost choked on my drink. He didn't just ask me that.

He shot me a full smile, showing his straight white teeth. "That was a serious question, not a pickup line. I promise."

"Sure. Well... I *don't* come here often, but that will probably change in a couple of weeks when I move in with Eli. I'm taking over Maya's lease, so I'll be in this neighborhood more."

He nodded. "Are you happy about that?"

"I am. Eli is one of my best friends, and I didn't really like living alone. I think it'll be a good change for me. I work a lot, and Eli has a way of helping me put things into perspective, I guess. It'll be nice to live closer to Maya too. Since she left the firm, I feel like I never see her."

Silence fell, and I immediately replayed my words, hoping they didn't sound as awkward and desperate as I felt behind them. Work was my life, and my friends were everything to me. I missed Maya, and Eli and I had grown a lot closer since she'd moved in with Cameron. I twisted a lock of my hair between my fingertips and released a sigh. "Sorry. It's been kind of a stressful few months for me. Lots of things changing."

"I get it. Cameron's not the same either. I mean, he's my brother. We'll always be close, but it's definitely different now. Maya is his first priority."

"Cameron's a good guy."

"He's the best of us. Maya's lucky."

I caught a slight frown marring the space between his dark eyebrows.

"So is he," I countered. Maya may have been a handful, but Cameron had put her through hell when he walked away from his half-baked marriage proposal years ago. She'd held up okay, all things considered. In the end though, they were both better people for having found each other again and for giving their relationship another try.

Darren flashed me a small smile. "Fair enough." He leaned close again, even though I could hear him fine. "So where's your lucky guy?"

I shook my head and stared down into my drink. "No lucky guys for me." Only lucky guy in my world was David Reilly, and I couldn't wait to be a country away from him. I lifted my glass to my lips. The distinct flavors of olive, vinegar, and vodka swirled over my tongue, and the promise of relief from my day at his beck and call loosened some of the tension in my shoulders. I held back a sigh.

"Good?" Darren flicked his gaze from the drink, up and down the length of my body, and back up to my face.

When our eyes met, I remembered how beautiful his were all over again. Light brown with flecks of green. Mesmerizing. Disturbingly so.

"It's perfect, just how I like it. I can't believe you remembered. It's been a while." I licked my lips, convincing myself that he wasn't really checking me out.

The smile in his eyes softened, and something darker came over them. "I'm pretty sure I committed that whole night to permanent memory."

I didn't know what to say. I wasn't even bumbling. I was lost for words. Darren was obviously hitting on me in a way that he hadn't before, and I had no idea what to make of it. My physical body was screaming at me to say something, to touch him, to give him some indication of how he affected me. But my brain was too smart for that.

Just when I thought I'd never win the battle between throwing myself at this over-the-top sexy man and talking him to death about my stressed-out existence, Eli appeared through the doors of the bar and came up to me. A few paces behind him was the guy Darren had been talking to earlier. Up close he was even more impressive. Tall and lean, light brown skin, with eyes a cool gray-blue. He looked like he was of mixed descent, but I couldn't begin to guess what origins could combine to make such attractive features.

Darren turned toward him. "Vanessa, this is Ian Savo. We're both on Ladder 9."

"And I'm Eli." Eli shook Ian's hand.

"Good to meet you. You too, Vanessa. Heard a lot about you." He pivoted toward Darren. "I hate to interrupt, but there's someone I wanted you to meet. Can I pull you away for a minute?"

Darren frowned slightly before taking the last pull from his beer and straightening his body away from the bar. The movement put enough space between us that I felt the loss of his warmth.

"Sure thing." He offered me a tight smile that seemed to reflect my own disappointment. "I'll be back in a few, all right?"

I nodded without a word and watched him disappear with his friend. I couldn't help myself. Watching him walk away was like seeing the sun go down and feeling the heat go with it. I turned back to Eli, determined to put an end to my little internal pout. Eli was staring at his phone, reading a thread of texts.

"What did Taylor want?"

"He wants to hang out tonight. I told him I'm getting drunk with you instead. He wasn't pleased."

Taylor was Eli's on-again, off-again lover. They were keeping things "casual" since Taylor was a photographer and traveled so often. Only problem was Eli wasn't the casual type.

"Is he heading out of town?"

Eli nodded. "London."

He'd never admit it, but he was completely head over heels for Taylor and burned every time he left town, knowing he could be hooking up with someone else. The result was Eli retaliating at times like these, to send a message that he too could have his own fun, even though as far as I knew, he'd been loyal to the "boyfriend" who wasn't.

I sighed, wishing I could say something to make him feel better. "I'd let you off the hook, but then I'd be that desperate-looking girl all alone at the bar."

"No, fuck that. Friends don't let friends look desperate at bars. Speaking of, you up for another round?"

I popped the olive in my mouth and nodded. "Sure, I'm going to hit the ladies' room. I'll be right back."

I maneuvered through the crowd and found the line to the ladies' room mercifully short. I took care of business and, on my way back to Eli, noticed Darren on the other end of the barroom. He was with Ian and two other women. Ian had his hands all over a brunette nearly as tall as he was. Next to him, a petite blonde was hanging on Darren's muscled arm, laughing as he spoke into her ear over the noisy crowd around them.

As if sensing my presence, he looked up and our gazes clashed. Heat rushed to my cheeks and disappointment flooded me. I wasn't sure how many seconds had passed when I realized how stupid I must have looked, standing in the middle of the bar fixed on Darren and his harem. I averted my eyes and carried on toward Eli as quickly as I could, cursing myself. Darren Bridge was definitely every bit of the player I'd been warned about, and I was stupid to believe anything different.

As soon as I found Eli again, a loud voice came through the speakers mounted on the wall.

"Ladies and gentleman. It's the hour you've all been waiting patiently for. We're ready to hear your best karaoke jams. Grab a friend, pick a song. Step up. Don't be shy."

Without ceremony, I grabbed the fresh drink out of Eli's hand. A song I knew pumped out from the bar's speakers following the announcement. Suddenly, the lyrics seemed to live under my skin. The need to sing bubbled up through my pores, replacing the unexpected feelings Darren had inspired in me over the course of the night. I welcomed the shift and chased it through half of my chilled martini glass.

"Whoa, what's up?" Eli stared at me wide-eyed.

I pointed to his drink. "Drink up. That's our cue."

DARREN

My face hurt from fake-smiling at the blonde who kept eyeballing Ian's advances on her friend. I wanted to get back to Vanessa, but I didn't see that happening anytime soon. Then, as if the universe answered my silent request, she came into view again. Stepping up onto the small stage in the corner of the room, she radiated. Dark auburn hair and soft pink lips. I hadn't been able to take my eyes off of her, and I still couldn't.

Somehow, she was the last person I expected to be on the stage. With a microphone in her hand, she stood there, twisting and untwisting the cord around her hand. Eli was bouncing beside her like he couldn't fucking wait to get started.

I stilled, anxious to see how she would perform. I wanted her to see me, but at the same time, I didn't. I hadn't fully recovered from the look on her face when I'd seen her moments ago. She wasn't the first girl I'd had to put on the back burner for one reason or another. But I couldn't remember feeling like such a jerk for it until tonight. No doubt she thought I'd ditched her for blondie.

And I had.

Thanks to Ian. I could have castrated him for pulling me away. Most nights I didn't mind being his wingman, but I had blinders on tonight. All I could see was Vanessa. Fittingly, she was on stage, for everyone else to admire the way I was right now.

"Do you know her?" the blonde shouted in my ear.

I winced and nodded, never taking my eyes off of Vanessa. Had I really blown it with her so quickly?

All for the brunette Ian had a hard-on for tonight. Pretty girl, body like a runway model, voice that would peel paint off the wall, but I didn't figure he was interested in her conversational skills. He just needed me to keep her roommate occupied long enough to make a play.

I shouldn't have cared either way. Not like Vanessa was the first female who'd had a physical response when I was inches from her. I reveled in the way her cheeks caught color when I touched her. Those small subtle touches that were easy to brush off as casual, but in my world, were tactical as fuck. I knew Vanessa was off-limits, but the second I'd laid eyes on her across the bar, nothing could have kept me from going to talk to her. I'd shown incredible restraint last time we'd hung out. In fact, I couldn't remember wanting to take a woman to bed so damn bad and denying myself. New York City was my playground, and I rarely denied myself of its pleasures. I worked hard, and I fucked harder.

I grasped my beer tighter in my hand, imagining Vanessa

on the receiving end of that mantra.

Meanwhile, she held the microphone close to her mouth and stared at the ground in front of her. She looked different tonight. Not like she was out on the town. No tiny red dress, stilettos, and messy hair from all the dancing we did at the club. Tonight she looked how I imagined she must look any day of the week. Her hair was soft and natural. Dark jeans hugged her hips, and a loose-fitting shirt fell over one shoulder, baring a single black strap. I wanted to grab that little strap with my teeth and...

The noise of the bar died down enough to hear the upbeat melodic intro of the song, and I strained to recognize the tune. A few seconds later, she belted out the first verse, her eyes closed.

Jesus.

It was hot as blazes with all the people jammed in this place, but goose bumps still rippled over my skin. She was incredible. Eli's off-key chorus wasn't doing her any favors, but even he couldn't detract from the raw talent pouring from Vanessa.

What doesn't kill you makes you stronger, stronger!

Every line came through more powerful than the last. She wasn't making eye contact with anyone except Eli and the ground, but every word that left her lips made me believe she was feeling it. The nervous way she'd been minutes ago had vanished. She was someone else on the stage, and how would I have ever known?

Blondie started to tell me something, but I held up a hand, silencing her until Vanessa finished the last verse and the song faded out to a roar of applause.

"Goddamn, she can sing," Ian shouted above the hoots

and hollers.

Hell, yeah, she could.

I smiled, clapping and whistling as loud as I could.

CHAPTER THREE

DARREN

"Vanessa!"

She moved from the front of the line to the ticket counter. I bypassed the train of people waiting and came up beside her. The timing couldn't have been better, and for some reason, an odd sense of urgency spurred me.

After her karaoke stint the night before, I had tried to find her, to no avail. Ian had totally screwed me on that. Took an hour talking with blondie about her postgrad internship before the brunette finally agreed to take Ian home with her. Took another half hour to convince her roommate to join them in the fun, and by then Vanessa was nowhere to be found.

I went home alone and slept like shit. I should have brought the blonde home to calm my nerves, but I had a feeling it wouldn't have mattered. I couldn't get Vanessa's voice out of my head. Every time I closed my eyes, I saw her up there singing her heart out. I couldn't remember the last time I'd laid eyes on a woman and hadn't run her looks through some sort of mental hot-o-meter. Tall, short. Nice body, too much makeup. Sweet ass. The list of assets or lack thereof went on...

Vanessa wasn't like that. She was more than a list of features. She was...beautiful. Naturally beautiful with a body I couldn't wait to get my hands on and size up in a much more intimate way. She wasn't all made up and ready for the club like she'd been when we first met, but for some reason, that made me want to take her to bed all the more. She wasn't trying to impress me or be more than who she was. She was...real. Real and disconnected enough from the scene that I'd been working for so long that maybe I couldn't help but be entranced by her.

She widened her eyes when I came up beside her. They were pretty, like the rest of her. A mix of color, pale green the most prominent.

"Do you mind?"

"No, of course not." She shifted her gaze away from me, setting her passport up on the counter.

"Are there any upgrades for two?" I asked. I shot the woman behind the counter a smile. *Curvy, older bottle blonde.*

She blinked a few times before looking down at her computer and tapping keys. "Let me see. Well, actually you're in luck."

"Darren, I can't—" Vanessa shook her head.

"It's fine. I'll get it." I reached for my wallet and tossed the woman my credit card.

Vanessa started fumbling with her own wallet. "I can't let you do that."

"It's four hours to George Town. I need a strong drink and good company. You'll be doing me an incredible favor by letting me."

She began to protest again, and I pressed a finger to her lips. Full and the lightest shade of pink, like a dusky sunset.

"I insist," I said.

I dropped my hand slowly, and when her bottom lip disappeared between her teeth, my dick noticed. Goddamn, I wanted to taste her. I blinked away the brief but potent vision of all the ways I could use those lips. And the soft pink tongue that darted out over them.

The bottle blonde handed us our tickets, and we hurried toward the gate where they were already boarding. I put our carry-ons into the luggage compartment, gave Vanessa the window seat in our first-class row, and we settled in. The flight attendant took a pass up the aisle.

"Can I get you a beverage, sir?"

I offered a tight smile and looked her up and down because I couldn't fucking help myself. *Killer lips. Stacked. Engagement ring.* Or according to her shiny name tag, *Ann*.

"Bloody Mary, please."

She lingered until I broke away and she looked to Vanessa.

"Ma'am?" she asked sweetly.

"Coffee, please."

When she left, Vanessa closed her eyes, resting her head back against the seat. Ann brought our drinks, but still Vanessa stayed quiet. Something had shifted between us, and I was pretty sure I knew what it was. I cleared my throat, trying to figure out how I was going to do this.

"Listen, Vanessa, I'm sorry about last night."

She lifted an eyebrow. "What are you sorry about?"

I ran my teeth over my lower lip, gauging her words, her mood. She seemed tired, and if I didn't know better, disinterested. I decided to go with some version of the truth.

"I didn't mean to ditch you at the bar. Ian wanted to talk to some girl. I didn't realize—"

"You don't need to apologize. Seriously."

She waved her hand, like it meant nothing at all, but I knew better. At least I hoped I did.

"I wanted to stay and talk to you. I looked for you, but you were gone."

She reached into her purse, grabbing her phone and earbuds. Shit, I was losing this battle a lot quicker than I'd anticipated.

"The truth is I wanted to get to know you a lot better the first night we hung out, but..."

"But what?" She pursed her lips together. Her red hair lit up with the bright morning sky shining in through our window. I couldn't help but wonder if she was red anywhere else. Now definitely wasn't the time to tease about cuffs matching the collar though.

I shot her a smile that I hoped would get her to relax. "But the truth is, I was told that you were off-limits."

That comment earned a small smile, though she tried to hide it by looking out the window. "Really," she said, though she didn't sound at all surprised by my admission.

"Cam didn't think it would be a good idea for me to pursue anything with you if it complicated things with Maya. I respected his wishes, very begrudgingly."

She turned, meeting my gaze. "And what's changed?"

I frowned. "They're getting married. Not an issue anymore."

"She's still my friend, and you're still Cam's brother."

I laughed and looked up at the ceiling. The seat belt sign was on. I had her captive for the next four hours. I could do this.

"There's got to be a statute of limitations on this sort of thing. We're adults. I think we can figure it out on our own, don't you?"

She stared down at her hands, picking at her fingernail and ignoring her steaming coffee. "Darren, I'm pretty sure I'm not your type."

I shook my head. "Completely untrue. Any man with a brain and who isn't dead below the waist would consider you his type, trust me."

Her cheeks turned pink, but she didn't soften. "I think Maya was probably right to not want us getting involved."

I nodded slowly, and Cam's earlier warning to stay away from Vanessa echoed in my ears. For some reason, it hadn't occurred to me that Maya would have issued the same warning to Vanessa. If she knew about me, she knew I didn't get involved with anyone.

"You know that just motivates a guy like me, right?" I tried to keep my tone light, but the challenge was spurring me almost as much as my attraction to Vanessa. Maybe it was a bad bet, but I didn't like the idea of my reputation getting ahead of me. "Plus, who's talking about getting involved? Nothing says we can't have fun and enjoy each other's company as friends."

I'd used that line before. It meant physical benefits with no strings and possibly no future at all, not even as friends. That's what I wanted, right? Make things a little interesting on the island, and Vanessa was exactly who I wanted to make that happen. Except she wasn't talking. She could hardly look me in the eye.

She twirled the stir straw through her coffee, staring at the swirls it made instead of me. "I'm sure you'll make plenty of friends while you're there."

I wanted to bristle at the comment, but I had no right. A hint of sarcasm laced her words, but there was something else in her voice that I couldn't pin. Disappointment, maybe?

The glimmer in her eye when I met her at the bar had vanished the second she saw me with Ian's twosome, and ever since then, she'd seemed to see right through me. Every line. Every play. Anyone else, I wouldn't have given it another thought. But for some reason, the guilt niggled at me. I was trying to make a play on a girl who was too smart for that bullshit.

Ten minutes later, Ann took our emptied drinks and Vanessa finally chanced a look my way. "I don't know about you, but I could use some sleep. I'm always restless the night before a trip. I slept terrible last night."

My jaw was tight, but I forced a polite smile. "Yeah, me too."

She crossed her legs, leaning away from me. Reaching for her earbuds again, she put them into place and closed her eyes.

I couldn't take my eyes off of her. I studied the small movements of her chest. Her breathing had slowed, and her eyelashes fluttered against her cheeks every so often. She was falling asleep. That's how riveted she was with my advances.

Maybe Cam was right and Vanessa had me pegged. Maybe I was incapable of getting to know a girl without the singular motivation of wanting to fuck her senseless.

Goddamn, but for the first time in a long time, I wanted to be someone better than the man Vanessa thought I was.

VANESSA

I switched out my yoga pants and T-shirt from the plane in favor of shorts and a tank top. I fluffed my hair and applied a little makeup, hoping it didn't melt right off my face when I stepped back out into the heat and humidity. I'm not sure why I bothered, but I wasn't sure who would be showing up at the beach barbecue.

Still unsatisfied with the vision staring back at me in the mirror, I went through three more outfits before settling on the first one I'd picked. My summer wardrobe had been lacking since I'd left home and moved up north. But that's not why nothing looked right.

Darren's handsome face flashed in my mind. I shouldn't care, but I did. I couldn't get him out of my head. He'd even crept into my dreams this morning, and waking up flushed next to the object of my unconscious desires was more than a little awkward.

I wasn't thrilled that he'd ditched me to chat up another girl at the bar, but I was more upset with myself for hoping for a minute that he was a man who would act any differently. His apology sounded sincere, but Darren was a player, and likely a good one. I didn't want to be the next girl who played right into his hands. I also didn't want to get hurt.

The truth was that Darren, on the outside, was a dream come true. A woman would have to be blind not to want him for herself. He was gorgeous, charming, and smart enough not to let any of the likely hundreds of women he'd taken to bed tie him down.

The physical attraction was real, no doubt. I could handle that. I hadn't been living a life of celibacy, but I wasn't going to be a conquest for someone who got around as much I suspected Darren did.

"Oh my God, I feel a thousand times better." Eli emerged from the shower in a fluffy white robe that seemed to swallow him up. "You look nice."

I smiled, grateful because Eli wouldn't lie to me if I looked terrible. "Thanks."

He moseyed to his suitcase and riffled through his clothes.

"How was first class with Casanova? He indoctrinate you into the mile-high club up there? You've been glowing like a candle since we saw him the other night."

I laughed. "Not even close. I'm sure he wished he could get his money back for the upgrade. I crashed as soon as we took off."

Eli stood up straight and tossed a black T-shirt and some denim cutoffs on one of the beds. "He seems like a persistent guy. I'm sure he's not done with you yet."

I had a nagging feeling that Eli was right, and if I was being honest with myself, I didn't want Darren to give up on pursuing me either. Crazy as that was...I was rebuffing his advances and wanting them all at once, which wasn't really fair.

Darren would be Cameron's best man, and I was Maya's maid of honor. I was going to have to figure out what I really wanted to have go down with Darren. Especially if I was going to survive the next week opposite him in all things wedding-party related. Before I could get into it any further with Eli, a knock sounded at the door.

Eli disappeared into the bathroom again with his clothes, and I went to the door. The second I opened it, Maya bounded across the threshold. I squealed and opened my arms for a big hug from my beautiful friend. I hadn't seen her in a few days, and with all the wedding prep, she'd been too busy for our regular lunches. I missed her and was all the happier to be here now, celebrating with her and enjoying some time to catch up.

"I'm so happy you're here," she said.

"Me too." When I pulled away, I noticed she wasn't alone. "Hi, Olivia."

If the Bridge brothers were dashing, their sister was the female equivalent. Dark brown hair and striking blue eyes that matched the cold way she treated Maya most days. Maya insisted they'd warmed up to each other the past couple of months, but whenever I was with them to coordinate bridesmaid details, Olivia had been short and to the point. Maybe a few days on a tropical island would loosen the stick up her ass. As long as she didn't mess with Maya's happiness and her big day, I'd deal with her frigid attitude and share my time with Maya when I had to. Like now.

Olivia smiled tightly, lifting her shoulders. "You made it."

"We thought we'd pick you up on our way to the barbecue." Maya glanced around the hotel room. "Where's Eli?"

"Present!" He emerged again with a grand sweep of his arm.

I laughed. Eli was somehow even more adorable and out of place than he usually was. His ghostly white legs were stark against his jean shorts. He had a twinkle in his eyes, and I sensed the sarcasm just waiting to break free at the first opportunity.

He hugged Maya, and after a few minutes, our small group made our way toward the beach where the festivities had already started. The sun had set, the air balmy and warm. In the distance, steel drums chimed and a little thrill went through me. The sweet sounds of vacation.

Maya hooked her arm with mine as we walked. "So how does it feel to be a free woman?"

No one knew my work hell like Maya did. Lucky for her, she'd escaped the world of suits and finance.

I took a deep breath, inhaling all the smells of my new environment. Spices and salt air and a hint of chlorine from the clear blue infinity pool we passed. "It feels...pretty awesome." Truth.

Briefly, I wondered how Reilly was going to survive without me on Monday morning. Then I promptly tossed the thought away. Not now. Not this week.

"How does it feel to know you're going to be a married woman in a couple days?"

"Feels right, in every way."

The glittering sunlight coming off the ocean waves shimmered in Maya's eyes. Something apart from her usual quiet excitement about the wedding passed over her expression. Maybe worry, or maybe a twinge of sadness. I couldn't know for sure, and I didn't want to ask and give whatever it was more energy.

I hugged her arm a little tighter. "You okay?"

She smiled quickly. "I've never been happier. I can't wait to be Cameron's wife. Honestly."

I was more excited for her to tie the knot than I'd ever expected to be. Maya deserved happiness, and I had no doubts that Cameron would be the knight in shining armor she needed. A rock, a place to call home.

I wanted a happily ever after for her, even as the headstrong person in me disputed whether marrying the man of your dreams in your twenties should be a goal for a woman of her talent and education. Half my friends back home had families already, but that wasn't me. I had a career, even if it felt like purgatory, and I lived in the greatest city in the world. I had a plan and a long way to go before I could slow down and think about how to achieve domestic bliss.

"Are you nervous?"

Maya shook her head. "Not really. I could marry Cameron tonight and I think it would feel like the most natural thing in the world. I already feel like we're married."

"You belong together."

She stared down our feet making a path through the soft sand. "Deep down, I've known that for a long time."

Other people staying at the hotel milled around the beach, but a small group of familiar faces gathered by the band. Nearby tables were set out with trays of food. Hints of spices and cooked meats wafted through the air.

I fixed on the two men standing several feet away, seemingly lost in conversation. Darren and Cameron were showstoppers in a crowd of fairly average-looking people. Gods among the masses. They were wearing even less clothing than usual, and I couldn't stop myself from sizing up Darren's physique, an occupation that I could probably devote several hours to each day. His biceps strained against the hem of his green T-shirt, and his calves were strong and sinewy, proof of the no doubt countless hours he'd devoted to his body at the gym. The overall result was a work of art.

"Maya."

A woman's voice interrupted my thoughts. The woman was Maya's future mother-in-law.

"Diane." Maya cleared her throat and gave me a tight look.

Oh. This was Diane Bridge.

"This is Vanessa. Vanessa, this is Diane Bridge, Cam's mom."

"It's good to meet you." I held out my hand.

She lifted her hand slowly and took mine, her gaze traveling the length of me as she did. Her careful appraisal felt nothing like Darren's. I stood awkwardly, waiting for her to say something. She let my hand fall after a moment and shifted her assessment between Maya and me for a moment.

"Vanessa is the maid of honor. Remember, I mentioned

her," Olivia chimed in.

I could see now where Olivia got her ice princess tendencies. Her mother carried an air of superiority that could not be missed. I was surprised it didn't knock people over when they passed her in the street. Still, she was beautiful and unmistakably elegant. I'd never seen someone look so refined on a beach in eighty-degree heat.

"Hey, beautiful." Darren came to my side, a welcome presence.

Diane frowned, and Olivia's eyes widened. The way they looked at me and the heavy judgment that poured from Darren's mother made me feel anything but beautiful in that moment.

"Mom." He leaned in and gave Diane a polite kiss on the cheek.

Her hard expression softened. A crack in her armor. Maybe she did have a heart in there somewhere.

"Where's Dad?" Darren asked.

She glanced over his shoulder. "Frank is arranging some tours for us this week. You know he can never sit still."

"Cool. Well, if you don't mind, I need to steal Vanessa."

"Do you?" Her voice was even cooler, and her perfectly plucked brow lifted a fraction.

"Important wedding party business." He shot her his dazzling smile.

I smiled and let him take my hand. Relief, warmth, and a giddiness I couldn't ignore coursed through me as he led us away. I glanced back, grateful that Cameron was doing the same now with Maya, and I hadn't completely abandoned her.

"Thank you," I whispered.

Darren smirked and threaded his fingers tighter into

mine. "You're welcome. I couldn't stand there and watch that much longer."

"Your mom...she's a little intense." I hesitated over the words. I didn't want to insult his mother. But I had a feeling "intense" was a kind word. In an instant, she'd made me feel so small and unworthy in her presence, as if she'd had a bird's-eye view of every insecurity I'd ever had.

He laughed. "You don't have to spare my feelings. She's my mom, but she's a freight train of judgment. I have enemies I wouldn't want to subject to her."

"Why is she so...cold?"

"I don't know." He winced, like something unpleasant had crossed his mind. "You hungry?" We'd meandered near the tables catered with food.

"A little." Several trays were piled with meats that were almost unrecognizable with all the spices caked on them. The smells stirred my faint hunger. Next to them were an array of fruits and pretty desserts cut into small pieces. I made a small plate for myself and took a bite out of one of the desserts first. Coconut and a fruit I'd never had. I moaned a little. Yummy.

"God, you're pretty."

I caught Darren staring intently at me. Something about the look in his eye, more wonder than seduction, had my heart skipping a beat. I warmed, and suddenly the tropical heat had become too much. Would I ever get used to Darren's compliments? Not likely. Still, I could spend a week listening to them, definitely. I didn't know what to say though. Thank you? I swallowed my dessert over the little knot that had formed in my throat. Being around Darren was doing things to my body, no doubt about it.

I stared down at my plate, my thoughts taking dangerous

turns. Seconds passed and no words would form. My hands wanted to do the talking, but deep down I knew that was a terrible idea.

"Darren..."

"Come on, dance with me," he said.

I caught my lip between my teeth and sized up the area around the band. Diane's unimpressed attitude wasn't making me want to put on a display with Darren. If her aim was to discourage me away from her son, she was doing a great job.

"No one's dancing," I said.

"Not yet. That's where you and I come in." He caught my hand and pulled me toward the music. "Come on, then. Let's show them how it's done."

CHAPTER FOUR

DARREN

The reggae playing didn't lend itself to any kind of beat that I was used to, so I pulled Vanessa close to me and we swayed together in a rhythm that was ours. I had to do something because watching her put exotic fruits in her mouth was giving me too many inappropriate thoughts. I was ready to kiss her, to taste whatever delights were on her tongue. I wanted to kiss her right now, but that was impossible. We were on display. Then Maya and Cameron joined us. Cameron's military pals and their kids posted up around us...watching, talking, drinking too much.

Vanessa sighed and settled against me. She fit nicely in my arms, like she'd been there many times, like she could easily belong there.

I caught a glimpse of my mother's face on our next turn. She was shooting me a look that was as predictable as it was irritating. Some of us thought we were here to witness two families coming together in holy matrimony. Not Diane. I knew better. She was losing one son this week. The idea, however unlikely, that she could lose me to Vanessa now was probably sending her into a full-blown tailspin.

I couldn't bring myself to care. I'd stopped caring about what she and Frank wanted a long time ago. My brother and sister had followed suit in their own time. One by one, they'd opted not to live under the superficial and unrealistic expectations that our parents had grown to believe were normal—white-collar jobs, debutante dating, country clubs.

Fuck all that. I wanted to *live*.

"What are you thinking about?"

I considered Vanessa's question a moment, wondering how I could explain what had happened to our family over the past fifteen years. Did I even know?

I tightened my hold on her and searched her thoughtful eyes. "I was thinking about you," I fibbed, but quickly turned it into the truth. One look at Vanessa and she'd stolen every thought. I'd been with plenty of beautiful women, but had anyone ever captivated me this way? I searched and came up with nothing, and I was suddenly compelled to know why. What was it about her that drew me to her this way?

She laughed. "Yeah, right."

"No, right now I'm thinking I want to know everything about you. Which is lucky because we've got the whole week together."

"Why am I suddenly so interesting to you?"

I didn't know how to answer that truthfully. I hadn't been able to stop thinking about her for the better part of the last twenty-four hours. Already I knew she wasn't like anyone else. Still, she looked genuinely perplexed. God, she really had no idea what she did to men.

I was determined to figure her out, and I was determined to get her under me.

"I think there's a lot more to you than meets the eye. Believe me, everything that meets the eye is driving me fucking nuts, but I want more. I want to see everything else."

She was quiet a moment. "From what I know, that seems unlike you."

I stared at her silently, not liking this reputation thing that kept coming between us. A little voice in my head told me I should let her off the hook. Like she said, I could make plenty of friends on this trip. But I couldn't bring myself to give up that easily. I wanted to know Vanessa, and I wasn't going to let my past get in the way.

"You know what? You've got a past too. I'm guessing you've got a life with some shadows that maybe you'd rather not see the light. How about we forget all that? For the next few days, let's just be us, without all the baggage. Let me get to know you, Vanessa, and I'll do my best to let you get to know me too."

"Okay."

Relief settled in my shoulders.

She took a breath, seeming resigned to the proposition, and simultaneously giving me a new spark of hope. I had a feeling she might have been overthinking her decision to devote any amount of time to me on this vacation. She'd be wise to, but I was determined to keep her talking.

"You want to go for a walk? Get away from all the prying eyes?"

After one glance in my mother's direction, she returned her attention to me with a tight smile and a quick nod. "Sure."

Together we walked away from the party and down to the water. The sky had gone from pink and purple to a deep magical blue that matched the darkened waves crashing gently at our feet.

I threaded my hand into hers and she didn't protest. Good sign, I thought, but also there was something comforting about the simple connection that had nothing to do with the great sex I hoped it would eventually lead to.

"So tell me about you. I want to know the real Vanessa Hawkins."

"I wish I had an epic tale for you, but my story really isn't anything special."

"I find that hard to believe. The woman I met at the club months ago worked a million hours a week and danced her ass off every weekend. I want to know that one who sings karaoke like a pro. Where'd you learn to sing like that? I've never heard anything like it."

"My mom. I never had voice lessons, but she and my dad were both musicians, so I guess it's in my blood. We didn't have much when I was growing up. For a while, we didn't even have a TV, so my mom and I would sing songs she'd learned on the road. She'd play her guitar and teach me the lyrics."

"So why are you working on Wall Street with a voice like that?"

She shrugged, her focus narrowing toward the melting colors of the sunset ahead. "I love to sing. Don't get me wrong. But it's not something to pin my future on. Didn't really work out so great for my mom."

"Why is that?"

"When my parents were still together, they were on the road a lot. Toured at different little clubs and bars all over the country. That kind of life wasn't really conducive to parenthood, so when my mom got pregnant, it came as a bit of a surprise. Her last stop on the tour was a little bar outside of Pensacola, not far from Callaway where I grew up. My mom was eight-and-a-half months pregnant, so she came home to her parents. My dad said he'd come back after a few more shows to be with her. He never came back."

"You never met him?"

"No, I've met him a few times, in New York when he was coming through town. He's a fun guy. Very charismatic. Talented too. I've seen him play a couple shows."

"So you get along. That's great."

She shrugged. "Sure. Talking to him is like talking to a friendly acquaintance. I know he's my father, but I don't think I feel the way I'm supposed to about him. The relationship we have is very casual. Disconnected in a way that doesn't bother me as much as maybe it should. That's weird to say, but he was never around. He has no idea how to be a parent. I guess I just accept that."

"Sounds kind of refreshing. Maybe Diane and Frank can pick up a few tips."

"Were you ever close with your parents?"

"Yeah, way back. Way, *way* back. I think I was nine when we started to see less of my dad. We moved out of the city but he commuted in. The more he worked, seemed like the less happy my mom was. For some reason it didn't bring us any closer, but Cam and Liv and I sort of bonded together from that point."

She leaned into me a little. "Seems like there's been tension between them and Cam, from what Maya's told me."

"Oh, yeah. They're uptight with too much money on their hands. The way my dad sees it, he worked as hard as he did so Cameron, Liv, and I could have the best of everything. Go to the best schools, marry into the wealthiest families, get the best jobs an Ivy League network can buy, and on and on and on."

"Doesn't sound like a bad life."

"It doesn't. But it's their life. Not mine." I couldn't hide the spite in my tone.

Why be a firefighter when I could be a banker? Why live in the heart of Brooklyn when I could have a house in the Hamptons? True enough, some people would give their left nut for the life of privilege that Frank Bridge wanted to give us. What those people didn't see was how the light left my mother's eyes a little more every weekend he stayed away working on a deal or schmoozing some new client. He lived and breathed work, and for my mother, no amount of vodka could replace the husband who'd left her to raise a family and keep up with the image of a banker's wife. For as long as I could remember, I'd wanted to be as far away from that life and lifestyle as I could get.

While my mind spun, Vanessa had grown silent beside me. I gave her hand a little squeeze.

"Truth is, I've never felt comfortable wearing boat shoes. I'd look terrible on a yacht."

Her jaw fell a fraction. "Your parents have a yacht?"

"No. Plenty of their friends do though. Keeping them staffed can be a chore, I hear."

We both laughed at that, and the sound instantly lightened the heaviness that had fallen with the subject of my family. Her natural beauty was amplified with the smile she wore. Sweet and genuine.

I wanted to see that more. She'd been so guarded with me since that night at the bar. I resolved then to keep her smiling on this trip.

We walked in silence for a few minutes. We were close enough to the party that the dim beat of the music could still be heard, but the nightfall had given us some privacy. I wouldn't have her devoted attention for too much longer.

"Tell me something about you that no one else knows."

"Like what?"

"A secret. An embarrassing story. A weird habit."

She smiled again, all the way to her eyes. "Why on earth would I tell you?"

"We're getting to know each other. Come on. There's got to be something."

A secretive smile curved her lips.

"What have you got?"

She shook her head several times. "No. Nothing. I can't tell you that."

"Spill it."

"Forget it. I'll think of something else."

I stopped walking, twirled her around, and brought her back into my arms. Why did she feel so perfect there? Like she fit just right, her lean torso molding to mine, her breasts soft against me. Her smile faded, and the quickening pulse at her neck caught my eye. She licked her lips, a little movement that didn't seem intentionally seductive at all. But I couldn't help but think about all the other ways we would fit. Of course, there was only one way to find out.

"Listen, you're stuck on an island with me. Like it or not, you need to get used to having me around interrogating you."

"It's a big island." A hint of a smile played at her lips.

I slid my palms up the sides of her ribcage, trying to memorize the feel of her. "Run, and I'll find you." My tone was a little more threatening than I'd intended. It was true though.

She licked her lips again and averted her eyes. If I held her much closer, she'd feel exactly what that little movement was doing to me.

"How about this? Tell me, or I'll kiss you."

She narrowed her eyes. "You wouldn't."

"I absolutely would. Right here, right now. Do you have any idea how badly I want to taste you?"

Her breath seemed to cease completely. She stared up at me, lips parted. Those pretty green orbs so open and asking. I pulled her closer, so her hips touched mine. I wouldn't mind keeping her this way all night, in fact. I had to figure out a way to keep her close this week. Call it the player in me. I was determined to win her over. For the sake of my increasingly evident physical needs, but also because I actually wanted to show her I could be more... More than what?

"So 'fess up. What is it?" Last chance. I traced her bottom lip with my thumb, counting down the seconds until I could have my mouth on it, nipping and sucking. Damn, I wanted to figure out what drove her crazy more than anything else.

"I still sleep with a teddy bear."

She said the words so quietly I barely heard them.

I laughed, and her pretty pink mouth turned down into a pout.

"I'm sorry, red. That's a good one."

She slapped my arm and tried to pull away, but I wouldn't let her. I liked her close like this.

"Fine. Do *you* have any deep dark secrets you want to tell a complete stranger?"

I could see now I'd opened Pandora's box. I'd have to maneuver this one carefully. I gave her my best innocent face. "No secrets here. I'm an open book."

"That's not fair. You need to tell me something." She trailed her fingertips over my forearms.

I leaned down, whispering in her ear, "I've got a weakness for redheads."

"That does *not* count."

"Sorry, red. I've got nothing. Nothing that can beat sleeping with a teddy bear anyway."

She was quiet, but I knew she wasn't mad anymore.

"I'll kiss you," she threatened.

"I dare you to."

"I will. Two can play this game, you know."

Her eyebrows went high, but I knew I could beat this girl at poker any night of the week.

"Then do it." The taunt left me, but I'd decided that second I wasn't going to wait for her to follow through on that empty threat. Her hands, once soft against my shoulders, tightened. If I could get her alone, I'd be making her tight everywhere. I groaned at the thought, and all my better judgment flew out the window. I sifted my fingers through her hair and angled her for a kiss she'd never forget, so close I could smell the coconut on her breath.

"Darren! Buddy!"

I cursed and tore myself away from Vanessa's half-lidded gaze. One of Cameron's military friends was trudging through the sand and coming our way. Clearly, he couldn't recognize that I was far too busy for a reunion.

"Darren!"

Jeffrey's voice was like a fucking megaphone. He must have had hearing loss from all the gunfire when he was overseas with Cameron. "Man, I haven't seen you in ages. What the hell have you been up to?"

"I'll let you two catch up." Vanessa's voice was quiet as she stepped away.

"No, stay."

I reached for her, but Jeffrey slapped his hand into mine

and then slapped me hard on the back at the same time.

Before I could argue, she was backing away. Lifting her fingers to her lips, she blew me a kiss.

VANESSA

I shouldn't have done that. Blowing Darren a kiss was stupid because now it hung in the air between us like an IOU, and I had a feeling Darren wouldn't be forgiving the debt. With him, a kiss wasn't a kiss. It was a gateway drug into sleeping with him, and already I couldn't get the possibility out of my head. He'd crept into my dreams again, and suddenly I was wound tighter than I'd been in months, maybe years. I had several more days on the island, and chances were good that, at this rate, I'd end up in his bed.

Was that such a terrible thing? If his bed was anything like mine, it was soft and luxurious and smelled like the tropical flowers they put in our rooms every afternoon. Add the scent of Darren, and I was a goner. I might never leave.

Hooking up with Darren wasn't the problem. What worried me more were the stirrings I was already feeling around him—feelings that made me long for more, something that maybe had been missing from my life for too long.

But Darren wasn't on the market for *more,* and nothing with him would last for long. Didn't change the fact that one look at him made my ovaries hurt. Every time he shot me that perfect smile of his, the small-town girl in me wanted to cook him dinner and press his shirts for the rest of my life. For the first time in a very long time, that insane thought almost seemed worth considering. Except that domestic fantasy wasn't what he wanted, and that definitely wasn't what I moved seven hundred miles from home to do.

In a private room off the main dining area, our group of guests had gathered for a late breakfast. I scanned the long tables set with colorful juices, fresh flower arrangements, and clean white tablecloths. I found Eli and Maya and quickly placed myself between them.

A server poured me a steaming cup of coffee, and I knew the instant Darren had joined the party. He paused at the entryway when I met his gaze. I could feel his eyes on me like a sunray. Warm, and not entirely unwelcome. Still, I shifted my focus back to small talk with Eli, forcing myself to think about planning our day with Maya. Darren had overrun my thoughts, but I had a long day planned and I hadn't penciled him in anywhere. Spa activities with Maya and the girls and Eli, and the guys were going fishing or something. Maybe a good activity-filled day away from him would cool down this raging attraction I felt for the man.

After breakfast, I wandered to the balcony to admire the view. Turquoise waters lapped up on the soft sandy beach dotted with blue-and-white beach chairs. Paradise. The object of a lot of daydreaming lately, and here I was, a distracted mess. Every peaceful moment was shaken up with thoughts of Darren.

As much as my brain shouted at me to be careful, I'd wanted Darren to kiss me last night. Hell, I wanted him to stop talking to his cousins and come kiss me right now. I wanted to be back in his arms, a place that gave me more comfort than I'd ever expected.

We barely knew each other, but being near him felt right. And for some inexplicable reason, he was trying to get to know me. Maybe it was all an act, a good play by a master player. A warm breeze kissed my bare shoulders, and I closed my eyes, caring less and less.

Cameron came by my side. He was tall and thickly built, the same as Darren. They shared some features, but they were so different. Cameron was so serious. The only times I'd seen him smile were with Maya. They lit up near each other, like two halves that needed each other to become whole.

"How are you doing?"

I lifted my mimosa and gestured toward the gorgeous view. "Could be worse. This place is amazing. Great choice."

He leaned down and rested his forearms on the railing. "We thought so too. It's very tranquil here, this little spot." He was quiet a moment.

"How about you? Cold feet?"

He didn't appear to be in a joking mood. He barely cracked a smile. "Not a chance."

"Figured as much."

"Have you been able to talk with Maya much lately?"

"Not a lot, I guess. Eli, Olivia...you know, there's always someone around. Why, what's up?"

He straightened, and the seriousness of his expression had me concerned.

"I was wondering... Can you try to talk to her today? She's close to you."

"She's closer to you."

"Something is off. I don't know what it is, and every time I try to bring it up, she brushes me off and changes the subject to something about the wedding. I don't know if it's nerves or what, but I'm worried about her."

"I'm sure there's nothing to be concerned about, but I'll talk to her. Probably just pre-wedding jitters, you know."

"I hope that's all it is. I want tomorrow to be perfect for her. She deserves it. If there's something else bothering her, I want to address it now. I don't want anything getting in the way of giving her the perfect day. God knows she deserves this one day to go right."

I nodded and touched his shoulder. "I'll talk to her. In the meantime, try not to worry. Today's your last day as a bachelor. Enjoy it."

"I'll guarantee he does."

I sensed Darren's warmth behind me before his voice broke into my conversation with Cameron. We both turned toward him. Cameron's intensity seemed to soften in Darren's presence. He was so carefree. I envied that, and I wanted to be near it. Like a moth to a flame, his energy drew me in every time. Even knowing the feeling couldn't last forever, I felt that little bubble of giddiness rising inside me again.

Cameron eyed him steadily. "You better not have anything crazy planned for today."

"How crazy can things get on a fishing charter?" Darren winked at me. "How about you, red? Have any strippers lined up for this afternoon?"

I couldn't help but laugh. Not Maya's style at all. Not to mention the fact that we'd be hard-pressed to find strippers whose hotness rivaled Cameron's and Darren's. "I'm afraid not. Manicures and massages are about as wild as we're getting today."

"Glad to hear it," Cameron grumbled.

Darren's beautiful eyes scorched my skin, and the air around us grew warm. The way he looked at me seemed too intimate for present company.

"Me too. Wouldn't want you getting too distracted."

"He's not bothering you, is he?"

A deep frown marred Darren's brow as he shifted to glaring at his brother. Cameron met his glare and then looked back to me.

Was Darren bothering me? Well, yes. But I'd sooner throw myself into traffic than ask someone to stop his advances.

"Of course not," I said. I straightened out the collar of Darren's shirt. "You know Darren. He's the perfect gentleman."

That got Cameron to crack a smile, but the tension between them lingered. I caught a glimpse of Maya chatting with Diane and Olivia again, so I figured I'd get on my way.

"You two have fun today. Hope you catch lots of fish. Don't fall off the boat, okay?"

Darren's jaw was still tight, but he'd relaxed a little. "Give me a little credit," he murmured, gently grasping my arm as I passed.

I glanced up into his eyes. That quickly I was at risk of losing any semblance of control being this close to him. Close enough to feel his energy. An invisible current pulsed between us. I felt it in places I wished I didn't.

"You'll have to earn it," I whispered, leaving him before my legs failed me.

DARREN

"What the fuck was that?"

Cameron pivoted away. "Stop taking yourself so seriously. It doesn't suit you."

I leaned in. "You think because you're getting married tomorrow that I won't bust your nose for being an asshole? Think again, Cam."

Cameron smirked and nudged me back a step. "Someone needs to say it. You going after someone like her is like watching a lion go after a gazelle on National Geographic. You know as well as I do she doesn't have a chance."

I couldn't rightly argue with him. I'd set my sights on Vanessa, and I had every intention of having her. All the signs pointed to success. The physical attraction was real, and the more time we spent together, the stronger it grew. I'd never once considered that we wouldn't sleep together on this trip. Before long, unless I did something really fucked up and unforgivable, she'd give in to me.

What business that was of my brother's was another matter.

"Why the hell would you care?"

"Because she's Maya's best friend. I told you to back off before. I didn't expect to have to remind you again."

"Listen, I was good." I jabbed my finger into his chest. "I played nice like you asked. Time's up."

"Not enough pretty girls on this island? You have to go for her again?"

"She's a fucking ten, and I want her."

He shook his head, glanced over to Maya, and back to the expansive ocean horizon. "You ever ask yourself why? Why does this one mean so much that you need to bed her and leave her more than all the others? Haven't you played this routine out enough?"

I ground my teeth down. "I know you love Maya and want to settle down and have a million babies, but fuck, what's with the judgment? This is my life."

He was silent. I wanted him to say more, argue with me some more. But he didn't give me anything else to work with.

"I... Listen, I want to be..." I shoved a hand through my hair and closed my eyes. Vanessa was there in my mind, smiling at me with those luscious lips. She was vibrant, a goddamn wet dream for any man. Why wouldn't I want her? The fact that some guy hadn't already stolen her heart and walked her down the aisle was a goddamn miracle. The mere thought of someone else claiming her for his own spurred something primal in me, an inexplicable need to make her mine.

"You want to be what?" Cameron was leaning against the balcony rail, his arms crossed.

I straightened slowly. "She knows my number, all right? If anything happens between us, she's going into it knowing I'm a bad fucking bet. And, maybe because of that, I want to show her I'm worth the risk."

"You mean she's more of a challenge now that you're working with a handicap. Nice."

"No!" I growled. I could have sucker-punched him.

Cameron snorted air through his nose and stared at me in silent challenge.

"I just want to see where things go. We're getting to know each other. That's not something I usually make time for. So who knows? Maybe there's a chance we'll see more of each other after this trip."

He shook his head with a sigh. "Whatever. She's an adult, so I guess she can make her own choices. I'd just like to see you not be so selfish with a woman for a change. If you're intent on getting Vanessa into bed, I'd like to see her be the one you give a fighting chance. That's all I'm going to say about it."

"Fine. You've made your point. Can we get drunk and go fishing now?"

"Sure."

"Prick," I muttered.

CHAPTER FIVE

VANESSA

After a lengthy massage, a French manicure, and more champagne than I needed in my already relaxed state, I found a spot beside Maya. She was lounging under an umbrella by one of the resort's pools. I hadn't had a chance to catch her alone all afternoon, and even now I hesitated to pry at Cameron's bidding.

"Come sit." Maya motioned to the lounge chair beside her.

I took the invitation and made myself comfortable. My muscles went lax. "That massage was killer."

"Agreed. The staff here is amazing."

"I never want to leave."

She smiled. "Maybe they're hiring."

I laughed. Only Maya knew how stressful my work life could be. The thought of staying on this heavenly island was tempting, if totally unrealistic.

"I noticed you disappeared with Darren at the barbecue last night. Any news to report?"

"Other than him pulling out all the stops trying to hook up, not really."

"Figured as much. He sure is nice to look at, though."

I chuckled softly. Couldn't argue there.

I fiddled with a menu left on the small table between us. "Are you hungry?"

She shook her head. "I shouldn't. I've gained like five pounds in a week. It'll be a miracle if I fit into my dress tomorrow."

"Don't worry. We'll make it fit."

"Yeah, I'm going to look like a stuffed sausage in white satin." Her hand went to her stomach concealed under her tankini.

"Is everything okay?"

She turned her head, but I couldn't read her expression behind her sunglasses. "Yeah, why?"

What could I say? *Cameron sent me on a fact-finding mission because he's worried about you?* I hadn't written off his concerns though. Maya had a way of keeping her feelings socked down deep enough where no one else could find them. She was private, and for the most part, I'd always respected that. It was her way, and who was I to make her put her feelings out there?

"Just wondered. You seem...thoughtful lately. I just want to make sure it's the usual wedding feelings and not something else."

She nodded quietly and took in a deep breath. A minute passed in silence before she spoke. "I'm pregnant," she said, her voice quiet.

My jaw fell, and I ripped my sunglasses off my face. "What... Wait. How? Have you been trying?"

"No. It's my fault. I fucked up."

"What?"

She took her sunglasses off and pinched the bridge of her nose. "I missed pills. Between everything that's happened these past few months. My mom, moving in with Cam, and pulling this wedding trip together, I missed pills, and here we are."

"How far along do you think you are?"

"Honestly, I'm not sure. I took tests, but I haven't seen a doctor yet. I've been putting it off. I didn't want to believe it could be true."

I was silent. Maya's life had been chaotic and at some points, extremely troubling. Maybe this wasn't what she was expecting, but still, this was news Cameron would welcome.

"You haven't told Cam." This had to be what he'd sensed her holding back.

Suddenly her calm exterior started to crumble. She winced, and her eyes became glassy. "This is a nightmare. I'm getting married tomorrow. How the hell am I supposed to keep this from Cam? He's going to freak out, but I can't tell him the night before our wedding. He's going to be a mess the same way I'm a mess and—"

"Okay, stop right there. Breathe. This is... Maya, this is a blessing. You both want a family, right?"

She sucked in an unsteady breath and exhaled, a slow tear traveling down her cheek. "Yeah, we've talked about it, but I didn't think it'd be this soon."

"Cameron is the love of your life. You made a baby. I can't think of anything more romantic. Tell him. He's going to be so thrilled. I just know it."

She shook her head, but I could tell she wanted to believe me. "I don't want him to be angry with me for being irresponsible." Her voice was a whisper.

I wanted to pull her into a tight hug. Instead, I reached for her hands and held them in mine, wanting her to believe me and take comfort in the words I knew to be true.

"Cameron loves you. No matter how it happened, it's happened, and it's something to celebrate now. Okay?" I wiped away her tear and smiled. Not for her sake, but because my happiness in that moment was too big to temper. I couldn't imagine what it would be like...to love someone as much as she loved Cameron and to be carrying proof of that love. To be taking that next step together.

She smiled a little, and my heart felt even lighter.

"When should I tell him? We're not supposed to see each other until the wedding tomorrow. I'll ruin everything. I don't want anything to ruin our day, but I don't want to keep this from him anymore either. It's been weighing on me. God, you have no idea."

I hushed her, smoothing my thumbs over the backs of her hands. "Maya, tell him tonight if you want to."

"Do you think I should?"

"Do what feels right, and don't worry about what anyone else thinks, okay? We're all here for *you*."

She nodded. "Thank you."

★ ★ ★

Maya had retired early for the night. Too restless for sleep, I hung around one of the outdoor bars at the hotel. The sky was a midnight blue, and the sweet smell of plumeria wafted through the warm ocean air. I twirled my half glass of pinot grigio by the base.

Maya's news was overwhelming. Not in the same way that it was for her, but an overwhelming reminder of how quickly life can change. Months ago she was barely living. Working hard every day, partying harder every weekend. Starting all over again on Monday. Not too different from my world, really. And now she was hours away from being married to the man of her dreams. In a matter of months, their family of two would grow.

More than anything, I was happy for my friend, but I couldn't ignore the sting of regret I felt under that happiness. I took a deep breath. Filling my lungs with the ocean air, I refused to let my thoughts linger too long on my own unfulfilled dreams.

I swallowed down the last of my lukewarm wine and did the one thing I promised myself I wouldn't do. I powered on my phone and checked my messages. Mom had texted a few times, asking me how things were. I texted her back, letting her know I couldn't stay in touch as regularly being out of the country.

Then I checked my e-mail, and dread quickly overrode all my other emotions. My phone loaded dozens of e-mails from work, many from Reilly, including a calendar invite for a review lunch scheduled for when I got back. Subtle. I stifled a groan and turned the phone off.

"Hey, beautiful." Darren took the bar stool beside me.

"Where's Cam? I thought you were going into town tonight."

"Nah. He turned in early. I'll give you one guess where he is."

With Maya no doubt. I grinned to myself, knowing better than Darren did why that was a good thing.

"Can I buy you another drink?"

"Actually, I should head back to the room. Big day tomorrow." I grabbed my purse and stood.

I may have been restless, and reconnecting to my work e-mail wasn't helping matters, but I wasn't sure my mind was in the right place to fight off Darren's flirtations.

Darren caught my hand, keeping me from leaving. "You look tense. What's going on?"

I hesitated. "Nothing. I'm fine."

"Come on. Take a walk with me." He tipped his head toward the dark shore that met the black horizon.

He smiled like he knew I couldn't and wouldn't say no.

"Okay." I slipped the tiny black strap of the purse over my shoulder and let him take my hand and lead me out to the moonlit beach.

"Talk to me, red. What's going on?"

"Just work. I made the mistake of checking my e-mail. Real life sucks."

He laughed and tightened his grasp around my hand. "I can't imagine getting thrown back into reality right now. Why on earth would you check in when you've got days left here?"

"I don't know. I'm a glutton for pain, I guess. Catching up is going to be a mess. I figured maybe I could get ahead of it."

"Does your job have any redeeming qualities?"

I stared down at the dark shadows our steps made dragging through the soft sand. "Probably not by your standards. I don't get to save anyone's life when I'm fetching my boss's dry cleaning."

"Does he respect you?" His eyes were serious now.

I shrugged. "I think deep down he probably appreciates all I do, but on the surface, he's too busy to really take the time to show it. I get it. It's part of the job. How about you? Is being a firefighter your dream job?"

His lips curved into a boyish smile. "I love it. Even when

it sucks. Sometimes it feels like it's in my blood or something— what I was meant to do. Every once in a while I'll have a few rough shifts in a row and start to second-guess things, but once I'm recharged I can't wait to get back. I find myself missing it."

"Do you miss it now?"

He stared down the coastline, a distant look in his eyes, before he turned back to me.

"I wouldn't want to be anywhere else than here with you right now. And that's the honest to God truth."

The more time I spent with Darren, the more glimpses I got of the man beneath the handsome, charming exterior. Despite all the warnings, despite my mind shouting at me to be careful, I was hooked. I wanted to know more. I wanted to unravel him and see him the way he'd never let anyone else see him before.

"Anyway. To hell with all that. We're on vacation. Let's do something crazy."

"Like what?"

I laughed and stared as he pulled his shirt over his head.

"Let's go skinny-dipping," he said in a hushed whisper.

My jaw fell open a fraction as he went for the zipper on his shorts.

"In the ocean? You're insane."

"Yes, and yes. Come on, don't be a prude," he said.

"It's against the rules. No swimming after dark." I pointed behind us to a sign I'd noticed when it was still daylight.

"We're on vacation. There are no rules."

He stripped his boxers off, leaving him naked in the moonlight. My jaw was gaping now, and I forced myself to look away. What I wouldn't give for a few minutes just to look...

"I'm not going in there naked," I insisted.

"Suit yourself." His voice rang out from a few feet away. When I turned back, he was making strides across the sand, his taut ass my only thought until he dove into the water.

"Water's fine!" he called out, his smile bright in the darkness.

I bounced in place, letting his infectious energy come over me.

Am I doing this? Yes. No. Yes. No way. *What the hell?*

I took a breath and stripped off the jersey sundress I wore.

Darren hollered from the distance. I couldn't believe I was doing this, but I couldn't stop smiling. Darren was crazy, but I kind of loved it. The truth was, no one else could make me do this but him. A fresh wave of terror hit me when I contemplated my bra and panties. I couldn't go in there stark naked. I had to draw the line somewhere.

"Come on, red. I'm getting pruned out here. Hurry up."

Without thinking, I unsnapped my bra, covered my breasts with my arm, and ran out to join him.

The water was warm, but still a shock against skin that wasn't used to being bare there. I swam toward Darren, trying not to think about all of the unknowns in the dark water. When one of those unknowns flickered against my foot, I screamed.

"What's wrong?" Darren swam close and caught my hand, grinning broadly.

"Something touched my foot. I'm freaking out." I looked across the dark water that I couldn't see through.

A wave pushed his body closer to mine, and then his hands were on me and he pulled me against him. "Don't freak out. I'll protect you," he murmured.

I swallowed over the breath that was caught in my throat. We were chest-to-chest, bare, and suddenly nothing had ever felt so perfect. My toes curled into the sand below.

"You know I'm more than my hair color, right?"

He traced a damp strand of hair that clung to my cheek. "So much more... You're like this streak of bright red through my head. Whenever I see you or think about you, it's vibrant. I can't think of anything else. Or anyone else."

I was speechless. If that came from his player toolbox of pickup lines, he deserved a medal. Silence fell between us, making my nakedness against him all the more tense.

A gentle wave crashed against us, but he held me solidly. His eyes were the darkest I'd ever seen them. He caught my face in his palms, caressing his thumbs over the apples of my cheeks.

"I still want that kiss you promised me."

My breath hitched. "That wasn't a promise. That was a threat."

"Then teach me a lesson."

I lifted my chin, saying yes in every silent way I could think of. I wanted him to kiss me. And I wanted a hell of a lot more than that. I slid my fingers into his wet hair in wordless assent.

"Vanessa."

My heart raced at hearing my name on his lips. Not a nickname, but my name. I gasped at the feel of his erection against me, his lips on me at the same time. I moaned into his mouth. I was instantly overwhelmed, consumed at the first touch of his tongue sweeping against mine.

I let my hands wander, exploring him. Down his muscular arms and back up his cool hard abs. I wanted this man. So did half of Brooklyn...and probably half the women at this damned hotel. But right now, I was the one in his arms. As much as he was lusting after me, I wanted him to be.

I caught a breath, but before I could think about breaking away from the heated embrace, he lifted me, hooking my legs around his waist. I went willingly. Desire for Darren raced across my sensitive skin, thrummed between my legs where the slightest friction between us made me dizzy.

"I know what you're thinking," he murmured, trailing slow kisses from my lips across my jaw.

He couldn't know, because all coherent thought was being overridden by the suddenly loud demands of my body.

He held my hips, caressing up and down my thighs like silk under the water. One more second like this, and I was a goner. I was going to sleep with Darren Bridge and enjoy every irresponsible minute of it.

"What am I thinking?" My voice was a whisper. If he only knew...

"You're wondering whether this is a good idea. Because you're smart and you see right through me, but you can't help but want this anyway."

His touch crept up my side, his wandering fingertips curling around my tight breast. I shifted my hips against him, wanting more of that delicious friction. I bit my lip, stifling a desperate sound that was crawling up my throat.

"Just give me one night, Vanessa. One night, and I won't let you regret it."

★ ★ ★

My back hit the wall of Darren's hotel room. We were tangled up the way we'd been in the water. Except our touches were no longer tentative. I was needy and frantic, ready to give in.

Bringing my thigh over his hip, he ground against me and

groaned. "God, I want you so damn bad."

I whimpered, tightening my grip on him. Our clothes were damp and sandy, and I wanted to strip away all the barriers between us again. He pushed his hands up under my dress, lifting it off and then unsnapping my bra. The cool conditioned air hit my bare skin, making my nipples and breasts tight and heavy.

"Beautiful," he murmured, trailing his fingertips over my pebbled flesh.

A whimper started low in my belly and rushed up past my lips.

Hooking his thumbs over the band of my underwear, he pulled my panties down to my ankles, planting soft kisses down my thighs. I pressed my palms flat against the wall as my knees weakened. I closed my eyes, relishing the heavenly feeling of his warm lips against my skin. Then his velvet tongue. Softly sucking his way back up, he stopped just shy of the place where I was wet for him, only him.

"I want to see all of you, Vanessa." The words were made of gravel and sex as he smoothed his palms against the sensitive inner flesh of my thighs, skimming up to my pussy. He parted my folds and my hips came forward an inch, seeking. I couldn't bring myself to be shy when I wanted him this much. Once we'd started this dance, all my inhibitions had flown out the window.

He exhaled sharply. "God, you're so wet for me already."

His touch fell away, and he rose slowly until he was all muscle and man towering before me. Agonizing seconds passed as he stripped away his own clothes. I watched, rapt, as more of his beautiful body came into view. The muted light of the room cast shadows against the sharp planes of his physique. Finally, he peeled off his black swimming trunks and stood before me, naked, proud, an unmistakable hunger dark in his eyes.

I'd gotten a glimpse of his cock as we'd left the ocean in the dark. Then and now it was fucking glorious. Half of me didn't want to stare and the other half wanted to get us to his room as fast as humanly possible. Here I could look all I wanted. And touch...

Before I could reach for him, he left me naked and trembling against the wall. Our gazes clashed, heated and full of promise. I was frozen, pinned in place as he moved with control. He retrieved a condom from his wallet and unwrapped it, carefully unrolling it down the length of his cock. The sensual movement nearly unraveled me. I closed my eyes, and behind them, I could almost see what it would be like. How deep he could be... Now that I'd decided, I couldn't wait to feel him inside me.

"Vanessa." My name fell from his lips like something precious.

I opened my eyes halfway, and my heart danced a rapid uneven beat at the sight of him. His skin was wrapped tightly over the most incredible physique I'd ever seen. He was a goddamn sculpture of perfection.

He reached out, and with his upturned palm, that simple gesture, I could move again. Like a magnet, I was drawn toward his heat, his energy. I walked to him on unsteady legs until we were nearly chest-to-chest. He threaded his fingers through my hair, sliding across my scalp as he lowered his lips over mine. I opened for him instantly. Then we were engulfed in another thought-shattering kiss. His tongue was soft and rough at once, deep and demanding, the very taste of desire.

I brushed my breasts against him, eager for his skin on mine again. I wanted him close, all around me and deep inside me. He pulled away, his breathing ragged, his grip on me no lighter.

"I can't get enough of your mouth. The way you taste..." He shook his head, like he didn't understand why.

I didn't either. I'd never wanted anything this badly. We hadn't even had sex, and I couldn't remember feeling this kind of frenzy before with anyone, ever. I couldn't believe it was the same for him, but the way he looked at me now made me wonder.

He sat down on the bed, pulling me toward him so my chest was at his eye level. Then he wrapped his lips around my nipple in a tight hungry kiss.

At the same time, he slipped his hand between my legs. He rubbed gently over my clit. When his touch went lower where I was incredibly wet, he released my nipple and went for the other roughly.

"I'm going to taste every inch of you, Vanessa. Every beautiful fucking inch."

His raspy promise vibrated through his chest and against my flesh as he tasted, licking and nipping at my breasts.

I gasped, gripping his shoulders to hold myself up. This desire was more than a fleeting wave of pleasure. It radiated under my skin, electrifying every nerve ending that met his touch, pulsing in the deepest part of me. The place I needed him desperately.

As if in answer to my silent prayer, he slipped a finger inside my pussy and began stroking and massaging. I could have come right then, easily, if I'd let myself.

"Darren." I arched into his touch.

I gripped him tighter, and he curled into me. Something

snapped. My patience, all those tension-filled moments of denying myself. All of it fell away. My jaw tightened, and I tugged at the silky hair between my fingers.

He gazed up at me, an animal hunger plain in his eyes. "You want me now?" His voice was soft and deep.

I'd wanted Darren for months, and these last days the ache had been so acute I could have flogged myself for ever denying his advances. Any heartbreak seemed worth the chance to sate this hunger. I nodded, because right now I didn't give a damn.

"Then come here, sweetheart. I want to feel your tight little cunt all around me."

His dirty words conjured a potent vision. Bringing his fingers to his lips, he licked my essence from them. A violent fever rushed over me, and I had a feeling that being with Darren wasn't going to be like any kind of sex I'd ever had before. He tugged me down confidently, straddling my legs on either side of his rock-hard thighs. With one hand on his cock, stroking over the condom, he used the other to steadily bring me down onto his thick erection.

We joined, inch by inch. My head fell back.

Good God...

My breath caught when I took the last of him. Tension lingered, but every part of me hummed with pleasure, his cock rooted so deeply. I felt only a faint sting against the fullness and the overwhelming sensations sizzling through me.

"You okay?"

His breath was a whisper against my neck, moving a wisp of my fallen hair. Strong, warm arms surrounded me, held me like a treasure that was bound to him. In this moment, I was. My body belonged to his, welcomed all of his.

"Better than okay."

Darren didn't need any more strokes to his ego, but I couldn't lie. He felt amazing. He was all the fantasies I'd played out in my head on lonely nights and more.

He moved my hips and brought me down again. That faint sting came again, right next to the incredible friction, and then melted into a kind of pleasure that took my breath away. He'd barely set the pace, and already I was climbing, overwhelmed with how he filled me, how right it felt being in his arms. I hadn't been with anyone in a while, and Darren was mastering my pleasure like no one ever had. I wasn't going to last long.

"Tell me how it feels, Vanessa." Tension and his potent need seemed to seep into me with his touch, firm fingertips pressing in my hips.

I reveled in his strength and was equally grateful for his control. Darren was this incredible mass of power, moving me at his whim. So easily he could become someone to fear. But one look in his eyes told a different story. I'd never felt safer or more cherished as I had in this moment.

I shook my head slightly, in disbelief of everything. Our closeness, a breath apart. That we were here, a place I never believed we'd be. The beginning of an orgasm crept up quickly, heightening that electric feeling that skittered over my skin, from my painfully hard nipples all the way down to my toes curled tight against his powerful thighs.

Tell me how it feels. His words echoed in my ears as I fell deeper into the feelings that had no name. I didn't have the right words except...

"I've never felt like this."

He brushed the hair back from my face, thumbing my cheek as he went. Shaking his head, he met my hazy stare. "Me neither."

I couldn't hold his gaze. I couldn't let myself believe what his look was saying. I brought my lips down firmly against his. He brought my hips down hard, lifting his so I felt his penetration in a new way. I moaned into his mouth, pleasure thick in my veins. A few more minutes and I wouldn't be able to speak. I closed my eyes and met his drives with more pressure of my own, joining us harder, binding our bodies tighter.

The shift in his pace answered my silent request, until every hard jolt ricocheted through me. I wasn't doing anything, just accepting him, letting him bring us to the brink. I held on tighter until the tension was too much to bear.

"Darren!" My jaw fell, a violent tremble taking over.

My thighs were damp and tight against his. Every muscle tensed, succumbing to this rush of sensation. He ruled my every movement. Even with my eyes closed, I could feel his on me, like a spotlight on this uncontrollable climb. I couldn't slow it down, and I didn't want to. I'd wanted him too damn long.

I broke, a loud cry leaving my lips. The next few strokes of his cock inside me brought me more pleasure than any man ever had. I rode it out, shaking from the intensity of it.

He took a handful of hair and arched my head back. A hot and hungry kiss met my skin.

"Beautiful when you come."

DARREN

I was seeing stars and I hadn't even come yet. I'd never been so enraptured in someone else's pleasure. And Vanessa was like a raw nerve. Like lightning you could touch.

Once she'd said yes, she'd held nothing back. She melted

against me, opened for me, moved with me, took everything I could give her. And the pleasure sweeping her features damn near took my breath away.

I was certain I could orgasm just from witnessing her come apart. Her pussy fluttered around me as she came down from her release. I turned us around and gingerly laid her on her back. I lifted off enough to see her better. She was so goddamn beautiful. I'd known that before, but now she was bare, naked and spread for me. Perfection if I'd ever seen it... and for the moment, all mine.

I surged into her, and she moved up the sheets with a gasp. I stifled a moan and went at her, harder and deeper. The delicious grip of her pussy on my dick had me right on the edge. Everything in my mind screamed for more, for release.

Her hands were everywhere. Every desperate touch spread fire over my skin, tugged somewhere in my gut as I fought the urge to bring our bodies closer. It was all too much. Something triggered inside of me. I caught her wrists, pinning them to bed on either side of her head while I thrust with abandon. Just needed to come...

Her lips trembled. She tensed around my cock, and I waited for her to come again, all the while chasing my own delirium. But she didn't come.

A quiet pleading glimmered in her eyes. "Let me touch you," she whispered.

Something tugged in my gut again. Without thinking, I withdrew and flipped her to her tummy. Hauling her hips up, I drove deep into her warmth. A throaty moan escaped her.

The reflection I caught in the mirror was a vantage only I had. She took every inch of me, over and over. It was an erotic sight. Satisfying and arousing. Enough to push me over. The sheets twisted into her fists, and she was there again. Seizing tight around me as she cried out.

I couldn't stop. Electricity flew down my spine. My balls tightened painfully, and I came, finding heaven inside of her. I released my death grip on her hips when I realized I was likely leaving marks.

With a heavy sigh, she wilted against the sheets. I covered her body with mine, inhaled her scent like oxygen I'd been deprived of. I sighed heavily. Relief washed over me—the relief of being close without having to see that look in her eyes.

Fighting the urge to stay buried deep in her heat, I slipped away. Had to catch my breath...

Moving off the bed and toward the brightly lit bathroom to deal with the condom, I left her to rest. I caught my reflection in the mirror. Warmth in my cheeks and a satisfied set of my shoulders. Something familiar and completely strange came over me.

You've done this a hundred times.

Fucked a girl. Got rid of the condom. Got rid of the scent of her, the taste of her.

I shook my head and turned on the faucet. I splashed cold water on my face and inhaled the smell of Vanessa on my hands. Blood rushed to my cock, but this wasn't right. That little voice was like metal in my mouth and made me uneasy all over.

I shut the bathroom door and turned on the shower.

The water poured down, and I washed quickly, mechanically while my mind went to war.

She's not like the others...

Vanessa was different. Everything about her revved me up. The way she moved, the way she brushed me off because even if she might have wanted me, she didn't need me.

But tonight, the way she touched me and reached for me screamed intimacy. I knew then without a doubt that she wanted more from me than a quick fuck. Whether or not she'd admit it out loud or even knew it, I could tell. As if I'd been programmed to take caution at the first sign of intimacy, my brain was suddenly on high alert, overthinking everything seconds after I'd had an incredible orgasm.

I was getting hard at the thought of being with her again. I wanted her tonight and tomorrow, all damn week, every different way until she couldn't walk back to her room.

I toweled off, ready to make good on that thought. Tucking the towel at my waist, I walked out of the fog of the bathroom and into the hotel room, expecting to see her still warming my bed. Except she was gone.

CHAPTER SIX

VANESSA

I'd had the best and the worst sex of my life last night. Eli's suspicions had been spot on. No doubt about it. Darren fucked like a god. His prowess between the sheets was aligned perfectly with his physical perfection. He was so far from anyone else in the sex department. Comparisons were an absolute waste of time.

Maybe intuitively I had known it would be like that all along. Incredible. Mind-blowing. Multiple-orgasm inducing.

Except, at the end of the day—or night—it was all about sex.

I knew the feeling. I'd felt like this before. Sure, it had been a while for me, but I wasn't a stranger to the occasional hookup. I knew what it was like to get caught up in the physical moment and then have reality set in after the fact. Along with that twinge of feeling a little bit used and a little bit cheap.

For some reason I had fooled myself into believing things with Darren would be different. But why would they? He was the ambassador of cheap, casual sex. And who was I but the next patron?

I'd come more than once. I could hardly complain, but the way it all ended had made me feel so empty. Like he wanted to keep as much distance as possible between us after we'd been so close seconds before.

Deep down I'd wanted something that didn't feel quite so...blunt. I was alone with that thought as he walked away from me. Then the sound of the shower he was going to take, alone. No amount of sex-scented hotel sheets could keep the unwanted feeling from creeping over my skin. I couldn't get out of there fast enough.

Even if I'd been up half the night regretting it.

"Are you listening?"

"What?" I blinked several times, and Eli's face came back into focus before me.

"I asked if you wanted to bring a purse to the ceremony or if you want me to keep your things for you since I'm wearing pants."

I shook my head. "I'll bring my purse. Thank you, though."

I held my teal chiffon dress up against me as Eli carefully worked the zipper up the side. The bridesmaid gown was a pretty strapless number that came up to my knee. Light and airy, perfect for an island wedding. Olivia was nearby, putting makeup on Maya, who was still in her negligee under a loose satin robe. Simple white lace that was going to be well appreciated by the groom tonight no doubt.

Eli looked stellar in a white collared shirt and a teal vest, his hair styled so his black locks were slicked back and out of his eyes. He'd be standing next to me on Maya's side. He had a hand on his hip. "You look exhausted. You need more concealer. Did you sleep last night?"

"Not really," I murmured.

He handed me a tube of makeup. I dabbed some more under my eyes, trying to make it blend over the many freckles that had cropped up on my cheeks the past couple of days.

He shot a quick glance to Maya and Olivia and then back to me. "Darren?"

His voice was low, and for that I was grateful. Last thing I wanted was Olivia knowing I had slept with her brother. I'm sure the news would make it to Mommy Dearest in record time.

I nodded.

"Is he a stallion or what?"

I shrugged. I didn't know how to answer that. It had been amazing. Textbook amazing. It could have been something even more if he'd showed an inkling of intimacy afterward. Instead I'd left his room feeling like the hookup that I'd worried I'd be if I gave in to him.

A knock sounded at the door, and I went to it, eager to escape Eli's line of questioning. Except Darren was on the other side. A flush of warmth crept over my skin in seconds. He was donning the same wedding attire as Eli, and the bright white shirt and vest contrasted beautifully against his olive skin and dark hair.

Idiot. I was an idiot for letting myself feel the way I did about him. The pope could have warned me, and I would have blindly followed my stupid heart right into the arms of this master player.

"I have a gift for the bride." He handed me a long thin box.

"Oh, thanks. I'll give it to her." I took the box and tried to look anywhere but into Darren's eyes.

"Can I talk to you for a minute?"

"Well, we're kind of in the middle of getting ready." I studied the ornate carpet floor of the hallway to avoid his stare. Why did I have to sleep with him hours before the wedding?

"You're stunning."

"Thanks," I said, so quietly I barely heard it.

"Vanessa, please. Just give me a couple minutes."

He slid his hand into mine, and I let him guide me through the doorway into the hall where we were alone. I closed the door behind me and chanced a look at the man who'd blown my mind and wrecked my night. He was cleanly shaven, tanned from the island sun, but he didn't look at ease. His jaw was firm and his lips were tight. He looked a little bit like how I felt. All made up, but restless and unsettled under it all.

I chewed the inside of my lip a second before speaking. "What did you want to talk about?"

"Why you left me last night..."

My heart twisted at his words, at the hint that maybe he cared. But I played it off like I didn't. "I was tired. I didn't figure you needed me hanging around." That was at least half-true.

He shook his head, seeming no lighter. "I'm sorry."

"Why?"

"I was an ass last night, and you know it. Stop pretending that you don't care, Vanessa."

I searched his eyes, wanting to believe him. The truth was I didn't want to care. I really didn't. But maybe this was the time to own up to it.

"Darren... This is my fault. I knew what I was getting into with you, and I let myself get too emotional about it."

He hesitated long enough for me to regret the admission. I should have stuck with my not-caring facade. I'd already let him into my body. Why bring him into my heart and show him without a doubt why I wasn't the kind of girl he could want for more than a night?

He threaded his fingers more tightly with mine, and hope fluttered in my chest.

"I freaked out. Okay? I care about you, and I'm not used to caring about the women I'm with. That reality hit me at an odd moment, and I didn't handle it well. I wanted you to stay, truly. I was..."

He winced.

"What?" I whispered. My heart was thrumming back to life, hope and unexpected feelings for Darren riding over the disappointment I'd left with last night.

This time he looked away. "I was hurt...seeing the bed empty, when all I wanted was to come back to you. But more than that I was pissed at myself because I knew I deserved it." He lifted my hand and pressed a soft kiss to the back. "Believe it or not, I don't want to be a cold-hearted bastard."

"It's fine," I lied.

"No, it's not. Last night was exceptional. I've never wanted someone so goddamn bad and then..." He hesitated. "Maybe it wasn't the same for you."

I shook my head. "It's never been like that for me. I was telling you the truth."

"Give me another chance, Vanessa. I'm asking, but you have to know me well enough by now to know that I'm tenacious as a motherfucker. I am not letting you slip away this easy, and I'm not giving up on whatever this is between us."

"What can there possibly be between us?"

"Whatever we want."

"You can't possibly want—" I couldn't finish my own sentence. The words died in my throat.

"Believe me, I want."

Then he melded his lips over mine, silencing my doubts and filling the space between us with all the fiery tension that had plagued me for days. He pulled away abruptly, leaving me panting and overwhelmed.

"I want it all," he said.

I caught my breath, and the seriousness in his eyes leveled me.

"I'll see you tonight."

And with that, he disappeared down the hall.

DARREN

The ceremony went off without a hitch. Watching Maya and Cameron say their vows against the sunset was nothing less than postcard quality. I'd never been a hearts and flowers guy, but even I couldn't deny the beauty of the moment.

The guests all meandered into the reception hall. I caught up with some of our extended family, cousins, and friends I hadn't seen in ages. A jittery kind of energy pulsed through me. Maybe it was watching my brother profess a lifelong commitment to the love of his life. Maybe it was the hope I saw in Vanessa's eyes hours before, hope that I'd dashed by being a heartless piece of shit last night. I still didn't know what it all meant. The foreign feelings this woman inspired inside of me.

She wasn't desperate. Not remotely. I'd had to gracefully work my way away from some stage five clingers more than once, but she wasn't like that. It was almost like she didn't want to want me the way she did. I'd gotten her to let go of that for a few precious moments last night, when I was inside her, taking her, making her feel things she could no longer deny. The physical connection had blown me away, making it easy for me to believe her when she'd admitted it had been the same for her. We had chemistry. That was undeniable now.

My thoughts spun around Vanessa, around the past few

days. Then my life, somehow easier to see from the outside in a place like this. An oasis from reality.

The setting sun basked the sand and sky in a pink glow. Cam and Maya were moving with ease on the dance floor, seemingly lost in each other. Maya was beaming, and hell if Cameron hadn't been smiles all damn day. As usual, he couldn't keep his hands off her, and why would he today, of all days?

I'd never known a guy to fall so hard and stay wrapped up in the same girl for so long. Through war, through two botched proposals, through a score of demons that Maya tried to put between them. His love for her had always been so foreign to me, but I'd admired it. Something equally foreign was the envy I now felt. Envy and a growing sense of having fallen short.

Not that it mattered what anyone else thought, but I could read it on people's faces around us. Wasn't I supposed to be the one taking the plunge first? I was the oldest, but Cameron had beaten me to it.

Putting someone else first and trusting implicitly that she'd do the same for you... That wasn't how we'd been raised. Was I even capable of it?

I couldn't even keep a woman in my bed after making love to her, if I could even call it that.

Maybe at first. I'd felt a connection with Vanessa when we joined that took my fucking breath away. Like our two bodies were made to accept each other, to bring each other to heights that no one else could come close to. Then, somewhere along the way, my mind went into autopilot and whatever spark of magic there'd been between us had been reduced to fucking. I'd fucked Vanessa, ultimately, the same way I'd fucked so many others. Like it meant nothing.

But she meant something.

I'd spent most of the morning by myself, lost in these thoughts, trying to sort things out in my head enough to figure out what the hell I was going to say at the reception. Me, of all people, ruminating on love.

Time was up.

I brought my knife up to my glass and dinged. I cleared my throat and glanced at the battered piece of paper on the table in front of me for a moment. When I rose to speak, the room grew silent.

"I'm not sure what Cameron was thinking when he picked me to be his best man. I think the love gods are looking down on us right now having a good laugh, wondering what this bachelor could possibly say to honor the sanctity of marriage."

Laughter rose up from the tables.

"I'll try my best though, because these two deserve it."

I'd never shied away from speaking in front of a crowd. I'd gotten my laugh, but now that I had to get talking about the nuts and bolts of love, I was stuck. The words...I'd written it all out.

Just fucking do it, Darren.

I forced the next words out.

"I've been thinking lately that love doesn't always come easy. Sometimes true love doesn't find a person for years and years, despite searching and any number of obstacles put in their way by others or by themselves. Seems like people can find love and forget its magic too."

I found my mother's face in the crowd. Schooled in detached politeness. Cold and hard, like her heart. Between her and Frank, it seemed like all three of us kids were damned. The fact that Cameron had found love among us was a miracle.

I looked away, not wanting to dwell on the loveless union

of our parents and what it had been like to grow up surrounded by that empty shell.

"What Cameron and Maya have found... I've never seen anything like it. They're two halves of a whole. Two hearts meant to find each other. Their kind of love runs deep and lasts a lifetime. It's a love to look up to, to fight for, to hold onto if you're lucky enough to find something so precious."

My voice wavered a bit, and a strange emotion gripped me, tightened my gut. Was I fucking this up? One glance at the tears in Maya's eyes told me I wasn't. Then Vanessa beside her, a rapt expression on her face. I swallowed hard. "Either way, seems like love can be a fragile gift. Something to be treasured once found. I know that Cameron and Maya will always treasure it in each other."

I smiled and raised my glass.

"Cheers, to the happy couple. Wishing you every happiness together."

VANESSA

Maybe it was the pink champagne, but now that all the formalities had passed, I felt lighter...relieved. Even if I was still reeling a bit from Darren's speech. I had a hard time believing that those seemingly heartfelt words had originated from some sort of canned speech he'd found online. That moment of hesitation...recognition...when our gazes had locked was still haunting me.

Something inside of me wanted to believe our time together had inspired some of those thoughts, but the fact was, we'd been in each other's lives for a matter of days.

Love took years. And sometimes years weren't enough.

Seemed like he understood that too.

Maya turned in her seat beside me. The nonstop traffic at the wedding party table had finally died down a little. I had wanted to ask her if she'd spoken to Cameron, but the day had flown by.

"Has Cameron's family worn you out yet?"

She laughed. "No, I'm actually enjoying meeting everyone. Thank God not everyone is like Diane." She sipped from her water glass.

"Did you talk to Cam?"

She smiled widely and happiness glittered in her eyes. "He came to my room last night. You were right, as usual. He was over the moon. I don't think I've ever seen him so happy."

Suddenly the news hit me all over again. I leaned in and hugged her tight. "I'm so happy for you, Maya. I truly am."

She pulled back and held my hand. "Thank you, Vanessa. For being a true friend, through everything. I know I haven't been around as much lately."

"Totally understandable. And for the record, I'm not going anywhere."

"I want this for you too." She gestured to the room that was alive with celebration for her and Cameron. "One day."

I smiled and cast my gaze to the floor. I wanted that too, but I had a long way to go.

"Eli told me about Darren," she said quietly.

I rolled my eyes, annoyed that he'd mentioned it. But among the three of us, few secrets were ever kept.

"Don't be mad. I asked him about it. He said you didn't really seem like yourself this morning. Is everything okay?"

I sighed. "Everything's fine. I'm just not sure what to expect. There's chemistry between us. No doubt about it. And he says things… Sometimes it feels like this could be more than just a fling. But it's hard not to be guarded with him."

"I know his reputation isn't promising. But maybe you should give it a chance."

She had no idea how much I wanted to, especially after my encounter with him this afternoon. Before I could say more, Cameron came up to her. He stood tall, towering above us both. She gazed up at him, stars in her eyes and glowing with love.

"Can I steal you away for a dance?" He held out his hand.

With that wordless gesture, she rose. "Of course." She glanced back to me. "I'll catch you later."

I waved her off and tipped back the last of the bubbly in my glass. I was ready to make my way to the dance floor, shake these thoughts, and have some fun. The party guests were starting to loosen up, and I was too.

Diane came up beside me as I rose. "Having fun?"

"Of course. What an amazing day."

She drifted her gaze to where Cam and Maya now danced. He was whispering something in her ear, grazing the slight swell of her belly. My heart swelled for their newfound happiness.

"Assuming you knew about the pregnancy?" Diane did a poor job of masking a grimace. "Cameron told us the news this morning. Makes sense now why they were in such a rush to get married."

"I think marriage has been on their minds for a long time."

"True enough. He's been lovestruck over that girl for years. I have to admit, I never understood the infatuation."

The way she said *that girl* grated over my nerves. How could she talk about Maya that way, especially on the day she became a true part of her family? This woman was cold beyond comprehension.

"I suppose they're the only ones who really need to understand it. It's their relationship." I seethed under my forced politeness.

She narrowed her eyes and then relaxed. A crooked smile curved up the corner of her mouth, and she glanced over at Darren sitting at the other side of the long table set for the wedding party.

"Darren will never make that mistake. He's not like Cameron."

"How is that?" I couldn't hide the edge in my tone. Somehow, the conversation was beginning to feel very personal.

What if Darren could fall in love? What if he fell in with someone like me? Would this witch still look down her nose at me the way she did Maya? What would that do to her high hopes?

"He's never let himself get swept away."

"Don't you want him to be happy?"

"Believe me, marriage won't make him happy." With that she turned, moving swiftly in the opposite direction away from me.

Relief and rage coursed through my veins. One day someone would make Darren happy. Who cared if I entertained a little fleeting fantasy that it could be me? I wanted Darren to find love even if it wasn't with me. I wasn't sure who or what had warped this woman's heart, but if any of the Bridge siblings had trouble finding love and keeping it, I wouldn't hesitate to place a fair share of the burden on the example she'd set for them.

Emboldened, I walked to Darren. He shifted from his conversation with the man who'd interrupted our almost-kiss on the beach and looked up at me from his seat. Heaven help me, one look at the man made my skin tingle.

His lips curved into a grin as his friend chatted away, and all the pleasures from the night before seemed to flicker in those beautiful brown eyes. Something had passed between us beyond ecstasy. Whatever that was had thrown us both off, and as long as we were here, together, I was going to live it and feel it.

"Want to dance?" I mouthed, not wanting to interrupt the conversation that was looking a bit one-sided.

He turned to his friend. "Hey, Jeffries, this is Vanessa."

The man had big eyes and a genuine smile. "Nice to meet you, Vanessa. You keeping this in guy in line?"

"Doing my best. He doesn't make it easy."

He laughed. "I bet."

"Can I steal him away for a few?"

"Sure thing." He slapped Darren on the back and winked in my direction before leaving us alone.

Darren rose and took my hand, gently tugging me to him. "This is a slow song. You know what that means, right?"

I lifted an eyebrow.

"Means as long as that song plays, I get to put my hands on you, and I can't guarantee I'm going to be a complete gentleman about it." The way he looked me over, I guessed he was only half joking.

I ran a finger down his teal tie and smirked. "Well, we're not in middle school. I think you could probably cop a feel without serious consequences."

The edge of his teeth dug into his bottom lip, and he

brought his arm around me. I closed my eyes a moment, tempted to skip the dancing part and get right to the ungentlemanly part...in his hotel room.

But the night was young.

I took his hand and pulled him toward the filling dance floor. "Come on, Casanova. Let's dance."

Once there, he pulled me into his arms. I melted into his embrace, one I was soon becoming addicted to. I rested my cheek against his solid chest and breathed him in. The cool and uniquely male scent that hit my lungs became a sixth sense. No doubt about it, I was attracted to this man on a level that felt primal and beyond my control.

He roamed his hands over my back, along the edge of my dress where satin hit bare skin. "Good speech," he said against my ear.

"Thanks, you too. Where did you dig that up?"

"The speech?" He arched an eyebrow and a knowing grin curved his lips. "That was all me. Trust me, I surprised myself."

"I'm impressed. Love isn't the easiest thing to talk about in front of an audience, I guess. But it was beautiful."

"Thanks, red."

He stared down into my eyes, making my heart hammer the way it always seemed to when I was around him. Would that ever go away? Would a day go by when I was with him and didn't feel that addictive pull? No matter if my brain knew better, my body wanted him. A kind of unseen magic lit up under my skin and made me want to take chances with this man.

The song changed, and the slow sway of our bodies seemed out of place. Darren spun me away, pulling me back close. We moved together to the faster dance beat, and I giggled, loving the way my soul came alive around him.

If I was being honest with myself, I didn't care enough if this tryst with Darren only lasted one more night. I wasn't going to let a minute pass me by without making the most of this time. Who knew what real life would throw at us back home? For the first time in a long time, I was really happy.

We danced until we were out of breath and I was nearly boneless from keeping up with his crazy moves. We finally took a break and grabbed some water at the bar. He loosened his tie, and I fanned myself.

"You're quite the dancer, Darren Bridge." The cool water slid down my parched throat.

"What can I say? You inspire me."

I laughed, unable to keep from smiling like a fool.

"You do. You're an amazing woman, Vanessa." He reached up, softly touching the flowers in my hair. Emotion flickered behind his light brown eyes. "I don't want this trip to end."

I closed my eyes because I didn't want him to know how true that was for me too. I took a snapshot in my mind. The music, the noise of people laughing and talking, the periodic whoosh and clinks of the bartender filling drinks behind us. I wanted to stop time. Make this day last forever. Make the trip last long enough to know if this fling with Darren was just that, a fling, or something that could take root.

"And I hate that I lost your trust last night. I want to show you that I can be better than that. I messed up. And I'll spare you the suspense, I do that occasionally."

"And I'm supposed to...what? Forgive you every time you pull some douchebag move on me?" I joked, trying to keep the mood light. Last night seemed like a distant memory, and the more time we spent together, the more ready I felt to move on and try again.

The light in his eyes darkened a bit. He lowered and took a less than chaste kiss. I sucked in a breath, and the cool scent of his cologne filled my lungs.

"People are watching."

"You're not my dirty little secret, red. I don't care if the whole world knows you're mine tonight."

"Who said I'm yours?" The challenge was baseless because I wanted nothing more than to be his. Claimed, possessed, if only for a night.

He kissed me again, softer, his breath sweet like champagne against my lips. "I say. And I'm not taking no for answer."

"You asked for one night, Darren."

"And now I'm asking for another one."

Every night I spent in Darren's bed was a night that brought me closer to falling for him. Still, I couldn't bring myself to care enough to say no. "Then what?"

"Then give me the next one," he whispered. "And the next. Call me crazy, but right now I want them all."

Beautiful, intoxicating words. "I'm pretty sure that's the champagne talking."

"No." He shook his head, his gaze steady on me. "I can hardly believe it either, but I want you like I've never wanted anyone before. I can't promise you forever, but I can't walk away from this either."

"I want to believe that's true."

"I can try to tell you everything you want to hear right now. I could search for the right words and hope they'd be enough to convince you of how I feel, what this craving feels like gnawing inside of me. But I'm all through with words today. All I want to do is touch...and taste..." he whispered against my lips through another kiss. "I want to feel and fuck. And I'm ready to take you upstairs and show you what you do to me until the sun comes up."

The heated look in his eyes left no doubt.

"Then take me upstairs."

CHAPTER SEVEN

DARREN

I devoured her, and heaven help me, she tasted like apples and champagne. I kissed her until her lips were swollen. Until her nipples were so hard I felt them through her dress. I explored every sweet crevice of her mouth until my cock was ready to explode if it didn't get some relief inside her.

We were on the bed, necking like teenagers. I loved her taste. I sucked at her skin, restraining myself not to make marks. I wanted the whole goddamn hotel to know she was mine, but she probably didn't. I trailed my mouth everywhere her dress didn't cover. Over the graceful curve of her shoulder, to the tops of her breasts, to the tips of her fingertips.

The little moans she offered up seem to short-circuit my brain every goddamn time, like I was wired in to her pleasure in a way I'd never experienced before. Suddenly nothing was more important than eliciting more of those sounds until she was screaming my name.

I exhaled slowly, trying to get a handle on my desire. Every instinct wanted to fuck, to rut so deeply inside her she'd never be the same. But tonight had to be different. I didn't want to leave her with the memory of a good fuck. I wanted to get under her skin and make her see me as someone different than anyone else had. Maybe even as someone different than

I saw myself.

I found the zipper on her dress and dragged it down, appreciating every inch of skin the motion revealed. I forced myself to go slow, stripping her down only to claim her in new places with my lips. I moved down the bed, taking her panties off as I went. She kept her legs together, and I fixed my gaze there. I wanted to spread her, tease her, lose myself in the beautiful body laid out before me.

She arched her back off the bed and unclasped the strapless bra she wore, tossing it away. I stood before her in complete fucking awe. Her deep auburn hair lay in a stark mass against the white sheets. She was stunning.

"Do you have any idea how beautiful you are?" I couldn't hide the raw appreciation in my voice.

"You have a way of reminding me." She slid her legs against each other seductively, revealing nothing. My cock ached to be between them.

I undressed swiftly, never taking my eyes off her. God, she was a fucking sight. I thanked my lucky stars that she'd agreed to give me another chance, because I wasn't even close to tired of this view. I wasn't sure I ever would be. I grabbed a condom and rolled it on.

Wasting no time, I crawled over her, kissing my way to her mouth. I delved deeply, unable to harness the lust that had built up. I sucked her tongue, her lips. I tasted her desire, silently promising her what was in store.

She tangled her fingers through my hair, tightening her grip. I repressed the urge to thrust into her right then. Her legs were parted around my hips, but I only grazed her. I shifted my hips so my cock slid through her wetness, up against her clit. She moaned into my mouth, and my vision went nearly white.

"Do you like that?" I asked.

"God, yes. There's no way you can touch me that feels wrong. It all feels right." She skimmed her hands lightly down my chest before she stopped and looked up at me. "Do you want me to touch you?" Her voice was breathy.

I lifted her hand to my mouth and pressed an openmouthed kiss to the well of her palm. "I'm going to put my hands on you, Vanessa. Everywhere. No restrictions. It's only fair I let you do the same."

I guided her arms around me and settled low so our bodies molded hotly together. Chest-to-chest, skin against skin.

I put my hands on her everywhere I could reach. Memorizing her. Worshipping every curve and freckle. Because in another minute I was going to be lost to instinct, completely at the mercy of the moment. I was ready to take her to the stars and then drown in the depths of her body.

"I want to worship you. I've thought of nothing else all damn day. But the savage in me wants to fuck you, Vanessa. I don't know if that's what you really want, and I don't want to scare you off again."

Her half-lidded gaze spoke of her approval. She touched my lips lightly, dragging her finger over the top and then the bottom. "I like the way you fuck," she said softly.

The way the last word rolled off her tongue made me want to come, made me want to stop talking and claim her body with one violent thrust after the next.

But... "I don't want you to leave again."

"I won't. I promise."

I hoped it was true, because my need for her was bordering on frantic.

Any patience I'd been able to hang onto disappeared. I

spread her thighs farther apart and pressed the head of my cock to her heat—slowly, painstakingly, until we were completely joined, my cock nestled deeply within her.

A desperate sound left her trembling lips.

I wanted to say something, but I could only think in sensation. Her heat, her surrender. She was so tight around me already.

I kissed her and thrust again. "Vanessa. Beautiful Vanessa. Your body is heaven. There are no words..."

My head was spinning, and I resisted the urge to unleash hell on her.

The energy had built up to a frenzy, and I felt it in every limb. A fever on my skin, an unexplainable ache in my chest. I stared into her and set a pace that spoke of my restraint. She coiled her legs around my waist, holding me to her—as if I'd had any intention of letting her go.

I could have come at any moment, but I had to see her let go. I had to hear her cry out again. Over and over until she was right there with me. The sensation wasn't complete without her.

Maybe this was more than fucking. Maybe for the first time in my life I was making love to someone, and I'd been too ignorant up to this moment to realize what that really meant.

VANESSA

Already tonight wasn't anything like the night before. Darren seemed to be hypertuned in to my needs, reacting to every sound, every touch. Minute by minute, he overtook my senses. Nothing existed outside of this moment.

The welcome weight of him against me was heaven. The

way my whole body tensed around his thick penetration. The heat that rolled over me in waves.

He brought his lips to mine. Hungry and rough, like the way he was making love to me.

Because this wasn't just sex. Not now, at least not for me. This man was under my skin.

I held him to me. His muscles, damp with sweat, flexed with every motion. I slid my hands lower, gripping his ass as he pumped.

His teeth met my skin, and he bit gently. I sucked in a breath and tightened around him.

We climbed higher. He went deep, withdrawing fully and shoving harder with each stroke, again and again. I felt everything. No one had filled me this way, made me so aware of the act.

"Darren...you're so deep."

"I can be deeper."

He caught me by the knee and pushed my thigh up against my chest, hitting me deeper and harder. I gasped and held his muscled shoulders as he took me over and over. No one had ever been this deep. As badly as I didn't want this moment to end, I couldn't stop the climax rapidly taking over.

"That's it. Come apart for me, Vanessa. I need to feel it, baby."

The words and the husky way he said them hurtled me straight over the edge. I bowed against him, flying toward the phenomenal feeling. Everything seemed to spin. Time suspended as the orgasm took over like a storm, thick and sweet and heavy in my veins. I shattered against him.

He hauled me against him tightly, sheathing his cock with one last powerful thrust. The cry that tore from his throat mimicked my own.

Seconds passed, only the sound of our ragged breath in the air. No words but an echo of those we'd spoken in the heat of the moment.

"That was incredible." He exhaled a shaky breath. "You're incredible."

He brought his lips down to mine with a kiss so soft my heart ached from the tenderness of it. I swore in that moment something passed between us. Something I'd never felt before. Something I didn't want to let go of...

"I have to take care of this condom," he said quietly.

"Okay."

He shifted off me and sat at the edge of bed. "*Don't* leave." He reached over and touched my hand.

I laughed lightly. "I won't."

Truth was, I was too boneless and wiped out to leave this time, even if I'd wanted to. And I didn't want to. I could drown every day in this kind of bliss and never come up for air. I melted into the sheets, warm and sated, the memory of Darren still pulsing inside my tender flesh. Heaven, indeed.

A few minutes later, he was curled up behind me, nuzzling my neck. I smiled in the dark, taking his arm and hugging it around my chest.

DARREN

I drank from a bottle of water and watched her sleep across the room. She was lying on her side, the sheet spilling off at her hips.

Last night had been...exceptional. No, *she* was exceptional. I'd replayed the night in my head a half dozen times since waking up to her. I was half-hard already but forced myself to let her rest.

I hadn't let anyone sleep over in a while. Of course, this wasn't home. Even if it were, I could picture her in my bed, tangled up in my sheets. Making everything smell like her.

The clock on the desk read ten o'clock. Sunshine streamed in through the cracks between the curtains. I stood and opened them a little wider.

I plucked a flower from the vase on the bedside table. The bed dipped under my weight. I ran my nose against her soft skin, still warm from sleep. I trailed the flower's silky orange petals across her shoulder and down to the small of her back.

She moaned and turned, giving me a glorious view her perfect breasts. Soft nipples that I wanted to suck until they were firm under my tongue. I licked my lips.

"Good morning, red." I continued to take her in, making no effort to disguise my lascivious appraisal of her.

"Good morning," she murmured. Smiling, she reached for the flower. She brought it up to her nose and sniffed. "Mmm, I love these."

"What are they? I see them everywhere."

"Plumeria. One of my favorites."

"I'll have to remember that. I've started a mental list of your favorite things."

"I think last night makes the list."

I moaned softly, remembering how good she'd felt under me. "Last night might have been at the top of mine."

She brought the sheet over her chest and rolled to her side. Had a woman ever looked more gorgeous straight from sleep?

I could have ravaged her again, but as addicted as I was

to her body, I was more and more intrigued by the woman underneath. Her heart, her past, her quirks. I wanted to know what made her tick, as if somehow collecting all of those little things could make her a little more mine. Vanessa had given me another chance last night. I wasn't sure I deserved it, but I wasn't going to make the mistake of letting her slip away again.

I took the flower and inhaled its sweet fragrance. "I want to know more of your favorites. Dirty martinis, plumerias, me, of course."

She laughed, a musical sound that filled the room and made me smile. "Of course."

"Let's see. What else? Favorite food."

She hummed. "I love comfort food. Chicken and biscuits for me."

"I keep forgetting you're a Southern girl. Which begs the question, where is your accent? Sometimes I hear a hint of it."

"I think I lost it in my travels. Only comes out when I've had a few drinks."

"Okay. Favorite song."

"Impossible question. Far too many to pick just one." She took the flower and traced it down my chest. "Enough about me. Tell me about you. What's the best thing about being a firefighter? I'll admit I'm fascinated that you run toward danger when everyone else is going the other direction."

"That's part of the appeal. Every day is different. I never know what to expect. Bringing people back to life is pretty great too."

Her gaze flickered up to mine. "You like to live on the edge."

I shrugged. She wasn't wrong. "You can probably tell by now I'm a little impulsive."

"I'm not sure if that's a good thing or a bad thing." Her voice was playful and light.

"No?"

She smirked. "No. I haven't decided just yet."

"Maybe I can make up your mind for you."

"I have my own mind." She lifted her chin.

I warmed at the challenge, that little spark of fire that drew me to her. "You do. But I think I know a thing or two about your body."

I tugged the sheet down, baring her breasts to me again. Her eyelids lowered, and she made no effort to cover her nakedness. I swept in, taking her nipple in my mouth and sucking until it was hard. I grabbed her other with my hand and squeezed firmly.

She gasped as her body shifted under the sheet.

Goddamn. My willpower shattered.

I'd asked for one night and taken two. Still, it wasn't enough. I wasn't nearly satisfied, and I wasn't certain when I would be.

I shook my head slightly, terrified and completely intoxicated by the way being in her presence made me feel. How could one person take control of me that quickly, without even meaning to?

I skated my palms down her torso like I was claiming my domain, taking away the sheet to clear my path. Down her thigh, over the handful of freckles on her knee, down her calf to her manicured little toes. I pushed her knees apart, and she relaxed, giving me the best view on the island. Her smooth pink pussy.

I brought myself closer, like a starving man desperate for a taste. Tugging at the little patch of auburn curls above her sex, I slid my tongue lightly over the slit that led to her opening. The taste of Vanessa. Apples and vanilla, sweet and addictive, just like her.

She gasped when I traced her slit with my fingertips. With her taste on my tongue, I inhaled her essence. My cock turned to stone, and every thought that didn't center on her went fuzzy. Fuck me, the things I wanted to do to this woman.

I grabbed her thighs, spreading her as far as she would go, preparing to lick her until she begged me to stop. I imagined diving in, fucking her with my tongue and then my cock. Making her cry out, over and over. All damn day straight into the night.

Then someone knocked on the door.

"Fuck." The curse came out with enough force that Vanessa jolted.

I stood, and she pulled the sheet back up, covering up her luscious body.

I wiped my mouth and tried to get my raging hard-on under control as I went to answer the door. I opened it a crack. Eli stood there, arms crossed.

"What?" Wasn't the most amiable greeting, but I had a beautiful woman in my bed and I wasn't thrilled to be pulled away.

"Is Vanessa in there?"

I frowned. "Who wants to know?"

"Well, half the wedding party will probably want to know when she doesn't show up for brunch. It starts in ten minutes."

"Oh, shit." Vanessa's voice rang out from inside the room.

I shut the door on Eli and turned. She was already up and scrambling to get her clothes on. I watched her, desire and disappointment swirling. My dick was still throbbing, and I wasn't ready to give up yet.

I stood between her and the door as she walked toward me dressed as she had been last night, but looking like she'd been thoroughly fucked since. I stretched my arms out, touching either side of the short hallway, blocking her exit.

"Don't run out yet."

She blinked up at me with tired thoughtful eyes. "I want to stay. Trust me."

"It's a brunch. What about me?"

She smirked. "What about you, Darren?"

I ran my tongue against my lower lip. "I'm trying to think of something clever to say, but the truth is I want to eat your pussy so fucking bad right now I can't think straight."

She made a breathy sound as I took a step closer to her.

"You know I want to say yes."

"Then say yes," I murmured softly, tucking back an untamed lock of hair.

"I'm going to be late as it is. I'm a mess."

"But I made you that way, and thinking about that is making me even harder."

The smudge of makeup around her eyes, the tangles in her hair, and the wrinkles in her dress were all satisfying reminders of night before.

"I can be quick," I lied. I pushed up the hem of her dress hopefully.

"But I don't want you to be. I like when you take your time with me." Her lips twisted into a coy smile.

I pulled her to me, looping my arm around her waist possessively. "Come right back."

She laughed and slapped my shoulder. "They're expecting you too. Get ready, and I'll see you there."

I groaned and nipped her earlobe. There was no denying it now. I was seriously addicted to this woman.

CHAPTER EIGHT

VANESSA

The last few days on the island flew by. Maya, Eli, and I wandered off to do a few excursions together. I couldn't remember when we'd had so much fun together laughing and goofing off.

Most days Darren found his way to me, at my side, a place where it seemed he'd always been. Our eyes spoke a language only we knew. Our hands found each other at the same time. Something invisible existed and grew between us that completed a dangerous fantasy...the fantasy that somehow this amazing connection between us could survive in the real world.

And when the night came, he didn't need to ask. I was there. Knocking on his door, falling into his arms, ready for everything he would give me for the short time we were going to be together.

When we were finally alone, we were desperate for each other. Tearing at our clothes, kissing hungrily, eager to be connected again. My body was tender from having him every night, but my hunger for him couldn't wane. He took me someplace else, and the faraway look in his eye when he followed me into sweet oblivion was one I'd never tire of giving him.

Our last night together was bittersweet. He made love to me slowly, drawing out every sensual touch. I trembled from being so on edge, but I didn't want it to end either. Something about that last night felt final. Meaningful, but heavy with all the things we weren't saying.

We didn't let sleep take us until the sky outside started to lighten. When I woke a few hours later, Darren slumbered beside me in the bed we'd shared night after night.

I took another snapshot in my mind. Our little slice of paradise.

But nothing could last forever.

I leaned over and kissed his shoulder. He didn't rouse.

Feeling sad and blessed and not ready to leave, I dressed and crept out to my room to gather the last of my things before we left for the airport.

★ ★ ★

The journey home seemed shorter. Maybe I should have been ready for the shift, but I found myself hating every minute that passed, taking us farther from our island escape.

We touched down after a rocky descent. Darren's hand warmed my tight grip on the armrest. I finally let go and took a breath, but the relief was short-lived.

Through the tiny window, the New York City sky was a dull gray, as if I needed the extra contrast to remind me of the inevitable. I powered on my phone, which promptly blew up with missed texts. I gave up trying to catch up after a few minutes and tossed the phone in my bag.

Darren and I made our way to the taxi line, our group scattered in various stages of arrival. I could barely look at him, because somehow I knew this was it. The dread in my gut told me before he could. No matter what we really wanted, things would change. We couldn't bring paradise home with us. Life didn't work that way.

The cab pulled up, and Darren loaded my bags in the trunk, saving the driver the task. I opened the door, eager to move on but not to say good-bye.

"Hey, wait."

I held onto the door, as if that could keep me grounded.

Darren turned me to him, brought us close, like we were precious to each other. He cradled my cheek and lifted my gaze to his. I steeled myself against the emotions that threatened to unravel me. My throat burned with all the things I wanted to say, all the things he'd made me feel on this trip that I was terrified of never feeling with someone else again.

I was falling in love with Darren. The truth of it stung even worse because I knew this could be it. He hadn't promised me forever. Didn't change the fact that I wanted a chance at it.

"You okay?"

I nodded. "I'm fine. Tired, that's all."

He hesitated, and I hated every tense second between us. I wanted to tell him how I felt, but I couldn't bring myself to do it now.

"I'll call you," he said after a moment's silence.

I smiled weakly and accepted his lips when they swept across mine.

Maybe he would. Maybe he wouldn't. All I knew was that in a matter of minutes we'd be farther apart than we'd been in a week, and already I was missing him like a hopeless fool.

The nights we'd spent together were already memories. Every time our paths crossed, I'd remember this bliss. How could I ever forget it?

I suppose it was better than never having had it.

I closed my eyes and pushed down all the wishing and hoping. I couldn't know right now what the future would bring, and now wasn't the time to ask him. We'd just have to see how things played out.

DARREN

I took another pass through the gym. I checked the machines in each room, straightened the weights, and ensured everything was in its proper place. This was my usual routine, but somehow everything felt off. Familiar but strangely lacking. Like something was missing.

I'd traveled all over the world when I was in the service, and still I couldn't remember feeling this off balance coming home.

I moved over to the pull-up bar, letting it take my weight for a second. The rough texture of the metal under my palm, the periodic clink of the machines, and the breathing of the people using them—everything faded into the background and my thoughts floated to Vanessa. Spread out for me, peach skin against the clean white sheets. Saying my name like a prayer as I made her mine, night after night. I tightened my hand around the bar and fought the surge of arousal at the erotic vision.

I closed my eyes and something happened. Emotion curled up around the physical feeling. A mix of excitement and pure terror. A combined sensation I couldn't name, couldn't touch because it flew too fast over me, rocked me, forced Vanessa back into my mind. Her rapture, arching under me, clinging to me like she couldn't live without me. And I'd felt the same. I'd needed her physically, yes. Desperately. But more. I craved her in a way that was beginning to scare the shit out of me. It'd only been a couple of days, but already I couldn't stop thinking about her.

"Earth to Darren."

A throaty female voice tore the intoxicating visions from my mind. My eyes shot open. The sounds of the gym came back in a rush. Delilah was beside me, her dark toned body displayed proudly in her tight gym outfit.

"Hey...sorry." I let out a breath and released my aching grip on the bar.

"I haven't seen you in a while."

She didn't just mean the gym, though she saw me here plenty. Delilah and I had enjoyed a few rendezvous, but more often I knew her as "DJ," Delilah Jackson, a seasoned and skilled medic we occasionally worked with on emergencies.

She grinned. "Want to spot me?"

I inhaled another deep breath and nodded. "Sure."

I followed her to the weight rack, and she stacked up an impressive pile of weights on the bench press.

"How have you been? You seem distracted."

"Just getting back into the swing of things since the trip. Brain is still on vacation."

"Cry me a river. Last week was hell. You missed some real winners. Just enough warm weather for people to start stabbing each other."

I chuckled, almost jealous. Shifts weren't the same without people like Ian and Delilah talking shit and going through hell right beside you. I liked that about Delilah—that we'd seen some shit together. Working together on as many emergencies as we had seemed like a lesser version of war.

That we'd slept together on occasion didn't seem to matter. If either of us ended the night with one too many, horny as hell, the invitation was always open. Until she met a girl a few months ago and we were back to being colleagues. We hadn't skipped a beat.

"How's the new girl?"

She smirked. "Wouldn't you like to know?"

I did and I didn't. "I'd like to know how you can you switch teams like that. You have no idea what that does to the egos of the men who've been to bed with you."

She laughed and reached up to start a new set.

"How do you screw a new flavor every week, Darren? Or are you so single-minded that you think all women are the same by way of their shared anatomy?"

I shook my head. "Not all the same. Definitely not."

Vanessa wasn't like anyone else. Something about her, or maybe the whole package, called to me, got under my skin the way no one ever had.

Delilah finished her set and sat up. Wiping her forehead with a towel, she looked up at me. "So who is it?"

I frowned. "Huh?"

"Who's got your head in the clouds, Casanova?"

"I'm not talking chicks with you, Delilah."

"Why not? You know I'm not the type to get catty. I know you a lot better than the girls who get tangled up in your web of abs and charm. I know you mess around."

I hesitated, but who the hell was I going to talk to? Cam? Definitely not Ian.

"I met someone a while ago, and we've... I guess we're..."

"You're sleeping together," she interjected matter-of-factly.

"We did, yeah."

"Okay. And now what? Are you dating?"

"She was on the trip. I don't think that counts as dating. We were inseparable all week. But I haven't seen her since I got back, so I can't really say what we are now."

"But you can't stop thinking about her."

"I guess so."

I drew in a breath and fixed my attention on Delilah's eyes, one of her best features. She was a pretty woman. Confident, fit. But she wasn't Vanessa. No one came close.

I hadn't been able to think straight since I'd seen her last. Once she'd decided to give in to me on the island, everything had been amazing. Pure magic between us. And then she'd gone cold the second we landed in New York. She'd barely said a word, yet it seemed like, in the silence between us, she was telling me it was over. Our little tryst had ended.

And that's what I'd wanted. I wanted to fuck around while we were away and come back to my life.

This life. The gym. Long days at the station. Nights out with friends. With women who meant nothing to me.

Except I didn't want them. I wanted her.

"I texted her to see if she wanted to get together. She's busy moving apartments this week."

"She's moving apartments, and she doesn't need your help? Sounds like she's blowing you off. Also, texting her sounds like you want to hook up. They're not all like me, Darren."

I met her smile. Delilah wasn't typical, but I could see her point.

"So what do I do? Show up out of the blue? Force her to let me take her out?"

"Well, I don't know this woman, but I'm guessing one of

two things. Either you—Darren, the player of all players—got played, or—"

"I'm not a player," I interrupted. "There's always an understa—"

"Oh, shut up. There will always be an understanding when a girl can't help but want to drop her panties for you. Doesn't mean she's never going to want a relationship. You can delude yourself into thinking everything is cut and dried every time, but trust me, you've broken hearts. Takes one to know one." She stood and draped her towel over the bar and faced me. "The second scenario is that she knows you're a selfish dick when it comes to women, and while you may have had fun together on your trip, she doesn't want it to go any further and get hurt."

I didn't necessarily consider myself a selfish person. I saved people's lives after all, some of whom barely warranted saving, but I did it all the same. Then again, I'd seen how fleeting life could be. How one day everything could fall apart for someone.

Life was short. Maybe I was selfish, and I couldn't justify devoting my life to someone who could compromise my happiness for a single minute. The question was whether I was capable of being true to a woman like Vanessa. Could I promise her something more and keep that promise, after years of never letting myself get tied down? What we'd shared on the island had been amazing, but could I change everything for her...just like that?

I thought of Vanessa and how I'd been drawn to her, over and over again. She challenged me, sure. But I wasn't unhappy for it. I was barely annoyed when she called me out on my shit. I probably registered relief more than anything. A breath of fresh air. Not the toxic air of a bar, filled with perfumes and body heat and sweet liquors that came off the girls who I knew damn well would get on their knees and do whatever I asked after three martinis.

Not Vanessa. She was light, and real, and brought an intensity into my world I'd never known.

"She's not a player. I've never met anyone like her before. We connected, and not just physically."

"Do you think she feels the same way?"

The look in Vanessa's eyes, the way she smiled at me, touched me, came for me. Yes.

I gave a slight nod, as if saying the word out loud might jinx everything.

"If she does, deep down she wants to see you as much as you want to see her right now."

"So what do I do?"

"You've never struck me as the kind of guy to let an obstacle come in the way of what he wants. Maybe it breaks all the rules in your playbook, but chase the damn woman. Do what you've got to do."

I racked more weights, switched places with Delilah, and pushed through a set with Vanessa dominating my mind. What did I really want? What the hell was I made of? The more I thought about the life I'd been living, the more I wanted to change it.

I'd broken away from my parents' expectations to live my own life, and here I was barely living it. I wasn't getting past the first course every day of my life. I hadn't even given myself a chance to get to the entrée. And Vanessa was the whole package. Something rang deep in me, like a voice I trusted that had been silent for way too long.

VANESSA

Piano, the tinkling of water glasses, and the not always quiet murmur of wall-to-wall suits. Those were sounds of the Theodore, an upscale restaurant several blocks from our office. Reilly was coming from another meeting, so we'd agreed to meet here.

I slicked my hands down my navy-blue sheath dress. I hadn't seen Reilly all morning, and I'd been too bogged down with trying to catch up to guess what he wanted to discuss with me today. I maneuvered between tables, my black pumps clicking on the dark wood floors.

Even knowing the maître d' would lead me right to Reilly, I scanned the room, trying to spot him first. He was a few feet away, drinking his seltzer water with lime, looking bored. A flash of worry that I'd kept him waiting too long sent heat to my palms. But when I arrived at the table, he managed a smile and rose.

"Vanessa. How are you?"

I sat and let the waiter pour my water. "I'm doing well, thank you."

He studied me a moment, and I briefly wondered if he'd ever looked at me that way before. Everything seemed strange being back. Achingly familiar yet oddly foreign at the same time.

"I trust you enjoyed the break."

I nodded quickly. "I did, very much. It was...rejuvenating." Not sure if he could comprehend it, but mere mortals needed a recharge every once in a while.

"I believe it. You look different. More rested, maybe."

I couldn't help but laugh a little. Nights with Darren had

taken a bite out of my sleep, but he was no doubt the reason for any lingering glow. I missed him more than I wanted to admit.

"You were missed, of course."

"Thank you. I've been doing my best to catch up today. I can't say that I was really prepared to dive right into a review today, but—"

"It's not what you think. I want to offer you a job."

I lifted my eyebrows. "A job?"

"I'm leaving the firm. An old colleague of mine, Bill Donovan, and I are starting up a hedge fund. Someone else will be taking my place, and you can either come with me or stay with them. The choice is entirely yours."

"Oh...wow."

He canted his head, as if he expected me to make a decision that instant.

"Well, I guess that brings up a lot of questions about the job you're offering me. Can you tell me what would be expected of me?"

"Much of the same."

A fresh wave of dread mixed in with the anxiety this conversation was already creating for me. Was he going to make me decide right now?

Maybe I didn't hate David Reilly per se, but I hated working for him. That wasn't the vacation talking, I assured myself. But what if I said no and lost my job?

He was driven, possessive, and cutthroat. I never wanted to get in the man's crosshairs. I didn't put it past him to be vindictive in any way that suited him.

The waiter came and delivered two endive salads.

Reilly thanked him curtly and nodded toward me. "I ordered for you. I hope you don't mind."

"Thank you." I fiddled with my napkin. "Would anything be different?"

"We've secured an office in Midtown, so your commute would be a bit longer. We'll be traveling quite a bit too. I'll be keeping my finger on the pulse of the major foreign markets. I'll need your support for that."

I chewed on my salad, delaying any response.

"The most significant difference in the job, outside of the travel, is the pay. I'm no longer limited by the firm's policies. I've discussed your salary with my partner, and we're prepared to double what you're currently making."

I coughed and vinaigrette stung my throat. Double. Jesus. "Wow."

"That's the second time you've said that. You're either completely stunned or you're stalling. What are you thinking?"

"I'm thinking..."

"Vanessa."

I swallowed carefully and took a drink of my water, buying myself some precious seconds before I spoke.

"I came into this position at entry level. I was never sure what to expect from it for the long-term. What you're proposing now sounds like I'd be turning it into a career."

He chuckled. "Well, what else would you do, Vanessa?"

His words stung. I knew I was capable of more than catering to his every whim and want, but I also didn't exactly have a lot of other opportunities lined up. I moved to the city on a wing and prayer, grateful that a college friend had hooked me up with Reilly. He'd kept me too busy for me to think of anything else.

"I'm not sure. I hadn't really thought about it."

He leaned in, forcing my attention to his shrewd gray eyes.

"Let me be completely honest with you. You were missed this week. By others, but no one missed your presence more than I did. I'm not trying to win you over by telling you that this is an enormous opportunity I'm offering. It's the truth. Executive assistants are a dime a dozen. I'm choosing you." He pointed at me with his fork and then returned his attention to the salad in front of him.

"I'm flattered." Not really, but hearing those kinds of words from him was unusual. Also he was offering to double my salary, which was a raise I badly needed.

"Then say yes. Say you'll come with me."

I wanted to think about it. This was all too fast, but that's how Reilly worked. Everything always moved fast, and most days I could keep up without hesitation.

But not today. Today I was overwhelmed, and I wasn't in the right mind-set for any of this. My head was still on an island, and my heart was aching for the man who'd worked his way into it.

"Vanessa?"

Thoughts whizzed through my mind in an unintelligible blur as I struggled to find the right words. But there was only one word.

"Yes." I offered a tight smile. "If those are your terms, I'll come with you."

"Excellent."

He smiled, a genuine smile that almost gave me hope. Maybe this reenlistment would mean a better working relationship between us. Maybe with more money came more respect. Then again, maybe not.

CHAPTER NINE

VANESSA

"Wait!" Eli's voice went high-pitched as we approached the first turn up the stairs.

I took a few seconds to catch my breath, even if the muscles in my arms burned from holding the heavy end of my chair. It was old, made of a burnished orange fabric. When I saw it at the secondhand store, the price was right and I knew it could be a chair that I could love, even if it didn't earn many compliments. Especially now as Eli and I struggled to get it to the second floor without killing ourselves. Ugly as it may have been, it was heavy as hell.

"Okay, go," Eli said.

Together we took slow steps up the narrow stairway.

"Hey, let me help with that."

Darren's voice echoed up to me, and then he was next to me, easily taking the weight that I carried.

"I've got this end," Eli grunted.

"Just let go and get out of the way, Eli. I've got it."

Eli lowered his end, and that quickly, Darren hoisted the old heavy chair above him, narrowly avoiding the stairway ceiling. Balancing it on his shoulders, he carried it swiftly the rest of the way up and through the doorway into what was soon to be *my place*.

He dropped it gently in the corner of the living room and stood, looking barely winded.

"Thanks," I said, wiping invisible dust off the chair. "What are you doing here?"

"You said you were moving. Figured you needed some help."

I shrugged, trying to ignore the pinch in my shoulders from the boxes I'd already carried up today. "We're good. Thanks though."

Eli shot me an exasperated look. No one ever wanted to be the one to help with a move, but hell, that's what friends were for. Maya and Cameron weren't coming back from their honeymoon for another day, so it was just us.

Having Darren in the space already made me uneasy. Never mind his blatant show of brawn. Never mind the way his shirt rode up, giving me a glimpse of the body that I'd had all to myself not so long ago. A few minutes ago, I'd felt the apartment, even in its haphazard mid-move state, was becoming mine. Now all I could think about was how Darren's presence changed how I saw everything. My bed wasn't just a place to collapse after a long day. It was a haven I wanted to share with him. This was a place to start over, but one night in my bed, he'd be here forever in my mind.

"I told you I could handle it."

"Vanessa, seriously. We've been at this for hours already." Eli had gone from exasperated to pissed.

Darren's gaze skated between my new roommate and me. "Eli, you hungry?"

"Hell, yes."

"Me too." Darren pulled out his wallet, fished out a few bills, and offered them to Eli. "Go grab us some pizza at Tony's down the street. I'll take care of the rest of this."

"Deal. I'll get the pizza. Least I can do." Eli waved away the bills and slipped past me.

He disappeared down the corridor, leaving us in the silence of the half-furnished apartment.

"What are you doing?" The edge in my tone surprised me, but I was hungry and confused and already wiped of energy from getting back into the swing of things at work.

"I told you, I'm helping you move."

"I don't need your help."

His jaw tightened, and his stare burned into me with an intensity I hadn't seen in him. Stalking closer, he pinned me with that look.

"I'm here, and I'm not going anywhere until you're moved in. You want to kick me out then, fine. I don't know what the hell happened between that last night on the island and now, but I'm lost."

My jaw fell a fraction, that last word catching me off guard. I knew what he meant. I'd done a complete one-eighty since the trip and didn't bother telling him why. But that word... lost. That was a good word for the emotional scrambling I'd done, trying to convince myself that Darren didn't want me for anything more than a casual hookup.

Every minute that passed, I convinced myself a little more that all those unspoken moments between us weren't as powerful to him as they'd been for me. Every careful touch, every way I'd broken myself open and given myself to him.

His tipped my chin, lifting my gaze to meet his. "Talk to me," he said gently, his searching stare no less determined.

"You came here to talk?"

He winced. "What the hell does that mean?"

133

"We spent half that trip in your bed. I figured you'd show up wanting more than a friendly chat."

Not that I would have minded a hookup. But that wasn't the routine I wanted to get into with him.

I wanted a relationship. Yes, I realized that now. I'd been missing companionship for too long, and maybe with the right person, I could make it work with my insane schedule working for Reilly. But Darren wasn't my happily ever after. He was my off-the-charts-happy-until-it's-over. My heart couldn't take that.

I walked away from his touch, trying to ignore how the air went cold around me the farther I went.

"I miss you."

"I miss you too." I stared down at my hands, trying to brush the dirt from them. "I'm sorry if I've been distant."

"You've been unreachable. I have to admit, I'm not used to being ignored so completely."

I closed my eyes a moment and released a tired sigh. "I knew things wouldn't be the same, and I just needed some time to come to terms with that."

"Just because we're back in New York doesn't mean things have to change. I mean, I want to see you. I want to..." His lips fell open, but no more words came.

"As much as I wish I could, I can't be the kind of girl you go for, Darren. Maybe because I find it nearly impossible to say no to you, I let myself go further than I normally would have last week. I pushed myself out of my comfort zone and let myself care about you even knowing that it wasn't going to last. But the truth is, I can't be with someone and then flip a switch and pretend like it didn't mean that much."

"I'm not asking you to. The time we spent together meant

something to me too." He walked closer, and his voice became quiet. "I have a colorful past, okay? I don't deny it. But that doesn't mean I'm not capable of anything else. When I met you for the first time months ago, I wanted you. It was physical. I had no idea all of this would go down. That I'd want you the way I do, that I wouldn't be able to look at anyone else the same. I wasn't expecting any of this, but I'm not going to let it pass me by without giving it a shot."

"If you're talking about a relationship…"

"Yes." He swallowed hard, and tension lined his face, as if this were so far from his practiced pick up lines.

He cuffed my wrist with his hand, and his thumb settled over the place on where my heartbeat could be felt.

"What are you doing?" I whispered.

"Making sure your heart's doing exactly what mine is."

I shook my head. My heart was flying. I couldn't believe Darren Bridge was saying these things. That I believed him. "I don't know what to say."

He brought my wrist to his lips, softly kissing the flesh. "Say you'll see me. Say that you'll try to make this work with me, against all your better judgment."

I struggled to bring air back into my lungs. "I want to say yes."

"Then say yes, for fuck's sake."

"I don't want to be a hookup, Darren. My heart can't take it."

"You were never a hookup. Never were and never will be. Understand?"

Before I could answer him, his lips were on mine, soft and determined all at once. I surrendered to the kiss and his touch, melting against him like I'd always belonged right there.

Between my schedule and his past, I had no idea how we would make it work. But it'd been so long since I'd let my heart feel this way. All the tiny shreds of doubt I'd been clinging to fell away in his arms. The perfect way he kissed me was a reminder that if we could find a way to bring that week of paradise home, maybe we could have it all.

DARREN

The weekend seemed too far away, but that was all Vanessa could completely commit to. Her boss kept her running pretty hard, and she had a lot of catching up to do. The whole thing sounded stressful and reminded me too much of the life my dad led.

Ian and I arrived at the gym just as Olivia was approaching the big glass double doors. A few strands of her long black hair swept up with the wind as we came in. She smiled brightly. For a split second, I saw the little girl who'd looked up to me her whole life, who'd trusted me to protect her and take care of her when our parents weren't around. And of course tease the shit out of her.

"Hey, I was just taking off. Are you coming to dinner tonight?"

"Dinner?"

"Cam and Maya are cooking a feast." Her blue-eyed gaze wandered to Ian and lingered there a little too long. "You're welcome too, if you want."

He shot her his signature smile, the one that made models fall on their backs. "Sounds great. I'm Ian, by the way."

He shook her hand, and her cheeks grew pink.

I frowned between the two of them, but neither seemed to

notice. "Actually, Ian and I might be hitting the bar later. I'll let you know if we're going to swing by though."

She glanced back to me. I probably did a shitty job of schooling my discontent because her smile fell away quickly.

"Okay. Sure. I guess I'll see you later."

She waved without looking back at either of us and passed through the doors.

"What the fuck was that?" My tone was clipped.

Ian raised his eyebrows. "What?"

"Touch my sister, and I'll slit your throat. Got it?"

Last thing I needed was someone like Ian setting his sights on my sister. I didn't know how innocent she was, but suffice to say she'd always be innocent to me. And Ian was the furthest thing from innocent.

He glanced back toward Olivia's figure disappearing down the street and out of view before returning to me with a nod. "Got it."

I stared a second longer, making sure he understood I wasn't kidding. I liked Ian. I didn't want to have to kill him.

His face split with a smile. "Dude, you need to get laid. You're turning into an uptight motherfucker."

I sighed, because I couldn't lie. "Yeah. I know. That's why I'm here every day."

True enough, life hadn't been the same since the trip. Work was the same, but when it came to unwinding, I ended up blowing off steam at the gym.

We walked into the weight room, and I scanned the room for familiar faces. The only one I wanted to see was Vanessa's. I had to find my way back into her world, one that was proving to be increasingly difficult to breach with her schedule. I didn't think I had an addictive personality, but when it came to being with her, I was hooked. And I needed my fix.

Maybe patience wasn't a word in my dictionary, but I was willing to find some when it came to her. I could have called up a dozen women to satisfy the physical need that gnawed at me a little more every day, but Vanessa was the one I wanted. And as much as I ached for her, I didn't want to make her feel like the hookup she worried she'd become to me.

"We'll fix you up tonight, man."

I shook my head. "Nah. I'm good."

I racked up my bar with weights and did a set. The rush and the burn and the slight fatigue that hit my muscles were all welcome sensations.

"You strung up on someone?"

Hell, I was going to have to break the news to Ian eventually.

I sat up and thought back to the only time they'd met. "You remember the girl at the bar?"

He chuckled. "You're going to have to be more specific."

"The singer."

He lifted his eyebrows. "Oh, *that* girl at the bar. Yeah. She was smokin'."

"I wasn't sure you'd remember. You were pretty distracted."

He laughed. "Oh, yeah. We had a good time. All three of us. Thanks for the back up." He winked.

I rolled my eyes. Further evidence that I needed to keep him a mile away from my sister.

"So how was she?"

I could reminisce in my head all day long on the mind-blowing sex we'd had, and I often did, but I wasn't going to regale Ian with the nitty gritty of our more intimate moments.

The devil knew he had plenty of his own fodder to work with, anyway.

"She's incredible," I said simply. "I want to take her out. Do something special. All she does is work lately, and I can't exactly tell her to stop."

"Sounds familiar."

I smirked. "It's not work when it's your dream job, man."

"True. I'm guessing she's not at her dream job."

"Not exactly. She's someone's personal assistant."

He wrinkled his nose and switched places with me at the squat bar. "So what? You're going to try dating her?"

"Yeah."

He shot me a wary look, full of doubt and probably fueled by his own ignorance.

"What's wrong with that?"

"Seems like a lot of work when we could hit the bar after work and you could have your pick. Or just take a spin through your contacts."

As he said that, my phone dinged with a text.

One of the girls I'd trained at the gym last month, Ellie.

Did you have plans tonight? I'm free.

I shot off a quick reply. *Not tonight.* Of course, the answer was not ever, but I didn't know quite how to word that yet. When I glanced up, Ian was staring at me.

"How are you going to clear the bench, Bridge?"

I shrugged. "I'll figure it out. I'm more worried about making this work with Vanessa right now."

I changed the subject quickly, simultaneously ignoring the problem that I could feel taking root a little more deeply.

CHAPTER TEN

VANESSA

Today wasn't exactly bittersweet. Tomorrow my commute would be longer and my paycheck would double. I could only hope I'd made the right choice. My knowledge of hedge funds was limited, but I was confident that with Reilly's background in finance and his broad connections with other wealthy investors, he would find a way to succeed with the new venture. Hopefully I'd be given an opportunity to grow as the new company did.

As I was packing up the last of my office supplies, a young man arrived with a dolly stacked high with boxes of documents.

"Boxes from Kevin Dermott's office?"

"Over there," I said, pointing to the corner of Reilly's old office.

Dermott was inheriting Reilly's position at the firm, a healthy jump from what I could tell. He'd been Maya's boss before she left. I didn't know him well beyond the fact that he and Maya had never really gelled very well. She'd left the company abruptly. She never told me exactly why, other than to imply that Dermott had played some part in it.

My phone began to vibrate on my desk. A Florida number came up that I didn't recognize. I let it ring, and a minute later a voice mail alert popped up. I listened and froze when I heard a voice from my past.

"Vanessa, it's Michael Browning. Long time. So your mom gave me your number. Hope you don't mind me calling you out of the blue like this, but I'm going to be up in New York City next week for a conference. I was hoping that maybe we could catch up. I'm not sure if you come back to Callaway much, but if you do, I guess I always seem to miss you. Anyway. Give me a call sometime and maybe we can get a drink or something. Talk to you soon. Bye."

I ignored the next person who brought in another dolly of boxes and moved to the window overlooking the street. I dialed my mom's number and pushed the phone to my ear. Two rings and she picked up.

"You gave Michael my number?" My words came out hushed and angry before she could even say hello.

"Wh— Well, hello to you too." There was an edge to her voice.

I'd caught her off guard.

"Why, Mom?"

"He wanted to catch up with you while he was in town, and it seemed harmless enough. Is that a crime, now really?"

"You had no right to do that without my permission."

"You're being a little bit dramatic, don't you think?"

"What if I sent Dad over to your house out of the blue?"

She was silent a moment. "That's different."

"Why?"

"Because... For one, I'm a married woman now. I'm not sure that would be entirely appropriate."

"I may not be married, but I'm seeing someone. And I don't need you pushing Michael on me and giving him the wrong idea."

"You're seeing someone? Who is he?"

"He's..." How did I describe Darren? "He's a firefighter here in the city. He also happens to be Maya's new brother-in-law. We spent a lot of time together on the trip."

"Oh. You never told me."

"Things are still really new. I'm not sure where it's going."

"That doesn't sound promising."

I rolled my eyes, bracing myself for the lecture that was coming. "He's fine. I just haven't had a ton of time lately."

She sighed. "You need to make time for a relationship if you want one to work. How long has it been since you've dated? It's your schedule that's always pushing people away."

"Mom, please don't lecture me right now."

She wasn't wrong, but I also hadn't been looking for a relationship either. Not until my heart started doing unexpected things around Darren. Impeccable timing too, when my professional life was getting turned upside down.

"I know I couldn't give you the father you really wanted, Vanessa, but I didn't raise you to live without love in your life. Maybe we don't always see eye to eye on the choices you make. I accept that. It is your life, and I respect that. I just want to see you make it a happy one."

I closed my eyes and rested my head against the window. "I don't need a man to be happy."

Yet being with Darren had made me happier than anything had in a long time.

"I know you don't. But you're not happy, sweetheart. Something's missing, and you know it. I'm your mother. I can sense it, even from this distance."

I hated when she was right. She'd go straight to the heart of something. Strip away all the noise.

I didn't know what to say to that.

Then a woman entered the office. She didn't look like someone who'd been hired to move boxes. She wore a tight black pencil skirt, a silky lavender blouse, and chunky square diamonds sparkled on her ears. Her dark hair was pulled into a twist.

"Mom, I have to go. I'll call you later."

I hung up quickly as the woman walked toward me with a smile. "I'm Jia Sumner. I work with Kevin Dermott."

"Nice to meet you. Can I help you with something?"

"Yes, actually. Kevin's not going to be fully operational in this office for a few more days. But he needs something from his files here. I'm just going to grab it for him quickly. Do you mind?"

Something about her manner gave me pause. She was all smiles and politeness, but I had an odd feeling that facade didn't fully represent the woman in front of me. Still, I had nothing to lose by letting her poke around. As of five o'clock today, I didn't work here anymore. I gestured to the stacks of document boxes that lined the edge of Reilly's old office.

"They've been putting everything in there. Let me know if you need any help," I added, because I was programmed to help anyone in a suit, it would seem. Thus was my lot in life, thanks to Mr. David Reilly.

She moved to the boxes, sifted through the files, and extracted one. "Here is it. That was easy."

She turned and paused, holding the file to her chest. *NYC Youth Arts Initiative* was typed on the tab. I knit my eyebrows together. That was Reilly's charity. Or at least the one that he and his wife had been heavily supporting all the time I'd known him.

"That's David's nonprofit, right?" I pointed to the folder.

Her smile froze. "It is. Dermott supports it as well. They're both heavily involved in donor management. Something came up and he needed a quick peek at this."

Just then, my phone rang. I saw Darren's number. Jia offered a small wave as she disappeared out of the office.

I swiped the screen and answered. "Hi."

"Hey, beautiful. Can you talk?"

Even his phone voice was sexy. Like thick syrup over a warm pancake.

"I can. Today's my last day here at the office so I don't have anyone hovering over me for once. What's up?"

"I want to see you tonight."

"Oh. I thought we're going to make plans this weekend."

"I know, but I can't wait anymore." He paused a moment. "Just miss you, red. It's been too long."

The tenderness in his voice tugged at my heart. I thought about him every day. He was the last thought as I drifted off to sleep, and the first that floated into my mind in the morning. I missed him too...more than I'd ever thought possible. But life had kept me too busy to do anything about it.

I'd been waiting until we had time, real time to spend together. But my life was made up of huge blocks of working hours and a scant slice or two of freedom that wasn't overtaken by sleep or other less interesting adult obligations. If I waited for too long though, we'd never spend time together again. My mom's warnings echoed in my ears, and in this moment they rang true. I could lose Darren if I didn't make time for him.

"If I get everything wrapped up here, I should be able to get out on time."

"Great. I've got a couple appointments here at the gym. I

can meet you at your place around seven o'clock?"

"That works. I'll text you if anything comes up."

"Perfect." His tone had changed into a happier one. "I can't wait to see you."

A smile tugged at my lips. I closed my eyes, and for a minute, I was back on an island.

"I'll see you soon."

DARREN

I left the locker rooms, freshly showered and ready to head to Vanessa's. She was running late, thanks to her dick boss sending her on a last-minute errand, but I wasn't going to let that get in the way of the night I had planned.

"Hey, stranger," Raina called out as I passed the doorway to her studio.

I slowed to a stop and backed up. Dread fell like a stone in my gut. My life would be a lot easier if I never had to see her face again. Of course, that wasn't her fault. I plastered on a friendly smile and leaned against the doorway.

"You survive without us?" I teased.

"Without you two brutes? Absolutely." She moved toward me, winked, and then gave me a quick once-over, wetting her lips.

I cleared my throat and tried to burn out the memory of what happened last time she looked at me like that. "I hope you didn't have too much fun without us."

"No," she murmured, coming uncomfortably close. "I figured I'd save all the fun for when you got back."

I nodded, eating all the words I wanted to say. She dragged her hand down my chest, slowing at the band of my jeans. This was escalating faster than I'd expected. Goddamnit.

"Not here, Raina."

I tried to take a step back, but she tucked her fingers in just over the band, effectively holding me in place.

A coy smiled played on her lips. "Yeah, you're probably right. Let's meet up after work."

I swallowed over the knot of regret in my throat. I closed my eyes and took a breath. I'd never been good at this part— the putting distance between me and someone I was over part. Mostly because I never had to be good at it. I'd never done something this stupid. The terms were usually much more clear. This was muddy and all sorts of fucked.

"How about we just keep things casual?" I finally said.

"I'm good with that. Your place or mine?" She slid her hand lower, over my fly, grazing my cock.

Any other day that might have done something for me, but I felt nothing. Suddenly I couldn't put distance between us fast enough. I backed away until I was out of reach.

She frowned. "Is something wrong?"

"This, specifically, is kind of wrong." I gestured between us, cursing inwardly. How had I gotten myself into this fucking mess? "I shouldn't have made a pass at you. I wasn't thinking about how awkward it could make things at work."

Her eyebrows lifted. "Darren, I'm totally fine with casual. I mean, I think I made that pretty clear last time."

I glanced down at my watch, desperate for anything to get me away from her. "Listen, I got to run. I'll see you around, okay?"

She closed the distance between us again. With every step toward me, tension coiled in my stomach. Not the sexual kind.

She grabbed hold of my shirt, tugging it toward her though

my body didn't move with it. I harnessed the urge to shove her back. Inherently I hated the idea of being tied to anyone. Now, I only wanted to be tied to one woman, and she sure as hell wasn't Raina. Not remotely. I had no idea how to dash her hopes of hooking up again without it blowing up in my face.

Before I could disconnect her, she was molded against me, planting her lips on mine. Lips, tongue, hand in the hair. I winced against her, masking my disgust as she pulled away.

"Call me later," she breathed, biting her lip as she backed into the yoga studio and disappeared out of view.

I ground my teeth down hard, holding my position and biting my tongue. I wanted to lock her in that fucking room and throw away the key. For someone who touted the spiritual art of yoga and meditation all day long, she was about as intuitive as a brick.

I pivoted to leave, anxious to get as far away from her as possible. Then I froze. Several paces ahead of me stood a beautiful blonde, her eyes narrowed, hands on her hips, mouth agape. My heart thudded in my chest as I walked toward her. A pound of regret compounded onto my growing mountain of self-loathing.

She turned to walk away, but I ran to catch up to her.

"Maya, wait... It's not what it looks like."

I felt her reply first—a hard slap across my face. I reached for the sting that she left, but I had a feeling she was just winding up. She worked her jaw, disappointment so clear in her soft brown eyes.

"I can't believe I told Vanessa to give you a chance. We're not home a week, and I catch you rubbing up on someone else."

"I didn't... I wasn't..."

"No? Then what the hell was Raina's hand doing on your

crotch? You're a fucking pig. Cam warned me and I—"

"I made a mistake." I ended up shouting it to halt her rant.

She paused, and we both stopped talking long enough to catch a breath. I shoved a hand through my hair, hating everything about this fucking moment.

"I hooked up with Raina way before the trip, and it was a huge mistake. I have no interest in being with her. I care about Vanessa."

"Apparently not. Looks like she was just another hookup."

"She means a lot more than that to me. This thing with Raina happened before. Things are different now, but I haven't had a chance to talk to either of them about it. I have every intention of being exclusive with Vanessa."

She set her hands firmly on her hips, her expression tight. "Then you'd better come clean with her, or I'll do it for you."

I studied her, gauged if she'd really do that. I couldn't gamble that she wouldn't. It'd be over with Vanessa. I knew it.

"Maya, Jesus, don't tell her about this. It would ruin everything."

"If you care about her, she needs to know what kind of man you are, so she can decide whether you're worth the risk. Because I can tell you right now, she doesn't have time for this shit. And she certainly doesn't deserve it."

"I know what it looks like, but I swear to you, this isn't me."

"Prove it."

"I plan to. Give me a chance to talk to her."

She shook her head, seeming no less pissed than she had a moment ago. "Vanessa is one of my best friends. I'm not going to watch you disrespect her this way, do you understand? You tell her, or I will."

"I will. I will find a way to make this right, but you need to let me do that."

"Fine."

"And Cameron..." I hedged.

"If I tell Cameron, he's going to kick your ass. So for the sake of the business, I'm going to spare him the dirty details."

I nodded, grateful for the sliver of mercy my new sister-in-law offered me. I didn't deserve it, but I was thankful for it all the same.

"Thanks."

CHAPTER ELEVEN

VANESSA

I'd texted Darren half a dozen times. I was running late. Reilly had sent me on a last-minute shopping errand. Tracking down his favorite designer pens that hit the expense account at four hundred and fifty dollars a pop had taken more time than I'd expected. By the time I finished, it was nearly nine o'clock.

I had to be at the new office fresh the next day. No way could I squeeze in a date with Darren, much as I wanted to.

I turned my key in the door and walked into the apartment, ready to curse for the next half hour straight over a glass of wine. Except Eli's music wasn't playing like it usually was when I came home, and the savory aroma of garlic and butter wafted over me.

I turned past the small hallway into the living room. Darren was lying on the couch, his bare feet propped on one end. He held his phone in his hand and the light glowed against his flawless skin.

I dropped my bags on my orange chair. "What are you doing here?"

He tossed the phone on the coffee table and rose with a dazzling smile. "I was trying to surprise you with dinner. I could have timed it better though. Sorry. It's probably not so great now."

He gestured to a few feet away where the small kitchen table had been set for two. Several bowls and dishes were covered with aluminum foil. A single candle burned in the center of the table.

"How did you get in?"

"Eli. He's sleeping over at Taylor's, I guess." Darren shrugged.

"This is crazy."

He laughed. "Why?"

Warmth flowed through me. I was overwhelmed with the thoughtfulness of what he'd done. And here I couldn't even show up on time for it.

"I'm such a jerk. I feel awful." I brought my hand to my mouth.

He came close, circling my waist with his strong arms. "I think your boss is the jerk. I'm just happy you're finally here."

I sighed and folded my arms around his neck, resting my cheek against his chest. He was so solid against me. Nothing in my world seemed as important when he was near. It was so easy...falling for him. Falling harder, faster.

"Are you hungry?" The quiet murmur vibrated through me.

Truth was I was starving, but Darren's kindness had completely captivated me. No one had ever done anything like this for me before.

I had no words for that.

His eyes glimmered, and my chest ached with all the things I hadn't said. Things I wanted to say when the time was right.

I was too tired to overthink it. I pulled my body—and then my mouth—tight against his. He was in my lungs, all man and musk, his skin heating me through my clothes. Then the taste that was only Darren on my tongue.

The earthy growl from his chest hit my ears and sent shock waves of pleasure straight to my core.

"I'll take that as a no," he said, as he lifted me off my feet and took us to my bedroom.

He lowered me at the foot of the bed. I caressed down his chest slowly, over his pectorals all the way down to his well-defined abdominals. Sliding my palms under his plain white T-shirt, I marveled anew at his incredible physique. And he was mine. This breathtaking man wanted *me*.

My touch went lower. He was already hard, his arousal obvious through his faded blue jeans. I caught my lower lip between my teeth. Nothing but a layer of denim between me and more pleasure than I'd ever known. I molded my hand over the outline of his erection, and he caught my wrist.

He clucked his tongue, and a flicker of mischief glinted in his eyes. "You made me wait, beautiful. Now you can wait a little."

I pouted my lip and leaned in to get closer to him. More contact. More heat. He punctuated the gentle order with his mouth over mine. His tongue plunged deeper. Sweet velvet strokes.

I moaned, rubbing myself against him. I cursed my clothes...and his patience.

"Easy, sweetheart. We have all night."

Smiling against my lips, he eased back, which only created more pressure within me. I was wild for the man, for his touch and his dirty words in my ears. I was ready to do anything to recapture the pleasure we'd found before.

I didn't really have all night, not if I was being responsible.

I was starting my new job in the morning, but suddenly I didn't give a shit. Staying up all night tearing up the sheets with Darren would be worth it, any day.

With one hand still around my wrist, he spun me so my back was to him.

He licked and nibbled up the column of my neck, sending a thousand tiny sparks of desire over my skin. My tits were suddenly heavy and tight, outgrowing my bra in my mind.

"Love your taste...the way you smell." He moaned softly, nuzzling into my hair. "You're a gift, Vanessa. I want to unwrap you."

I grinned like a girl about to get her wish. I craved his skin on mine and so much more. "Then what?"

"You want me to spoil the surprise? Or do you want me to tell you all the filthy things I'm going to do to you?"

My breathing sped up. I'd never been great at dirty talk, but Darren was different. He was bad and uninhibited, and I loved it. I wanted to hear him promise me ecstasy in slow explicit detail.

"Tell me everything." I rolled my head back on his shoulder and shifted my ass to tease the prize in his pants a little more.

He sucked in a sharp breath. "Bad girl," he growled. He seized my other wrist, binding them both behind me with one firm grip. The circumstance put unwelcome distance between our bodies. Then he turned us together so we faced my mirror.

His dark gaze met mine. "Okay, Vanessa. Here's what's going to happen. I'm going to strip you down. First your clothes." He nipped at the place where my neck met my shoulder and started slowly zipping down the back of my sheath dress. "Then your modesty. I'm going to spread your legs and take my time admiring the paradise between your thighs. I've been fantasizing about your beautiful little cunt, Vanessa, and all the things I want to do to it."

I arched back against him.

"Then I'm going to make you come all over my hand. I want you loose so I can fuck you hard." He yanked my dress down over my shoulder.

My eyes rolled back, and the blood in my body seemed to double. I was pulsing. Heavy. Overflowing with desire. He was single-handedly doing this to me with words, and only his touch could rescue me.

"How does that sound, sweetheart?"

I released a whimper. "Yes... God, yes."

He released his hold on my wrists and my dress fell at my feet. Unclasping my bra, he let that fall away too.

My chest heaved under uneven breaths. My need for his hands on me was outrageous. But he touched me only to drag my panties down to the floor with the rest of my clothes. I stood there, naked everywhere he was still clothed. Vulnerable. Aching so badly for him.

I sighed as his hands traveled the contours of my back, all the way down to where my ass creased against my upper thigh.

"And this pretty little ass of yours. I'm going to do things to that too one day. I'm going to make you come a thousand ways. That's a promise."

Anticipation turned into an unbearable heat under my skin. I was so wound up, I might have said yes to anything. Even things I'd never done before.

No one had commanded my pleasure the way Darren had. He turned sex into something so much more for me. There was nothing repetitive or simple about the way we came together. I'd go anywhere with him. Say yes to any invitation.

Foolish maybe, but a part of me wanted to be the best he'd ever had too. I was determined to give him more than the other women who'd had him.

He leaned down, softly kissing my shoulder. "Spread your legs for me."

I swallowed and moved my feet apart a comfortable distance.

He lifted his head, and I met his hungry stare in the mirror. I knew then that he was going to make good on his dirty promises. Right in front of this mirror.

A different kind of warmth eased any lingering tension in my muscles. The whisper of his breath on my skin and the comforting heat of his body behind me. I was vulnerable, but I felt safe and treasured above everything else.

Curving his hand to my front, he slid over my wet slit. I was throbbing for his touch. Situating my hypersensitive clit between the lengths of two fingers, he pinched gently.

I sucked in a breath and held back the cry that lodged in my throat. The action hadn't brought me pain but made the ache in my clit all the more acute. Then, with slow firm strokes, he gave me the touch I'd been aching for, and my body climbed with every caress.

Even with the erotic vision staring back at me, I couldn't keep my eyes open. Stars lit up the darkness behind my eyelids, and I chased the incredible sensations his talented fingers were inspiring.

He released my wrists and used the hand that wasn't pleasuring me to toy with my breast, squeezing and pinching. I thrust my hips into his touch, racing for more contact. He kept going at my clit, and I was edging closer to that sweet release.

"I want your pleasure more than I want mine, Vanessa. I

want to see your face when you come for me. Watch."

I opened my eyes and made a small sound of protest when he halted his ministrations. He swept a hand from my breast to my pussy, dragging his fingers through the moisture that had accumulated there.

Then he was back at my clit, anchoring my body to that delirious pleasure center. Behind me, his fingers slid between my cheeks.

I grabbed his forearm, bracing myself, no words. Then he pushed a single digit past the tight circle of my anus.

With a gasp, I rose on my toes, but his penetration only went deeper, again and again. The pressure on my clit went harder. My cheeks and chest were red with heat. My eyes were glossy with lust and need, wide open as Darren continued to assault all my senses. His fingers were in me just about every way a lover could be, but my shock melted almost instantly.

The orgasm I'd been running toward crashed over me like a tidal wave. Fast and hard and crushing.

"Oh my God!"

The cry that came out of me was pure ecstasy. I quaked in his arms. My legs buckled under the incredible release. My body went slack against him, and he held me as pleasure hummed through me.

"What are you doing to me?"

He whispered a kiss against my neck and held me a little tighter.

"I'm ruining you for anyone else but me."

DARREN

All the days without her melted together, stacked up like a heavy weight. I needed relief.

Lying on the bed, waiting and wanting, she was perfection. Smooth skin curved around a body that had my dick aching every time I saw her. The slight plane of her belly. Breasts that fit perfectly in my palms. The glistening lips of her bare pussy, spread for me, waiting for my cock.

This hadn't been part of my master plan, but I sure as hell wasn't arguing. We could sit and eat and talk and try to get on the same page with my screwed up past another night. Right now, all I cared about was burying myself so deep in Vanessa that nothing else existed.

I wanted her rough and sweet, feisty and loose. I wanted her mouth, her pussy, and any place else she'd let me in. I'd consume her, pleasure her, and use her until neither one of could see straight.

Even as the thought entered my mind, I wondered if it would ever be enough. In my nearly thirty years of living, I could barely remember the faces belonging to the bodies that had given me release. I'd craved that pinnacle moment, but never the person. Nothing like this.

Now I doubted whether I could ever stop needing to sate myself inside Vanessa, this beautiful incredible woman, over and over.

I tugged my T-shirt over my head and shucked off my pants and boxers. I found a condom in my pocket and rolled it on. I wanted her so goddamn bad I was shaking. The bed dipped under my weight as I nudged her thighs apart around me. I caressed up her thigh and hip and over her belly.

I trailed down to her mound and spread her open...pink and sweet and ripe. My mouth watered, and I resisted the urge to lick her straight into another orgasm.

Slowly, I pressed into her pussy with my fingers, exploring the wet velvet flesh. She gasped and gripped me when I grazed her G-spot, the place I knew would put her over the edge again and again.

"This pussy is mine."

She answered with a sigh.

The need to consume her, to physically lose myself to her in every conceivable way, overwhelmed me.

Maybe I could lose the man I'd once been. The one who'd wasted time with too many others who weren't her. I could just be hers. Pleasure her, comfort her, and show her things about her body that no one ever would.

I wanted to be that man.

She spread her legs farther and lifted her hips into my slow torturing touch.

"I'm going to fuck you harder than you've ever been fucked. Tell me that's what you want."

Her eyelids fluttered to half-mast. "I want that."

"No one's ever going to have you the way I will," I said, my words heavy with the promise. I dropped down, hovering over her supple body.

She lifted her torso and brought me to her at once, kissing me hard. "Take me. Ruin me."

I groaned against her mouth and met her passion with all of mine. I guided the tip of my cock into her and then shoved into her so hard her breath rushed out.

"Mine."

Her lip trembled, and a single affirmation came out in

whisper. "Yes."

I cupped the back of her neck and circled around her hips, holding her in place. Then I pounded into her. She dug her nails into my sides. I didn't care. I welcomed the pinpoints of discomfort. She took me completely. Her pussy was tight and slick around my cock. I slammed home again and again.

"Vanessa..."

I said her name over and over, and together we created an erotic symphony. The sound of our bodies crashing, becoming one. Breathless adorations mixed with her cries as they grew louder and longer.

I couldn't tell when she stopped coming and started again. Still, I felt her climbing higher with me all the way. Everything was too intense, like an electric storm between us—dangerous and overpowering.

My pulse hammered in my veins. With every desperate touch between us, a strange emotion raged through me, mingling with the ecstasy I felt being inside her body.

I didn't want it to end.

Her cunt rippled over me, and she pressed her head back into bed with a loud cry. My control shattered. Pleasure fired through me like a hard drug. The orgasm rocked me, and I slammed my hips against her one last time. I fused us together tightly, embedding myself into her so completely and came.

As the seconds passed, the tension in her body released and her touch fell away. The sweat on my skin cooled, but my head was still buzzing.

As I slipped from her body, a satisfied smile curved her lips.

"You certainly know how to keep your promises, Mr. Bridge."

I laughed softly and kissed her. I had the distinct feeling that no one had ever fucked Vanessa quite that thoroughly, and I was glad for it.

Begrudgingly, I left her to take care of the condom. When I came back, she hadn't moved an inch. I lay beside her on the bed and admired her.

When I pressed a kiss to her belly, her stomach growled.

She laughed and put her hand there. "Sorry. I guess I am hungry."

"I'll get you a plate." I moved off the bed and grabbed my jeans in case Eli decided to come back unexpectedly.

"I can get it." She lifted to her elbows, still glowing and flushed. She was a beautiful sight.

"Relax, I'll be right back."

Damn, running after that boss of hers all day and she expected me to let her serve herself.

She lay back, looking thoroughly blissed out. "This is too decadent."

I zipped up my jeans. "Yeah?"

She sighed. "I feel like I'm living on a fantasy island where all the gender roles are reversed. A breathtakingly handsome man is going to prepare me a home-cooked meal after giving me one of the most intense sexual encounters I've ever had."

Pride curled through me. I planned to give her so many more encounters like this one, and I'd cook for her every damn night if she kept working herself like this.

I shook my head, feeling more and more pissed about the way her boss treated her. No respect for her time, and from the small hints she'd given me, her intellect too. She was little more than an indentured servant to him.

That someone as smart and talented as Vanessa could

justify that kind of treatment blew my mind. I resolved to talk to her more about it.

"Anytime, red."

I went to the kitchen, plated some chicken and biscuits, and warmed up the gravy.

She ate and I watched, content that the night had gone as it had. I'd missed her, but I couldn't fully appreciate how much until she was there in front of me.

I'd had plenty of meaningless sex with women I'd never see again. But with Vanessa, each time felt new, like opening a door and discovering what lay within. Figuring out the key to her pleasure drove me, but the orgasms weren't enough. I wanted that hazy look in her eye afterward that told me what we'd done meant more to her.

Despite my past and all my stupid mistakes, I had to make her believe that it meant more to me too.

But tonight wasn't a night for confessions. My muscles felt too good. My cock was still humming with the memory of being tight inside her. She was glowing and happy. I didn't want to ruin any of that right now.

CHAPTER TWELVE

VANESSA

I woke up to the unwelcome sound of my phone alarm. I turned it off. As I blinked away sleep, my room came into focus. I sighed and stretched. My muscles ached a little from being up late with Darren, but I didn't regret a minute of it.

Darren stirred beside me. I went to the bathroom to brush my teeth, and when I came back, he was sitting propped up against the bed frame, the sheet bunched at his waist. He was holding something in his hand.

"Who's this?" he said.

Heat rushed to my cheeks and I went to him. "None of your business."

I reached for the little brown bear in his hands, but he moved it before I could grab it. I sat beside him on the bed and crossed my arms, feeling slightly mortified. I was twenty-six, after all.

"Put him down, Darren."

"Listen. If you're going to have a guest in the bed I want to share with you, I should at least know the name of my competition."

I laughed and pushed at his chest. "He's hardly competition."

"No? You didn't light up like that for me when you got

home."

"Stop teasing me." I sat up on my knees, wrestled the little cloth creature from his grasp, and tossed it out of sight on the other side of the bed.

Truth was, I lit up every time I thought about Darren, let alone shared the room with him. Whether he could see it or not, I came alive with him in my life. That fact frightened me as much as it enlivened me.

"What's his name?"

I rolled my eyes because I knew he wasn't going to let up until I'd answered all his silly questions.

"Beau. Okay? Can we talk about something else now?"

His eyebrows arched. "And I'm not supposed to be jealous?"

"Beau is my dad's name. So, no. It was a gift from one of the times he remembered my birthday."

"Oh." His smirk faded a bit. "Sorry."

"Don't be. I'm not."

I shrugged, because, truly, I wasn't sad about it. Beau was my father, true enough. But he was also a man. A flawed human, just like the rest of us.

"Not everyone's cut out for parenthood. He could have stuck around, and maybe that would have been worse for me."

"Not everyone would be so forgiving," he said softly, tracing circles over my bent knee.

"We are who we are. Some people aren't capable of being what the world wants them to be."

"Did your mom ever remarry?"

"Yeah, Phil's a nice guy."

"You don't sound like you're thrilled with him."

I shrugged again. "He's fine. Beau was the love of her life.

What they had, she'll never have with someone like Phil, but they're happy together. I'm glad she's not alone anymore. And I know he'll never break her heart."

His eyes were serious, but he didn't say anything for a while.

Deep down I knew that Darren already had the ability to break my heart. Shatter it beyond all recognition. The passion we had between us was unrivaled. It was also dangerous. The men of my past were nothing next to a man like Darren.

As if he wanted to derail those unspoken thoughts, he reached for me. In a flash, I was under him, his warm naked body stretched over me. I released a breathy sigh when he pinned my arms above my head. Something inside me melted at the feel of him over me, holding me captive.

Then he spread his touch everywhere. Pushing my nightshirt up with one hand, he toyed with my nipple until it beaded under his touch. Then he flicked his tongue over the tip.

"Love your tits. Your body." He sucked my nipple into his mouth and released it with a pop. He trailed his lips over my breastbone, hovering over my heart where he placed a gentle kiss. "Everything," he whispered, his light brown eyes bewitching me.

I was falling for this man. Hook, line, and sinker.

I closed my eyes, letting the memory of last night wash over me, adding to the potency of what Darren's touch was doing to me now. Even being tender from our exertions last night, I ached for him again.

"And this..." He slid his hand into my underwear.

I bit my lip when he found my clit, rubbing it to life and sending pinpricks of heat over my skin.

"Darren, what are you doing to me?"

I didn't think we had time for a diversion this morning. Even so, I spread my legs wider to accommodate his touch. I shifted my hips forward, and he answered by slipping two fingers into me, his thumb barely grazing my clit. Just enough to keep me wanting more. He twisted gently inside me, teasing the walls of my sensitive inner flesh and then withdrawing. Over and over. Carefully at first, and then rougher. Every nerve ending was alive, pulsing with pleasure.

My cheeks warmed. The city was still asleep, the morning still quiet, and I was being hurtled toward an orgasm that felt bigger than my body. But it was the dark hunger in his eyes that pulled me out of my own pleasure and made me bold.

I reached for his cock. He exhaled in a rush before thrusting into my touch. That promise of the pleasure I could give him was all I needed to keep going.

While he rubbed me toward my release, I brought him with me, circling him and stroking him from root to tip.

His flesh was throbbing, hot to the touch. We were completely focused on one another, making everything I was feeling even more intense.

I was seconds from coming and sensed he was too. I fantasized about putting him inside me bare and coming together that way.

Not yet...

I closed my eyes with that thought and tensed everywhere. I soared, completely enveloped by the intense pleasure.

My entire body felt racked by the violence of coming so hard so quickly. I caught his tense expression as my hips undulated on the wave of my fading orgasm. His fingers, slick from my arousal, came around mine, adding pressure and strength to the strokes I'd faltered on with my own release.

Only a few seconds went by before he flipped us, so I straddled him and his back was flat on the bed.

His grip tightened and sped up. "Fuck, baby, just like that."

Strain marked his features, and his lips fell open. As his torso curled up, his cock jerked in my grasp.

His release spilled over my fingers and onto the sharply cut ridges of his abdomen.

"Wow." With a shaky exhale, he relaxed back, eyes to the ceiling.

I smiled, sticky and equally sated. The satisfaction of inspiring that face on him landed like a cherry on the hot fudge sundae of an orgasm he'd given me.

"That officially made my day." He grinned lazily.

I laughed and leaned down, kissing the sweet lips of that man who was winning me over, one mind-bending orgasm at a time.

I stiffened when I thought of the time. Damn it. I had to be on my way soon. I scooted off the bed.

"My shower was not built for two. You're messier, so you can go first."

I visited the bathroom, cleaned myself up a little, and turned the shower on to warm up for a bit. When I emerged, Darren hadn't moved.

"It's all yours. I'll get some coffee going for us."

"Thanks, red."

I rolled my eyes. Was he ever going to give up on that moniker? Maybe the feistier side of me wanted to rile every time he said, but then I thought about what he'd said in the ocean our first night together. That I was vibrant in his mind. I'd always remember those words because I felt the same way.

Darren lit up my life like no one else.

I went to the kitchen and poured a measured portion of coffee grounds into a flimsy filter. I hummed to myself, an old tune that my mom used to sing when she was in a happy mood.

The shower door shut with a thud, and I checked the time on the microwave, making sure I wasn't going to be late for work.

I set the coffeemaker to brew and poked around the refrigerator for anything I could make. I didn't have a lot of time, but the sexually satisfied female in me wanted to make my man some breakfast all the same. Before I could patch together a plan with the sparse contents of my kitchen, a quiet bell rang.

I glanced around. Darren's phone was set on the coffee table. I picked it up with a plan to take it to him. Instead, I froze in place when I saw the message lighting up the screen.

Contained in the message was a selfie of a woman lying in bed, barely clothed. The sender, "Ellie," was a beautiful brown-haired woman with bedroom eyes and enough cleavage to make me jealous. Another message quickly came in above it.

Ellie: Woke up missing you this morning. Call me soon xx

The words slammed right into me. Anger swiftly replaced all the warm fuzzy feelings I'd been enjoying seconds earlier. My jaw locked tight, and I swiped the screen. "Ellie" had texted him several times last night, inviting him to meet up at her place. His only response was that he had plans. I couldn't stop myself from scrolling down for more. Two other texts from single-named girls that had gone unanswered. Then one that made my empty stomach roil.

Raina: Just want you to know, I have no regrets about what we did. I had an amazing time, and I know we could again. Casual and discreet. Cameron never needs to know.

The soft shuffle of Darren's bare feet across my wood floor was barely audible over the blood pounding in my ears. I looked up, not recognizing the person in front of me. He wasn't the man I'd slept with last night. He couldn't possibly be the same man I was falling hopelessly in love with. How could I have been so stupid?

He frowned as I handed his phone to him, my hands shaking badly.

"What's wrong?"

"Who is Ellie?" No amount of composure could keep the heartbreak out of my voice.

He studied the phone for a moment and then looked up, an expressionless look frozen on his face. "No one. Just a girl I used to hang out with."

"And...Raina? Don't you work with her?"

His jaw tightened. "Were you... Did you go through my phone?"

What I'd done wasn't right, but I'd done it. Something inside me went cold. I moved around him, went to the bedroom, and started shuffling through clothes for work. I had no idea what I was doing, but it beat carrying out the total breakdown I wanted to have right in front of the man who was inspiring it.

"Vanessa. Baby, talk to me."

I whipped around. "I'm not your baby. I'm not your *red*. I'm nothing but another name in a long line of women who obviously know you better than I do."

"Those women mean nothing to me."

He tossed his phone on the bed and came closer to me. Heat and anger and all the love I resented feeling for him vibrated between us.

"*Nothing.* Do you understand? They aren't you." He cupped my cheeks. His eyes said more...said things I wish he'd say out loud.

I couldn't tell him I loved him. Not now, when I couldn't possibly mean as much to him as he did to me. I couldn't look any more pathetic, but I could hold onto that small piece of dignity.

"I don't fit in your world." I closed my eyes. "I shouldn't have looked at your phone. That was private. I saw a message come from one of those girls, and I couldn't stop myself. I felt... possessive, which was stupid. I obviously have no place feeling that way."

His touch fell away. "I wish you hadn't seen it, but in a way I'm glad you did because now I have to face something that I was hoping like hell I could avoid."

I waited for him to tell me something terrible. As if I could feel any more insignificant or broken, I waited for the words that would surely end whatever this was between us.

"I have a colorful past. You know this. I've been with other women. Never anything serious. But nonetheless, some of these women I've been intimate with—"

"Don't... Just...stop talking." I winced and retreated a few feet away. "All my instincts told me this was going to happen, but whatever you do to women, Darren, you're damn good at. Because I'm just as hopeless as the rest of them. The only difference is that I'm not going to do 'casual and discreet' with someone I care this much about."

"I would never ask you to."

"Then I suppose we're at an impasse." I shrugged like I didn't care, but inside I was dying a slow death. All I could see was a future without Darren, and it was bleak. I barely knew the man, but somehow he was so far under my skin I couldn't breathe, couldn't have a day pass without wishing he were in it. Even as I fought for those moments, incredible moments like last night, not having any of them was an unbearable thought.

He came close again. I wrapped my arms around myself, as if that could protect me from his next words.

"You're the only one I want to be with."

"If that's true, why haven't you told anyone?"

He exhaled sharply. "It's complicated. I have clients. Not everyone obviously, but a lot of these people are clients who come to the gym."

"Well, are you running a gym or a fucking escort service, Darren? I mean, why don't you charge them for the extras while you're at it?"

"You're getting too emotional about this."

I laughed because if I didn't, I was going to break down.

"Yes, I am. For the record, this is what it looks like to care about someone you don't want to share with the rest of the world. Take a good look, and maybe one of these days you'll meet someone who makes you want to see only that face. Not a thousand women with bedroom eyes and cute names like *Ellie*."

He grabbed his phone from the bed with a curse. "Do you want me to call her right now and explain to her in detail what my relationship with you means to me?"

"Don't bother. You're officially back on the market."

I tried to move past him, but he blocked me. In the small

room and with his large frame, it didn't take much.

"Like hell I am."

"Just go."

"I'm not going to cheat on you, Vanessa." He placed his hands on my arms.

The possessive touch gave weight to his words, but how could I believe him?

"That's reassuring," I said, unable to meet his imploring gaze. "Let me go. I need to get ready for work."

"Let's talk about this."

"I don't have time to talk to you, Darren," I snapped. "Now, get *out*."

I twisted out of his grasp, went to the bathroom, and locked the door behind me. Leaning against the door, I listened for him. As if I could hear his regret, his love, anything at all that might take some of this pain away. All I could hear was my heart beating angrily in my chest. All I could feel were painful wet tears stinging my eyes.

Inhaling a deep breath, I pushed off the door and turned the shower on. I stepped in and my tears disappeared, disguised under the spray of the water.

DARREN

I texted Cameron, letting him know we needed to talk. He was still at home so I walked in the direction of the brownstone he now shared with his bride. Maybe having Maya as a witness would help.

Because nothing could possibly be worse right now. I was a fucking idiot, and Maya was right. Vanessa didn't deserve to deal with this shit. And I certainly didn't deserve her heart.

Even as I sensed her becoming mine a little more each time we were together, this morning was a classic reason why she'd been right to be guarded. But I wasn't letting her go without a fight.

I cursed to myself as I walked, sometimes out loud, earning a few odd stares from strangers on the street. I didn't give a shit. This morning had been amazing and a total goddamn disaster.

For all my wanting to give her the perfect night, this was where I'd landed.

I didn't bother knocking but walked right into the apartment.

Cameron was sitting at the kitchen table, coffee in hand. Maya was on the couch with a book. I looked between the two of them before taking a chair across from Cam.

"I fucked Raina."

His jaw was tense, and his gaze seemed fixed on the coffee cup in front of him. "I know."

"She told you?"

Maya looked up from her book for a second.

"She figured it'd be better for me to hear it from her first." Cam's words were slow and deliberate.

I got the strong sense that he was harnessing a good amount of anger toward me. "And?"

He took a deep breath. "And she was right. Kept me from putting my fist through a wall. Not sure if she could have kept me from putting it to your face if you'd been there."

I nodded. "I deserve that."

"Now I need to address it with Raina."

I drummed my fingers on the table, trying to guess how horrible that was going to be. "Maybe you should let me—"

"No way."

"I wish we could just drop this. Pretend like nothing happened."

"That's obviously not working out." Maya rose and sat down beside us at the table. "Raina had her hands all over you, so she obviously thinks whatever happened can happen again."

"I'll explain that I met someone. It'll be good practice." I stared down at my hands. They turned into balled fists when I remembered Vanessa's devastated look when she'd read those text messages. "I've made a real mess of things. With Raina. And now with Vanessa..."

I shook my head and shoved my hands through my hair with a heavy sigh. I had to fix this somehow. But I had a lot of damage to repair to even come close.

"Did you tell her?" Maya's voice was calm, infused with concern that gave me a little hope.

"I was going to. We had..." I sighed again. "We got sidetracked. I was going to try to explain things to her, but I didn't. She saw some texts from Raina and others this morning."

"And..."

"And I'm pretty sure she never wants to see me again. Can't say I blame her."

The silence that fell over the table was loud with all the things I knew they wanted to say. Didn't matter. I was the master of my own self-loathing right now.

"I think I'm in love with her," I muttered quietly.

When I looked up, Cameron's eyes were wide. Maya's were softer.

Cam blew out an audible breath. "Wow. I guess I never expected to hear that come out of your mouth."

I stared blankly at the table. "No one's more surprised

than I am. But when am I ever going to find a girl like her again?"

"You should know, since you've sampled about half the available women in New York."

"What are you going to do?" Maya asked.

"I have no idea. I don't think she'll see me again."

Another minute passed before Maya spoke. "Okay. I have a plan."

I raised my eyebrows and waited for any hope she could give me.

"Cam and I have an announcement to make, and we wanted to bring everyone together for it anyway. Let me coordinate a dinner for tonight. I'll invite Vanessa and you, of course. I can't guarantee anything, but at least it gets you in the same room with her."

"She usually works late. How do we know she'll even show?"

"We'll do it close to her office so she won't have an excuse."

"I'm willing to do whatever it takes to get her back. I need a chance to make this right."

She stood again. "Don't make me regret it."

I nodded. Maya was giving me a chance I didn't deserve.

CHAPTER THIRTEEN

VANESSA

I arrived at the office of Reilly Donovan Capital with three minutes to spare. I was usually early to work. Despite the hellish morning I'd had, I was grateful to at least be on time this morning. I wasn't sure I could deal with Reilly's wrath if I hadn't been. I smoothed my hands down my black pants and straightened my blouse so the wide scoop centered on my chest.

The door was dark and imposing, its facade made of an ornately carved wood that seemed to belong in an older structure, like an early bank. I pushed it open and entered the reception area. Maroon walls were decorated sparsely with gold-leaf-framed artwork. Even the paintings seemed dark.

I approached one of two desks that faced one another. A woman my age, maybe a little older, lifted her head. She had big brown eyes, and her dark hair was short and curled against her scalp.

"Hi, you must be Vanessa." She rose and shook my hand.

"That's me." I lifted my shoulders, unable to shake the first-day jitters, even knowing I'd be providing much of the same support to David as I had before. Her friendly countenance was a reassuring start.

"I'm Adriana, Bill Donovan's assistant. They're on a call

right now, but I can show you around and give you the lay of the land."

"That would be great."

She spent the next ten minutes guiding me through the various rooms. The conference room was occupied for their call, but both David and Bill's offices were as lavish as one would expect—dark polished surfaces, expensive liquors nearby, and views to the street below. If I had a million dollars or more to invest, perhaps all of those details and the scary bank door would give me a measure of comfort.

Near the entryway, Adriana guided us back to our desks. Mine was already nearly obscured with stacks of paperwork. My head started spinning as I began mentally organizing it all.

"Looks like I'd better get to work."

She nodded. "I'll let you get situated, and we can go over whatever questions you have. I have a system, but since we're starting new with this venture, I'd like to get your input too so we can stay efficient."

"Sounds great."

I powered on my computer and started sorting through the paperwork on my desk. I threw myself into every task, for once welcoming the distraction of the thousand things I needed to do today. My appetite had vanished, so I worked through lunch, not pausing until Reilly called me into his office hours later.

"In my office now, please."

I scrambled for my notebook. Something was definitely wrong. I closed the door to his office and settled into a chair across from his desk. "Is everything okay?"

He slumped into his swivel chair. "My grandmother passed away a few days ago."

Only then did I notice the tired look in his eyes. "I'm so sorry."

"I have to go up to the Hamptons for her funeral."

"Of course. I'll hold things down here. Whatever you need."

He shook his head and fumbled through the papers on his desk, seeming distracted. "No. I need you there with me."

For a minute, I sensed something a little desperate in his voice, but quickly the hard-faced Reilly I knew too well met my concerned stare.

"There are some things that need to be taken care of at the summer house up there anyway."

The last thing I really wanted was to head out of town with Reilly, but my job was hardly on solid ground with this transition.

"Of course. I'll make travel arrangements."

"Good. No need for a hotel. We'll stay at the summer house."

I nodded and stood to leave.

"And a coffee, please."

"Sure."

In the office's little kitchenette, I prepped a fresh brew and brought him a cup. When I set his mug down, his hand grazed mine. I froze.

"Thank you...for everything." He looked up at me with those gray eyes that I'd grown to dread.

"You're welcome," I answered quietly.

He moved his hand away, and I left without another word.

★ ★ ★

Reilly had left the office earlier than usual, allowing me to do the same. Maya had insisted I make dinner with her and Cameron tonight. I was curious what her big announcement could be. I took the empty seat next to Eli. I hadn't seen him since his sleepover with Taylor last night and was surprised that he was solo again so soon.

"Where's the boy?"

"He's on a flight to Dubai. Photographing cityscapes." He sighed, and a faraway look touched his eyes. "Probably getting screwed by some beautiful sheik."

"You're letting your imagination run away a bit, I think."

He twirled his straw around in his drink. "Maybe I am. Would help if he stayed in town long enough to make me believe he cared."

"Have you told him how you feel?"

I was one to talk. I'd fully admitted to myself that I loved Darren but couldn't get the words out. Not that any of that mattered now. I shoved the feeling back down, but every time I imagined Darren's gorgeous face, it reared back up again, dominating the forefront of my mind. The amazing things he'd said to me the last time we were together. The way he seemed completely overwhelmed by our connection in the same way I did.

I loved Darren. And I hated that I did.

Eli shook his head, and a lock of his black bangs swept into his eyes. "I'm sticking with passive-aggressive and hoping he sees the error of his ways."

"You're not happy, Eli. You need to either tell him you need a commitment or move on. I don't like seeing you this way."

He shot me a sidelong glance. "You giving relationship advice now?"

"I'm not an expert, but I'm your friend. I want to see you happy. You deserve that."

"Thanks. Unfortunately, he's the only one I want right now. I just don't know how happy that's going to make me in the long run."

I took the glass of wine the waiter delivered graciously.

"I know the feeling," I muttered and took a healthy gulp that I nearly choked on.

Darren took that moment to drop into the only empty seat at the table. Of course Cam and Maya would invite him. He was family and Cam's best friend.

And as long as I was friends with Maya, I'd have to tolerate being in his presence from time to time. The thought was unbearable. One look at him, and I was a tornado of memories and regret, of remembered passion and fresh shame for giving him so much of myself. A known player. A man who'd never let a woman tie him down. I swallowed hard and let the waiter take my dinner order. I wouldn't be able to get anything down. I'd been sustaining myself on coffee all day and still had no interest in food. Not when I was sitting this close to Darren.

Leaving wasn't an option. I couldn't do that to Maya. I didn't want to be rude, but avoiding Darren's stare was becoming a losing occupation. I retrieved my phone from my purse and quietly loaded up new messages in my e-mail. I scanned through everything. Then a text came in from an unknown number. New York.

You're beautiful.

I frowned and texted back.

Who is this?

I waited, wondering if I should be engaging in text messages from an unknown number. Maybe this person was a total creep. Or a wrong number.

The guy at the table who can't take his eyes off of you.

I reread the text when the meaning dawned on me. I glanced up quickly, just as Darren lifted his gaze from his phone. I averted my eyes quickly, not at all ready for extended eye contact with the man who'd had me in tears all morning. I hesitated over what to say next. If anything. He hadn't reached out to me all day, but maybe this was why.

New number?

His reply came quickly.

Got it this morning. Time for a fresh start.

I went back to my e-mail and tried to focus on the mental checklist I was making for tomorrow's trip. Another text came in.

Give me another chance. Please.

Just then, Maya spoke up. "Okay, everyone. Thank you

all so much for coming. We lured you here with the promise of a big announcement. So without further ado, Cameron and I wanted to share with you that we're having a"—she grinned broadly and looked to Cameron—"boy."

The smile that spread across Cameron's face was pure joy.

Darren whooped, Eli and Olivia clapped, and I gave Maya a hug so tight she could probably scarcely breathe.

"Congratulations, Maya. I'm so incredibly happy for you both."

As I said the words, fresh tears hit my eyes. Out of nowhere. Damn. I was letting my personal problems leak all over Maya's beautiful news.

"Are you okay?" She held my hand, her expression tight with concern.

"Yes. I'm sorry. It's nothing." I wiped stupidly at my eyes, hating myself. "I'm going to get some air. I'll be right back."

I left the table quickly and walked a few paces past the entrance of the restaurant where no one was lingering or smoking. The night air felt cool on my skin and stung my tired eyes. Tomorrow would be better. I hadn't had twenty-four hours to get Darren even a little bit out of my system. No wonder I was a wreck.

"Vanessa."

I heard his voice, and my heart twisted painfully in my chest. I felt it in my gut where I'd lodged all my anger toward him. Then in my eyes where I'd tried to cry it all out. I closed my eyes, praying that he'd leave me be.

"Vanessa, look at me."

His voice was barely a whisper and his tender touch on my cheek sent a fresh wave of almost tears to my eyes.

"Why are you doing this to me?" I didn't recognize my

own voice. It wasn't strong and angry the way I wanted it to be.

One look into his brown eyes, seeing my own hurt reflected there, gutted me.

"Because I can't help you're the one I want. You're trying to come up with any reason to derail us. But I won't let you. I want this to work, damn it."

"I'm afraid it won't. I'm in so deep with you already. I'm falling for you, and I can't seem to stop it unless I believe the worst."

He came closer. I was trapped between his body and the building.

"You're falling, Vanessa. I've fallen too. I'm in deep. You had every right to be pissed at me over those texts. I never promised to be perfect because I'm far from it. But I promise to be loyal. You need to believe that."

"You've been with so many other women. Why would you change anything for me?"

"Every day you give me another reason. You're real. You don't play stupid games. You call me out on my shit. You may want me, but you don't need me."

"That's not true." I did need Darren. So much it frightened me.

"I know I don't deserve someone like you. But that doesn't change the way I want you."

I weakened against the building. "What do you expect me to do?"

"I expect you to kick me to the fucking curb the way you did this morning. But I can't give up that easily. Despite what you may think, I've been loyal to you. I can't even look at other women, let alone consider being with them. The way I feel when I'm with you..." He closed his eyes a moment before opening them again. "I want to be a better man. You make me want to be a better man. Someone who deserves someone like you. Give me a chance to prove to you that I can."

My walls broke down more with every word. I couldn't deny wanting to give him another chance. "I don't want to be your dirty little secret."

"You aren't. I can't promise that my past won't come back to haunt me at times, and it may hurt you. For that, I'm sorry, because I can't change my past and the choices I've already made. But I'll deal with those situations as they arise. I made my bed. I knew one day that mixing leisure with work was going to catch up with me. I think Cameron knew it all along too. Now that he knows the worst of it, I feel like I can deal with everyone else."

"You told him?"

"Kind of."

"What about Raina?"

"I talked to her this morning after I left your apartment. She knows I'm seeing someone. And everyone else is going to be texting the wrong number for a while. Doesn't solve everything, but hopefully it means that nothing like this morning ever happens again. I don't think I could live with myself if I saw that look on your face again."

I swallowed, reliving that terrible moment for about the hundredth time today. "I was devastated."

"I know you were. I hate myself for putting you through that."

"You have to know that I always want to give you the benefit of the doubt."

"I know." His eyes glittered under the streetlights. "Hey, want to go inside and I can announce to the whole restaurant that you're my girlfriend? That you decided to forgive my douchebag behavior because you can't deny how crazy I am for you?"

I laughed despite a little part of me wanting to stay mad. "Don't do that."

He slid his finger down my nose. "Either that or I could just tattoo your name on my ass."

The heavy weight that I'd walked around with all day slowly began to lift and I smiled. "You're crazy."

"You make me that way, Vanessa," he whispered.

Then he kissed me—a soft soulful kiss, like the first note of a slow song. The world went still save the wild beating of my heart. It was just us. I wrapped my arms around him, rose on my toes as he embraced me. The kiss deepened until, breathless, we broke apart.

We weren't exactly making a scene, but another few minutes and we easily could be. He feathered his lips over mine, restraint evident in his features.

"Come home with me."

I would have said yes in an instant. Because I couldn't manage to say no to Darren. But I also was in no position to say no to my employer.

"I can't. I'm traveling tomorrow. I won't be back for a couple days."

His dark eyebrows knit together. "Where are you going?"

"I have to go to the Hamptons. My boss's grandmother died unexpectedly, but we still have to work. So he's bringing me with him."

He rested his forehead against mine. "This isn't going to be easy, is it?"

"Nothing worth fighting for ever is."

"I'll always fight for you."

CHAPTER FOURTEEN

VANESSA

A driver picked us up at the jet way in East Hampton. I was even less thrilled about taking this trip than I was yesterday. We were scheduled to go to London next month, Hong Kong the month after, so travel with Reilly was going to be a part of my future. Like it or not.

Unfortunately, Darren was the only one on my mind. Every minute of the day I carried a bit of him around with me in my thoughts. The way I melted into his arms last night. The way he could make me laugh and send a long hard day away after a few minutes in his presence.

The town car brought us to Reilly's summer cottage, which was far from rustic. We pulled up the long driveway to an expansive home with cedar shingles. Inside, tones of seaside blue and earthy browns set the tone of the decor against bright whites—trim, furniture, and linen. Top to bottom, the place was reminiscent of the few glossy VIP publications I'd seen from time to time that celebrated the homes and social lives of the elite society that could use "summer" as a verb. For the rest of us, summer meant a few trips to the beach, sunning on someone's rooftop deck, or trying to stay cool in the unbearable city heat. Reilly and his family lived in a different world.

He dropped his keys onto the table in the foyer and

shrugged off his suit coat. "I'll be leaving for the service in an hour. I'll be in my office in the meantime if you need me. There are several bedrooms. Pick whichever one suits you." He gestured to the stairs.

"Thank you."

He disappeared into the ground floor office, closing the pocket doors behind him.

I brought my bag upstairs and poked around. To think this place was just sitting here, waiting for summer. Every room was perfection, like an unmade bed that was begging to be jumped on. I found the master and briefly admired its view of the ocean. Figuring I'd leave that room to Reilly, I picked a room two doors down that featured a less impressive view, but one that still put my apartment view of my neighbor's fire escape to shame.

A light rain had begun, and gray fog hovered over the rocky ocean waters. Perfect day for a funeral, though the patrons of said event might disagree.

I opened my laptop and worked through the afternoon. I started to get hungry for dinner and meandered downstairs. As I did, the front door opened and the sound of rain filled the large foyer, soft behind the loud noises of people's voices.

I followed the noise and found Reilly, smiling ear to ear, beside three others. One I recognized immediately as his ex-wife, Cheryl. The others were men his age, dressed in suits.

"Vanessa. You're here." Reilly turned his broad smile to me, a sight so rare I was immediately caught off guard. "Bring us some wine. The cellar is that way, through the kitchen." He pointed behind me.

I moved quickly in that direction. Cheryl's footsteps clicked on the marble floors. I paused at the stairway as she approached. She moved easily in her tall heels, her body outlined in a tight black paneled dress.

She smiled when our eyes met. "Come on. I'll help."

Together we perused the dozens of bottles lining the cellar wall. I lifted out a bottle that looked dusty enough to be good, but truthfully, I had no idea what was what. "How about this?"

She wrinkled her nose and motioned for me to put it back.

"No, no. Let me see if I can find something special for today to honor David's *nonna*." She scanned the rows of wines, pulling out a bottle here and there. "It's been ages since I've been down here. Oh, here. Lafite. He's drunk enough to let us drink this one, I think. Let's try it out."

She led us to the nearby bar and took two delicate bulbous glasses off a rack behind.

"So...Vanessa."

The way she said my name gave me pause. Maybe she didn't remember me.

"We've met before. Briefly at the company party last year."

She laughed softly and popped the cork from the pricey bottle. "Trust me, I'd remember a beautiful young woman working long hours next to my husband."

I swallowed. "Ex."

She smiled, with no hint of malice in it, and lifted her glass. "Cheers to that, darling."

I clinked glasses with her, feeling a little guilty as I did. What it would be like to be free of a man like Reilly, to be able to start over, to start fresh? She had done it. Of course, she was starting over with the benefit of a fair portion of their wealth in her bank account. Rich people problems.

I took a sip of the wine. It was so smooth. Wine would never be the same for me after this. "This is exceptional."

"David only ever wants the best." Swallowing another mouthful of the delicious nectar, she stared at me over the rim of her glass.

Funny that Reilly so rarely spoke of her. She was stunning. Of average height, but full and thin in all the right places. Dirty-blond locks curved into a long bob at her shoulders. Her dark blue eyes seemed to see right through me—a feature that no doubt came in handy when maneuvering the intense social waters of New York's mega-rich.

"I guess we should go up." I stood awkwardly, hoping we could get back upstairs soon, though Reilly seemed like he'd already had one too many. I'd never really seen him drunk before, and I wasn't really sure how we, or I, were going to deal with that.

Cheryl spun her wine glass by the base. "I'm not in a rush. This is a happy accident anyway. I wanted a chance to get to know you a little better."

"Oh... I'm just his assistant."

"You're the one he left me for. I suppose I'm curious, that's all."

I coughed and set my glass down, peering at her with wide eyes. "What?"

She lifted her eyebrows, looking genuinely amused.

"Maybe I should have worded that differently." She sighed and looked wistful for a moment. "I suppose technically I left him, but David would be furious if the world knew that. That was part of the agreement after all. Sometimes reputation management is more important than money. Thank God for that. So let the record state that we parted amicably, and mutually. Between us, I told him I wanted to move on." She shrugged and paused to sip again at her wine. "I didn't have anyone else exactly, but I'd had enough being married to a shadow, you know? He was either gone or perpetually unhappy. What's the point in having all this money if you're miserable all the time?"

Better to be rich and miserable than poor and miserable, I thought, but I kept it to myself. None of that explained why the hell she thought Reilly would leave her for me.

"I'm sorry things didn't work out between you two. I still don't understand what any of that has to do with me, though."

She offered a smile that I swore held a measure of sadness in it. "In the heat of the moment, when he was still intent on ruining me if I moved forward with the divorce, he admitted that he'd been falling for you, that it'd taken all his willpower not to act on it and make you his mistress. He was trying to hurt me, and at the time, it worked. Nothing should have surprised me or hurt me. Women like me, we're thrust into this life of security and possession. It's always understood that loyalty is a one-way street. No one expects us to be happy."

She emptied the glass and refilled it, pouring a bit more into mine as well. "Anyway. If he wasn't sleeping with you already, I figured it was only a matter of time. His words stung of course, but ultimately the truth gave us both another reason to move on."

"I'm not sleeping with him," I insisted. The mere thought of sleeping with Reilly made me faintly nauseous. I'd never see him that way. I was in disbelief that he could possibly want me that way. He couldn't possibly.

"It doesn't matter now."

"But I'm *not.* I work for him. We work long hours, yes, but I swear to you he was never unfaithful to you, with me or with anyone else that I knew of."

She flashed me a practiced smile. "I believe you. Thank you. Regardless, it's over now. We're friends, David and I. That will never change. I want him to be happy, but I don't know if he's capable of it, honestly. Maybe he can find that in you."

I bit down hard on my bottom lip. Was she giving me her official blessing to be the woman to replace her? I wanted to yell out that I didn't love her husband, that my only concern for his happiness was tied directly to my steady employment. I honestly didn't know what to say, so when Reilly called down the stairs for us, much as I didn't want to see him right now, I welcomed the chance to leave this conversation.

I grabbed some extra glasses, brought them upstairs, and quickly retired to my room. I wanted to jump in the car and drive straight back home, but I was here until the morning. With Reilly and this unspoken thing between us. Good God. I silently prayed that everything Cheryl had said was nonsense. Maybe she was only trying to bait me into admitting some imagined wrongdoing.

The noise downstairs died down after less than an hour, and footsteps shuffled up the stairs.

"Vanessa."

I turned in my chair. Reilly was in the doorway, tie askew, lips dark from the wine. There was nothing hard and fierce about his countenance. Drunk, he looked like half the man he was on a normal day. He stumbled on his first step into the room.

"I want to talk to you. I have things I need to say."

I stood and faced him, torn between wanting to help him stay standing and wanting to keep my distance.

"Reilly..."

"Call me David."

He lifted his gaze. Seeming to gain some composure, he made his way to me. I swallowed hard and tried to look away.

"Look at me."

I closed my eyes, a momentary escape from the nightmare I was certain was only just beginning. He put his hand on my cheek. I jerked away, his damp palm on my skin a shock and a violation at once. We so rarely touched.

"I want you to be mine, Vanessa. She was never really mine. I want to start over, with you."

He reached for me again, but I backed away a few steps until I was up against the wall. He slid his hands over my blouse, his bleary gaze shifting there.

"God, I want you."

I brushed his hands away and recoiled, panic prickling under my skin.

He reeked of wine and something else, a nervous odor that became more pronounced as he caged me in with his arms propped against the wall beside me.

"Stop it. You're drunk."

"Maybe. Doesn't change anything. You're everything I want."

"You should get some rest." I wanted to run, but I'd never seen Reilly this way. I had no idea what I was dealing with, and I didn't want this to escalate more than it needed to. We had to face each other, one way or the other, in the morning. Already it was going to be more awkward than I could imagine.

"I don't sleep. You know that. Unless maybe you come to bed with me. Take care of me. That's what you do, you know? We're perfect, you and I. I can give you everything you could ever want. You already give me everything I need. We're just missing this one thing…"

His hand strayed again, finding its way to the place where my blouse split into a V at my chest. When I pushed him away this time, he held on and the fabric ripped.

He groaned and pushed me hard against the wall. "Give me what I want, Vanessa. Goddamnit, I can't stop thinking about you. I need this."

Adrenaline spiked, and I pushed him off hard. He stumbled back against the chair I was sitting on earlier.

"Get out! Get out, or I'm leaving." I was trembling. How far would he push this agenda?

With some struggling, he found his way upright again. "Tell me you don't feel the same way."

"Reilly...David. You need to leave. We can discuss all of this in the morning. You're drunk, and you need to go to bed."

That perpetual need to get ahead of a potential problem propelled me out of my room, down the hall, and into his. I found a glass in the adjoining bathroom and filled it to the brim. Searching around the cupboard, I located some ibuprofen. I returned to the bedroom and Reilly had followed me. His face fallen, he dropped onto the bed. I pushed the glass and tablets into his hand.

"Drink. And go to bed. We can talk about this in the morning."

I turned and shut the door behind me. I hurried back to my room and locked the door. I hoped against hope that he was too drunk to remember any of this in the morning. But even the possibility of brushing all of this under the rug wouldn't stop the anxiety thrumming through me.

I stood in front of the window, my arms wrapped around myself. I waited for my heart to slow, for the panic to ebb away. Reilly was gone now, and I prayed I'd never feel him touch me that way again. Ever.

I stripped off the ripped shirt, wanting to rid myself of the evidence of his hands on me. I'd never had someone touch me that way. A few grabby guys in college but nothing I couldn't handle. Nothing had ever felt this unwanted.

I was angry that he'd put me in such an uncomfortable situation. He was drunk, but he had no right. I riffled through my small suitcase and pulled on a T-shirt that Darren had worn on the island and I'd claimed for myself. Sinking into a chair that overlooked the darkening sky, I inhaled deeply. His familiar scent filled my lungs and some tension released in my shoulders. I closed my eyes, wishing Darren were here with me, taking all this madness away.

I picked up the phone, trying to still my shaking hands. I didn't believe Reilly would really hurt me, but the entire evening had me rattled. Between Cheryl's blunt admission and then his...

How could I have known he felt this way when he'd only ever been cold toward me?

I called Maya. I cursed when it went to voice mail. I hovered over Eli's number and hesitated...

DARREN

The phone rang, jolting me out of sleep. I'd drifted off between calls. Vanessa's number came up on the screen, and I answered groggily.

"Beautiful."

"Sorry for calling so late." Her voice was small, like she was a thousand miles away. She wasn't that far away, but it reminded me that she was farther than I wanted her to be.

I stretched, trying to ignore the wood I was sporting that would love some attention from my favorite redhead. "I miss you," I said, not bothering to hide the suggestion in my tone.

"Were you sleeping? I can call back."

"No, it's fine. I was just catching a few winks before my next emergency. And I was telling the truth, I miss you. Miss hearing your voice."

She was quiet and the fog of sleep began to clear more. "Is everything all right?"

She let out a heavy sigh. "I don't know. It's been a strange trip."

"Vanessa. What's going on? Are you okay?"

"I'm fine now. Reilly came home from the funeral drunk." She sighed again. "I shouldn't even be talking about this. It's stupid."

"What happened?"

"He came on to me. I had no idea—" Her voice had that small faraway sound again.

"Did he touch you?" I sat up straight in my bunk. Every second she was silent was killing me.

"It all happened really fast, and I got him to leave, thank God."

Rage scorched through my veins. I stood up and looked around for my keys. I found them and went for my coat next. "I'm coming to get you."

"Stop. Darren, I'm fine. I'm just kind of rattled and wanted to talk to a friend. I just... I wanted to hear your voice too."

I hesitated, but every protective bone in my body wanted to get to her as fast as I could. "Should I be worried? I mean, is he in the house with you?" I'd learned how to keep my cool for a thousand emergencies, but the first hint that Vanessa was in trouble had me ready to fucking sound the alarm.

"I think he's passed out now. I'm pretty sure he's going to have a massive hangover tomorrow. Hopefully this will all blow over."

None of that comforted me in the least. "I can be there in a couple of hours. I can have someone cover my shift. It's not a problem."

"I'm fine. I promise. I'm sorry, I shouldn't have even mentioned it. I didn't want to upset you. Seriously, forget it."

I gripped my coat tightly before dropping it back on the bed. Maybe I was being rash, but the only thing keeping me from getting on the highway right now was the concern in her voice when I'd mentioned it.

"When are you coming home?"

Home. To me. Where you belong.

"We fly back in the morning. We have an event in the evening, so maybe I can come see you before."

Not likely, knowing him.

The thought of another man's hands on her was making me crazy. She was mine, goddamnit. Fuck, I didn't even want his eyes on her. She bent over backward for that asshole, and their first trip out of town he got grabby with her. My fingers curled into a tight fist.

"Promise me you're okay."

"I'm okay. I'm a thousand times better now."

"I'll stay on the phone with you all night if you want. You gotta talk me down though. I've got my keys in my hand, and I'm ready to come get you. Say the word."

"Just stay on with me a while. Tell me about your day."

I sighed. "I slept most of the day. Figured it would be a long night." I closed my eyes and had the vague feeling that I'd dreamed of her. "What if I don't want to wait until tomorrow to see you?"

The promise of seeing her, touching her, making love to her, was potent. Maybe the prick could walk in on us and know without a doubt who'd laid claim to her body. Her heart. If he heard the way I could make her scream, I'd remove all doubt.

"What did you dream about?"

I smiled. "You, of course."

She laughed.

"I don't like you being far away."

She let out a small sigh. "You sound like my mother."

"Maybe she's onto something."

"She hates when I travel, and she can't understand why I live where I do. I think she's scared for me every day of her life. She thinks Callaway is the safest place in the world."

I dropped my keys and settled back onto the bed. "What made you leave anyway?"

She was quiet a moment. "I never really felt like I belonged there, I guess. One day I realized I couldn't stay in that little town for the rest of my life and watch my dreams fall away."

"And what are your dreams?"

I knew I was living my dream, but I had a feeling she was far from it.

"I don't know. I guess I'm still figuring that part out. All I knew was I wasn't going to find them there."

"You have real talent, red. You should do something with that. I know I'm not the only one who'd pay to see you sing your heart out the way you did the other night."

"That's nice of you to say."

"Nice or not, it's the damn truth. Have you thought about it?"

"I don't know. Real life gets in the way. Bills to pay. Bosses to please. Plus it's hard to imagine the life of a musician turning out any better for me than it did for my mom."

"They're your dreams, Vanessa. Your dreams, your life. If you don't make sacrifices to make them come true, no one else will."

I knew that better than most. Of course, most of my family thought my life choices were one giant sacrifice. Didn't matter, because I *was* living my dream, and no one would ever convince me otherwise.

She was quiet and then yawned. "I should go. It's getting late."

I got angry again, thinking about her being there with her boss. I fought every instinct to respect her wishes and let her be. Besides, what would I do? Barge into the house and sweep her away? Seemed a little dramatic, and as much as she hated her job, she probably still needed it. For now. Still, I wasn't ready to let her go just yet.

"Stay on with me a little longer. I'll quit nagging you, I promise."

She laughed, and I smiled at the sweet sound. Damn, I missed her. I wanted her in my arms, her voice in my ears.

"Sing something for me."

She laughed again, a little more tentative. "What do you want to hear?"

"Anything. The first thing that comes to mind." I had a feeling she could sing me a TV jingle and I'd hang on every word. She had the voice of an angel. The sexiest redheaded angel this side of heaven.

She cleared her throat, and then her voice came through. Soft at first, and then a little stronger as she moved through the lyrics. I didn't recognize the song, but it was a sentimental tune. A little sorrowful, about falling in love, a bittersweet state of being. The way she sang it, with so much heart, made it something visceral and beautiful.

I wanted to answer the lyrics like she'd spoken them to me. If she'd been with me and not miles away, I swore I would have.

Her voice faded away. I could listen to her sing for hours. The saddest, sweetest songs...all day long.

"Sing me another one."

CHAPTER FIFTEEN

VANESSA

"I want her gone."

Reilly's voice echoed through the large kitchen as I crept down the stairs. The edge in his tone fell like a tight fist in my gut.

He's firing me. Oh God. This is it.

"I don't care how many street kids she's done finger paints with, my money fuels the whole damn operation. She's not sitting on that board with me. You vote with me, or I pull my pledge. See how long the initiative stays afloat without my donations."

I relaxed a little but stayed out of view. He continued pacing the kitchen floor. He looked pale and tired. No doubt the buckets of wine he drank last night weren't doing him any favors.

"Cut the bullshit, Nicole. I don't care that you and Cheryl are friends. Vote against me, and I take my investors with me. You'll be done. That's all I'm going to say about it. I'll see you at the meeting at the end of the month, and I trust you'll make the decision that's best for the organization."

He hung up and rested his hands on the granite countertop with a sigh.

I wanted to run back up to my room, but the house was

too quiet. I set my suitcase down on the landing and walked to the kitchen.

He lifted his gaze. "Morning."

"Good morning. Want me to make some coffee?"

"No, we'll pick some up on the way. Are you ready?"

"Ready when you are," I answered lightly, avoiding his gaze.

We didn't speak the whole way to the airport. Once we were in the air, I decided to break the awkward silence and get to work.

"We have the investor cocktail tonight. I have everything set with the venue so we should be good with all that. And then you have a lunch meeting with Dermott today. Do you still want to keep that, or should I move it?"

"Keep it."

"Okay." I tapped out a quick e-mail to Dermott's assistant confirming the time and location.

He exhaled heavily and stared out the window. "I'm sorry about last night."

I stopped typing. I didn't know what to say. Words failed me, as they so often did around Reilly. But he remembered, which was the last thing I'd wanted. My hope that by some miracle we could go on pretending it hadn't happened disintegrated.

What he'd done wasn't okay. I didn't want to forgive him, but I also didn't want to acknowledge it at all.

"I don't lose. All my life..." He shook his head and looked back to me. "You know I used to play baseball, back in high school? I was the best player in town. Then I went to Yale, played a little bit there, but mostly just studied my ass off. Graduated with honors. Then I came to Wall Street and the rest is history. I'm good at what I do."

"I know you are." No one could dispute that. In the greed-fueled game of making money, he was right up there with the best of them.

"I've never lost like I did with Cheryl. She woke up one morning and decided she wanted something different. Just like that. Somewhere on my way to the top, this piece of my life just failed. I never even saw it coming. I struggled with it for a long time. Then I started to think, maybe this wasn't really a failure. Maybe I didn't lose this round. Because I realized I wanted something different too. I wanted you."

I could hardly breathe. "Reilly, I—"

"David. Call me David."

"David." I swallowed hard and abused the inside of my lip as I searched for the right words. "I had no idea you felt this way. You've always been so..." Cold, unfeeling. The possibility that under all of that he wanted me sexually could not have been further from my mind. "You've challenged me a lot."

"All that would change," he offered quickly. "This new life, working on the fund, things are going to be different. We'll make a great team, the two of us."

He said it like he'd already decided for us both.

Didn't matter what he wanted, I was in love with someone else. Not to mention that I was not one iota attracted to the man who'd seemingly made it his sole mission in life to make my tenure in his office as unbearable as possible.

"I'm seeing someone."

He leaned in. "I'm a very wealthy man, Vanessa. You would have everything you need. Just about anything you could ever want."

His tone was unflinching, and an uneasy feeling came

over me, like the walls were closing in the same way they had last night, when he'd had me pinned. I didn't know what to say, but thankfully, he stopped me from saying anything.

"Think about it." He sat back in his seat and opened the newspaper that had been folded neatly beside him. "On second thought, let's move that meeting with Dermott to tomorrow."

And just like that, the conversation was over.

He'd decided. I knew him, and I knew this to be true.

Panic welled up inside of me, but somehow I managed to push it down. I'd get another chance to explain to him that I couldn't be a part of this vision he had for us. I couldn't ever be that for him. I just prayed that when I did, he'd really hear me.

DARREN

A beat-up hooker, a heart attack, three bums, and a kitchen fire. Good thing I worked all night because I couldn't have slept a wink if I'd wanted to. I couldn't stop thinking about Vanessa. We'd talked for over an hour, after I'd made her promise me a dozen more times that she was all right. My blood was still boiling with the thought of her prick boss coming on to her.

Ian and the guys on the crew tried goading me between emergencies, but I was in no mood for jokes. By the time I got off my shift, I'd made up my mind.

I'd called her office and got her flight information. An hour later, I was at the airport waiting for her at the baggage claim.

She came into sight through the security doors, and some of the tension from the night eased up off me. One look at Vanessa made the world right. Manageable. Better.

As if answering my silent call for her, she recognized me. She smiled, ran toward me, and bound into my arms.

I scooped her up and off her feet, burying my face in her hair, inhaling her sweet scent. Apples and vanilla.

"What are you doing here?" When she pulled back, her eyes were bright. Her smile was so sweet and genuine.

I stared into her eyes, felt her soft skin under my touch, and remembered the voice that had come through the phone last night. I'd wanted to say it then, but I couldn't bring myself to say the words over the phone. I wanted to have her in front me, in the flesh. Close enough that I could feel her...

"I have to tell you something." I caught her wrist and held it gently, felt her heart beating steadily. "Vanessa...I love you."

Her smile faded, and her breath caught. I reveled in the rush of beats thrumming under my thumb, because the same rush was beating through me too. Lip trembling, she opened her mouth to speak.

"Don't. Don't say it. Not yet. Because you're about to hate me."

I immediately hated myself for being the one who would ruin it all. Not just yet though. She frowned, a silent question. I couldn't give her the right answer now, so I just kissed her. I kissed her until the moment was broken by the sound of a man calling her name.

"Vanessa! What are you doing?" A second later, the man turned his angry stare toward me. "Who are you?"

The way he said it made it sound like I should drop to my knees and beg to shine his fucking shoes. What a smug dickhead. This was the guy barking orders at her all day long.

"I'm Darren Bridge. You must be the one who thinks he can put his hands all over my girlfriend."

"Let's go. I don't have time for this."

He reached for her, but she flinched back, as if her instincts gave her no other choice.

"What? Now I can't touch you?"

The incredulous look on his face put me over the edge instantly. He really thought he owned her. He was dead wrong. He reached for her again and yanked her arm, pulling her toward him and not bothering to give me a second glance.

No fucking way. I'd come here to give him a piece of my mind. Now he was going to get a hell of a lot more.

I grabbed his arm, squeezing it hard until he let her go. A flash of fear crossed his face. I was taller, more muscular, and way more pissed off. He was smart to feel fear.

Inserting my body between them, I wasted no time punching him square in the nose. He dropped to the ground immediately, which might have satisfied me if I hadn't already fantasized about him putting up enough of a fight to let me get a couple more shots in.

"Touch her again, and you're going to need to buy a new face. I'm just getting started."

"Darren!" Vanessa screamed and scrambled around me, following him down to where he now sat on the ground.

By now, we'd attracted a few stares, and people passing by were wisely giving us a wide berth.

"Vanessa, leave him. Let's get out of here."

Ignoring me, she fumbled around in her purse for a bunch of tissues and thrust them up to his nose in a desperate attempt to stop the blood gushing from his face.

"Are you okay?" Her voice was hushed.

"No, I'm not fucking okay. This goddamn Neanderthal is your boyfriend?" His angry shout was muffled and gargled.

"Vanessa, seriously." I hated being the second guy barking at her, but that she was still giving him any of her attention after what he'd done was ridiculous. "He'll live. Let's go."

"Leave us, Darren. You've done enough."

I grimaced. "You're going to stay and help this fucking guy?"

She turned her head to glare at me, still holding the tissues to Reilly's face. "He's my boss, and you just broke his nose. Just go."

VANESSA

I love you.

I couldn't get the words out of my head. He'd said he loved me. And my heart had nearly burst in that moment wanting to say it back to him. Because I did love him. More than I ever thought possible.

Buildings sped by us as we drove into the city. I was still in disbelief at what had happened. I cursed myself for calling Darren last night and giving him cause to worry. The results had been disastrous.

"You told him about last night?"

I chanced a look at Reilly, who sat beside me. "You caught me completely off guard. I needed someone to talk to."

"You could have talked to me," he snapped.

"You didn't seem like you were in the mood to talk."

He made a sound of disgust as he replaced new paper towels that I'd collected from the airport bathroom against his nose. "What's his name? Darren Bridge? I'm pressing charges."

If my adrenaline wasn't already shooting through the roof, it peaked then. I looked to Reilly warily. I hesitated over what I was going to say next. "Frank Bridge is his father. You might know him."

He turned his head, looking out the window, still holding his swollen nose. "I know him. I guess I can see the resemblance a bit. But I'd never guess he'd raise an asshole like that."

I bit my tongue. I wasn't excusing Darren's rash behavior, but he had done it in my defense. No one had championed for me that way. Ever. Even if it had been a stupid decision. He wasn't anyone's enemy.

"Obviously I'm not going to be able to go to the investor cocktail tonight. I can't show up like this. You'll have to go and work the room with Bill and Adriana."

"How will I know who to talk to?"

"Adriana will brief you. You'll do fine. Just...be who you are. Nice, professional. I'm sure you'll make friends fast."

"Okay." I exhaled heavily, closing my eyes as I leaned my head back against the cool leather of the town car. "I'm sorry," I said quietly. I wished none of this had happened. What a mess.

"You don't have to be. He will be though."

I turned toward him, ready to beg. "David...please."

He waved his hand. "It's nothing you need to worry about. I'm going to take care of it."

I'd never known Reilly to be the forgiving type. I clamped my jaw tight. God, if Darren weren't going to be in so much trouble as it was I'd call him and scream at him for being so foolish to cross a man like David Reilly.

CHAPTER SIXTEEN

DARREN

I'd just started my shift when the captain came into the kitchen.

"Bridge, there's someone here to see you. He's out front."

I rose and made my way through the truck stalls to the front of the station.

A man in a suit pivoted away from the street and came into full view. He took a small step toward me and then stopped.

"Darren Bridge. I'm David Reilly. We didn't get a formal introduction earlier." His lips were a thin line, and he was trying like hell to level me with his eyes.

He was the picture of Wall Street. I knew his type too well—the three-piece suits, the buffed-up shoes, the air of superiority that came with playing with other people's money all day long.

Only the bruises on his face didn't fit quite right. Dark purple streaked under his eyes and marred the place where his nose had been set.

"Come back for round two?" I wasn't joking. I curled my fist into a ball, even if my knuckles still ached a bit from busting his face hours earlier. I had a lot more insights I wanted to share with this guy.

The stony expression didn't waver. "Don't press your luck."

I crossed my arms. "What the hell are you doing here,

then?"

His glared twisted into a snide smile. "You know, Bridge, the only reason I'm not pressing charges against you is because of your father. We go back."

I wanted to ask how he knew my father, but the puzzle pieces fit together quickly enough.

"I let him know I wasn't impressed with being attacked by his son. He was more than glad to make it up to me though. He's invested heavily in the fund I'm starting. I'm sure Vanessa has told you about our new venture."

I ground my teeth down. "Glad it worked out for you. Hope it covers the medical bills."

He chuckled quietly and scuffed the sole of his expensive shoe against the pavement. "Oh, it doesn't make a big difference to me. Seemed like a fitting penance though. I've got all the money I need. I'm just killing time. You see, Bridge, you might be able to give her a nice tumble in the sheets, but as long as this is how you plan to spend your life, it'll never be enough."

He gestured toward the station, and his judgment speared through me, all the way down to my bones. I wouldn't let on, but he could have been my father in that moment. Didn't matter if the whole damn country thought I was a hero. I'd always be a disappointment.

"Vanessa's special," he said. "She deserves more, and I can give it to her. I can't imagine what you make here, but I can guarantee it's not enough to give her all the things she really wants."

"Maybe it's not, but I'm pretty sure she doesn't want you."

His lips curved up into a smug grin. "I don't need to chase women, Bridge. I don't imagine you need to either. It's pretty easy to tell when a woman is interested. I have a keen sense for what exactly they're interested in too. You've got a uniform. I've got a credit card with no limit. I think we'll find out soon enough what and who she wants."

Was he trying to convince me that Vanessa actually *wanted* him? Not a chance. She had been seriously rattled when I talked to her last night. Then again, she'd been quick to keep me from going out there and rescuing her. Reilly watched as the wheels spun in my mind.

"You don't believe me. Let me ask you this, Bridge. Why does a beautiful woman like Vanessa work for a man like me?"

"Pretty simple. She needs a job." *She's miserable with you. You treat her like shit, and the only reason she stays is to pay her bills.* But saying it out loud would only threaten her job more than I already had.

"If you believe that's true, you're dumber than I thought."

"Fuck you."

I took a threatening step his way. He stiffened but didn't move back. He withdrew his hands from his pockets and pointed to me.

"No, fuck *you*. And you touch me again, you're going to have some serious problems that even your dad won't be able to pay away. I'll make goddamn sure you're arrested, and I'm sure it won't sit too well with the department. You love this job so much? Be grateful you have it, because you won't have anything to fall back on after this."

He took a few short breaths, lowering his tone as he continued.

"I came here to tell you to stay away from Vanessa and stay away from me. That's what we both want." He turned without another word, walked a few paces down the street, and slipped into the back of a black Lincoln idling at the curb.

I paced around the station for a while, trying to get Reilly's words out of my head. That guy had real fucking nerve.

Finally, I fished my phone out of my pocket. Calling Vanessa right now would probably only add more fuel to the fire. Instead, I dialed my father's number. We hadn't spoken since the wedding, and I couldn't remember the last time I'd actually picked up the phone to call him. The rule was mandatory-only.

"Son, good to hear from you." His tone was even, professional, like I was a client, a good old boy.

I was a man now, but he was still my father. The sound of his voice elicited emotions that would probably never go away. The most pronounced being resentment, and maybe a twinge of remembered jealousy that he'd chosen to spend our childhood with bankers and boardrooms.

"You know why I'm calling," I said.

He cleared his throat and waited.

"I'm an adult. I can take responsibility for my actions."

"I've come to terms with your choices, Darren. I didn't expect you to start becoming violent. And over what, a woman?" Disappointment infused the calm, collected voice of a man I'd never truly know.

"That *woman* is Vanessa. The prick that you're investing your money with had his hands all over her. He had it coming."

"Sounds like that's something she needs to work out with him."

"As long as she's my girlfriend, it's something he'll need to work out with me."

He sighed quietly on the other end of the phone. "What do you want me to say? I can't have you assaulting people. Especially people who share connections with me in the industry."

I swallowed a string of curses and kept my voice steady. "Just pull the funds, Dad. I don't want you paying people off to save me trouble. It's not your job."

"I'm your father. It will always be my job to protect you, even if I don't always agree with how you've chosen to live your life."

I winced. I couldn't remember the last time he'd agreed with my choices. To enlist and start a career doing something that I loved. Nothing would ever measure up.

"Have you written the check already?"

"It's done, son. Just forget it and move on. A million dollars isn't going to break me, especially if Reilly and Donovan can do what they say they can. I'm interested to see how the funds perform."

A tone sounded, and my radio started going with specifics of the call.

"Dad, I've got to go."

"I'll talk to you soon, son. Don't worry about any of this. It's all taken care of."

VANESSA

The party was being hosted at the Terrace Room at the Plaza. With its ornately painted high ceilings and breathtaking chandeliers, the room was as opulent as any I'd ever seen. Then again, this event was about attracting money—celebrating it, enjoying it, and making more of it. I was confident Adriana had picked the perfect venue with that theme in mind.

I checked in with the hotel staff to ensure everything was on track. Adriana and Bill had arrived, and several guests had started trickling in. I'd spent most of the afternoon memorizing faces. Adriana had more experience with this sort of event and seemed to have enough confidence for both of us. My nerves were getting to me a little, but without Reilly snipping at me every five minutes, I actually felt more competent than I'd expected to.

I escaped to the bathroom, which was no less lavish than any other room in the historic hotel. I checked my appearance in the wall-sized mirror, reassuring myself that I could pull this night off.

I smoothed my hair, which fell down my back in loose curls. Black was the official dress code for New York, but I had gone off script with a deep red cap-sleeved dress with a plunging surplice neckline. The fabric had a subtle shimmer to it. I silently thanked Reilly's expense account for this one. He'd wanted me to look the part, and I thought I did.

Darren's voice echoed in my head. *Beautiful.* I closed my eyes and envisioned his handsome face, eyes that saw me like no one ever had.

I hadn't had a chance to talk to him yet, and heaven knew we had a lot to discuss. Boundaries when it came to work and our relationship were at the top of that list. I was more worried than angry, but I didn't have time to deal with the aftermath of this morning's drama until this party was behind me.

I checked myself over one last time and ventured back into the event room. I scanned the room for familiar faces when a cool hand touched my arm.

"Vanessa."

Jia was beside me, a lowball glass filled with amber liquid in her hand. She was stunning in a black cocktail dress that draped beautifully over her petite frame.

"It's good to see you again. I wasn't expecting you," I said guiltily. She hadn't been on the guest list.

"I'm here with Will. He hates coming to these things alone, so I figured I'd keep him company." She lifted her glass in the direction of a young man in a suit speaking with Bill and a few others. "Bill wants him to work the room. Making connections."

Will Donovan was Bill's son, and though we'd never met, Adriana had mentioned he'd be attending tonight. He was striking. Tall with dark blond hair and a chiseled, handsome face. No surprise that the gorgeous Jia was his date. They made a handsome pair.

"Where's Reilly?"

I drew in a steeling breath, reaching for my prepared excuse. "He came down with something. He was really disappointed to miss this."

"I'm sure." She pursed her lips and took a slow sip from her drink, looking me up and down. "You look lovely, Vanessa. I'm surprised Reilly can keep his hands off of you."

I'm sure the comment was meant as a joke, but I felt the blood drain from my face.

She paused a moment. "Oh, wow. Don't tell me he's already moved on from Cheryl?"

I shook my head. "It's not like that."

"Oh?" The black wing of her brow arched high.

I chewed the inside of my lip. Good God, Reilly shouldn't have left me here on my own. The event had barely started and already I was eating my words. I cleared my throat, desperate to change the subject.

"So is Dermott all settled in now?"

"I wish I could tell you." She shrugged, swirling the ice in her glass. "He intended to bring me up with him, but...there were some complications."

Her smile was tight. I couldn't read her well, but I sensed more to that story.

"That's disappointing," I hedged.

She lifted her chin, seeming to still whatever emotions embroiled within her. "We've been working closely for months. Reilly took care of him. Dermott didn't take care of me. Sometimes the women get left behind."

"Maybe it was for the best."

She didn't blink. "Maybe women like us shouldn't be underestimated."

The discontentment rolled off her in invisible waves. This woman was disgruntled. No doubt about it. I fidgeted with my clutch. Jia didn't strike me as someone to underestimate. I really should move on, work the room like Reilly wanted me to.

"You're friends with Maya, aren't you?"

I hesitated. "I am. You know her?"

"I mentored her a bit. Until she left, of course. Did Maya ever tell you why she left the firm?"

"No, she didn't."

Her expression was frozen in a quiet analyzing stare, as if she were studying my very pores. I got the strong sense that she knew exactly why Maya had left.

"Maya is a very private person," I continued. "I was sorry she left, but I knew she wasn't happy. She didn't want to talk about it, so I left it alone."

"I should probably leave it alone too. Let's just say... Dermott and Reilly have a lot in common."

This conversation was weighted with things I wasn't sure I should know.

She reached into her small clutch and handed me a card. "Let me know if you'd ever like to chat."

I took it, glancing at the card and back to her. "I will."

The rest of the evening was less eventful. I didn't stray much from Adriana's side. We played well off each other, and the people we spoke to seemed receptive to hearing more about all the great things Reilly Donovan Capital could do for their portfolios.

On my way home, I called Reilly.

"How did the cocktail go?"

"It went really well. I think we connected with some promising prospects."

"Good to hear."

"How are you feeling?"

"I'm fine."

Silence stretched between us, and I struggled over my next words.

"Have you rethought things with Darren? I feel terrible about all of this. He was being really emotional, which really is my fault—"

"I'm not pressing charges, if that's what's been worrying you."

"Thank you." I exhaled a relieved sigh.

"I'll see you tomorrow, Vanessa."

DARREN

I sat at the lieutenant's desk, working through the paperwork that was piling up when someone knocked.

Ian opened the door and paused at the threshold. Vanessa moved around him and into the room.

"She said she wanted to see you," Ian said.

"Thanks," I muttered.

Ian closed the door, but I barely noticed. I was too busy trying to pick my jaw up off the floor.

Vanessa was radiant. Sex and elegance and luscious legs in a sleek red dress. Hopefully no one had seen her come in because she couldn't have stuck out any more. We weren't supposed to have guests at the station, but if I was going to make an exception to the rule, this seemed like as good a time as any.

"What are you doing here?" I finally found my voice.

"I tried calling you," she said.

I patted my pocket for my phone, but I'd left it downstairs. I'd been ready to throw it at the wall after talking with my father.

"Sorry," I said, looking her over as she moved into the fluorescent-lit room toward my desk.

"Is this your office?" She ran a finger over the cheap metal chair that sat across from me.

"No. I'm covering for the lieutenant tonight."

She nodded.

"It's nothing special. Just a bunch more paperwork." I moved to the front of the desk, sat on the edge, and shoved my hands in my pockets. Needed to keep my hands off of her. Easier said than done. Watching her move around the room in those heels was giving me a hard-on.

Every time we were in the same room, I felt like I was in a tornado, wrapped up in emotions I had no idea what to do with, wanting the damn woman more than I wanted air.

"We're not really supposed to have visitors."

She turned to me and leveled me with those green eyes. "Do you want me to go?"

"No." *Hell, no.*

"I talked to Reilly tonight. He isn't going to press charges."

"Lucky me."

"It *is* lucky. It's not like him to let something like that go. You really shouldn't have done that." Her lips were a thin line.

I winced, remembering Reilly's unwanted visit and the resulting conversation with my father. I hated the whole fucking thing. All because I couldn't stand to see the way Reilly was treating Vanessa. Seemed like I cared more than she did, which pissed me off even more.

I straightened. "My dad is helping fund his little venture. Pays to know people with deep pockets. I suppose you know that."

Her brows wrinkled, but I was already winding up.

"Yeah, I saw your boyfriend today. He told me all the good news."

"My boyfriend?" She moved away from the chair, coming closer to me. Her heels clicked on the concrete floor. "What's that supposed to mean?"

"Means you're on your way up, red. And I like it right here where I am. If I wanted to compete with dirtbags like Reilly, I'd have done everything my parents wanted me to do. I'll stick to bringing the bums off the street back to life and running into burning buildings. Maybe that's not the life everyone wants, but it's my life."

"You're not competing with him."

I stood, ready to lay it all out for her. "No? He puts his fucking hands on you, and you've made it clear that's not a problem. I mean, what really happened with him out there? I feel like maybe I'm not getting the whole story."

"Stop it."

"Then tell me what's going on here. Explain to me how you justify working for a guy like that if you're not in it for something else?"

"It's my *job*." She leaned in and her skin glowed, turning from soft peach to a glowing pink. "You can look down on me all you want, but I'm good at what I do. I'm trying to build a career and—"

"And you could be doing anything else but this."

"I'm not like you, Darren. I don't have rich parents to fall back on. It's easy enough for you to turn your back on everything they offered you, but I never had that luxury. So don't judge me for finding my own way."

"You think you've got it all figured out, don't you?"

"And you do?" She put her hands on her hips.

"I like my life."

"Me too!"

A weak laugh escaped me. "Do you?"

"I liked it a lot better before you decided to punch my boss. You can't go through life doing whatever you want, Darren. The world doesn't work that way."

She was shouting, and I wanted to shout back. My blood boiled when I thought about what Reilly had said. I inhaled deeply. I had to get her out of here before I lost control and did something stupid like tell her I loved her again. Lot of good that had done for me.

But before I knew what I was doing, I captured her arms and pulled her against me. Heat and anger pulsed between us.

Her gaze flickered to my mouth as she swayed toward me. "What are you doing?"

"Whatever the hell I want."

CHAPTER SEVENTEEN

VANESSA

Before I could speak, his mouth came over mine in a bruising kiss. His taste was rough and masculine.

He was pissed off. So was I.

I met his fervor, burying my fingers in his hair and tugging him to me, even as his nearness made my senses spin.

"Damn it," he muttered.

He hoisted my dress up my thighs and shoved me up on the desk in one fluid motion. Something crashed to the floor behind me, but I couldn't see it and Darren didn't seem to care.

I was anchored to him by his savage kisses while he went to work, tugging down the sleeves of my dress. My breasts spilled out, and he squeezed them, pinching my nipples until I whimpered. Then hard sucks at my breast lit fire under my flesh.

I wrapped my legs around him until our hips met and his erection strained against my thigh. Heat arrowed to my core where I pulsed for him.

Reaching between us, I fumbled with the button on his pants. I didn't give a damn where we were or what the rules were. I had to have him. Right here, right now.

Every touch was intense, making me edgy and hazy all at once. The thin straps of my thong cut into my skin as he ripped it off. Then he was on his knees. He lathed his tongue over my aching clit, mingling my moisture with his. The sensation was heaven. My hips seemed to move of their own accord against his touch. Even as I wished this could go on, the torrent of desire pulsing through me demanded more.

"Darren. Now, hurry."

He left me long enough to fish a condom out of his wallet. Shoving down his boxers just enough, he hastily rolled it onto his thick length. He pushed the head against my slick entrance, and I braced myself to take all of him at once. If his tight grip on my thighs was any indication of what I could expect, he'd be fucking me hard and long this way.

With one hand steady at my hip, he curled the other behind my neck and tangled into my hair. He held me that way for a moment, gazing into my eyes. His lips were wet with my arousal, his breath a warm whisper against my skin. Then he began to push into me slowly, fusing us together.

I closed my eyes with a shaky sigh.

No matter how angry I was with him, I couldn't deny how we fit. Moments like these brought us together and convinced me that Darren was the only one I could ever love. He'd wanted to ruin me, and he had.

Liquid and molten, I was melting into him, becoming his...irrevocably. Warmth snaked through me as he rooted deeply, stretching my sensitive tissues until I trembled. A mist of sweat swept across my skin. Already I was on edge, craving the next invasion, ready to succumb to the intoxicating rhythm our bodies created together.

He pulled back and thrust, a measured stroke that had my sex rippling around him. He traced the bow of my mouth with his thumb before pushing it past my lips. I licked and swirled my tongue around the rough pad, sucking the salt from him.

He closed his eyes and shoved again so deep I cried out.

Holding me close against him, he set a rugged pace. "Tell me what you want. I'll give you anything. Anything, baby."

I clung to him, struggling to take him deeper, to find places where our flesh could meet and crush together. "Darren..." Every breath was a desperate sound as he pumped into me.

"Tell me...Tell me, Vanessa."

"Darren...I..." *I love you. God, I love you.*

The words rang in my mind, punctuated by the fierce thrusting of his hips against mine.

Now, even when my love for him seemed to move like honey through my veins, swimming with my desire, mixed up with my anger and frustration, I couldn't form the words out loud. I couldn't tell him like this, in the heat of it, when everything else was such a mess. My courage deserted me, and I fell back on the lust that was ripping me apart.

"Fuck me. Fuck me, please. I need you."

That need was a knot of heat buried deep. Only he could reach it and satisfy the violent craving that rocked me.

A flicker of emotion passed behind his eyes before he withdrew and turned me around to face the desk. He licked up the column of my neck and nipped hard at my ear.

"If that's what you want..."

With his hand firm on my back, he bent me forward over the desk. My thighs pressed hard against the cold metal edge. Hauling my hips back, he slammed home abruptly, reaching the deepest part of me.

A scream crawled up my throat. I found the edges of the desk to brace his punishing drives, but I was entirely as his mercy.

My desire climbed like a raging fire under my skin. When I thought I couldn't last a minute more, he withdrew.

His palm came down hard on my ass. I jolted, but the desk under me allowed no room to escape. The smack echoed off the walls. Heat radiated from the place where he'd made contact. My pussy tightened, aching for his cock inside me again.

Another one fell in the same spot.

The pain was sharp, sizzling through me all the way to my toes and lifting me higher. He slapped the spot again and the world spun. The higher I flew, the more I wanted.

"Darren. Please..." I said his name like a prayer. I needed release.

He answered by filling me again. Then a series of fierce thrusts that took me outside of my body.

I was lost. Free falling. Completely at his mercy.

"I'm coming," I moaned. Because, sweet Jesus, I needed to. My whole body buzzed, tensing around his penetration. He was everywhere. Incredibly deep.

He made a desperate sound and buried himself deep enough to set off one last wave of pleasure through me.

A quiet tone went off in the distance, and I remembered where we were. Must not have mattered because Darren didn't move. His breath was ragged like my own.

I was weak. Drained. Emotionally frazzled. Physically sated.

We'd resolved nothing. We'd only satisfied an ache that never seemed to wane.

DARREN

I tried to catch my breath. What the hell had just happened?

I slipped from her, and she turned in my arms. Christ. She'd walked into the room the picture of elegance, and I'd reduced her to this. Her bared breasts were mottled with dark red from where I'd sucked her, badly wanting to make the marks that could show anyone else who cared that she was in fact *mine*. Her ass wore the imprint of my hand. I'd nearly shredded the condom to come inside her. The need to possess her ran that deep.

I'd lost my goddamn mind. All sense of control and self-preservation had flown out the window. How had I grown to care for a woman this much?

Her cheeks were flushed. God, she was beautiful down to her bones. Even if she didn't love me, I loved her, past her skin and the physical attributes that had attracted me to her.

All her raw beauty, her fire, her kind heart. The whole of who she was had taken hold of me, challenged me, changed me. I couldn't help but want to fight for her.

Day by day, I'd fallen into this dangerous attraction, so consumed that I was losing all sense of who I was.

I'd risked my job this morning without a second thought. I'd let a few swings fly in the military, but those careless days had passed.

I slept with women, took and received physical pleasure, discarded any problematic feelings, and carried on with my life. I never tried to take their hearts. That had all changed with Vanessa, and I was in over my head. This was wrong. For her. For me.

In an instant, I saw everything differently—raw and more

clearly than I'd ever wanted or intended to.

I stepped away from her, immediately regretting the loss of her warmth and the memory of her tight around me. I buried the condom in the trash and tried to pull myself together. I could straighten myself out, but my head was a clusterfuck of emotion.

Nothing but the shuffling of shoes on the concrete floor and the quiet rustle of clothes coming back into place pervaded the sound of my heart beating in my ears. A heavy silence. Filled with all the things that were welling up inside of me. Things I didn't want to say but had to.

Finally I came to face her. "I'm in a world of shit if anyone finds out what happened here. You should go."

"I'm sorry."

Hurting her now would be easier than hurting her later. "I'm sorry too."

She froze for a second and then blinked as if she'd caught the true meaning of the words.

"I'm sorry I let this get so out of hand." I steeled myself to say what I needed to say. I went to war inside, but reaching for the man I was before she came into my life was easier than I'd expected. "With everything that's gone down...maybe we should take a break."

A hint of glassiness swept her eyes. A cold mask tightened my expression as I guarded myself for the worst. I'd cut things off with women before, when they started wanting a relationship, expecting that I could be capable of one. It was never easy, never something I welcomed or enjoyed in the least. I didn't want to hurt anyone, but I had to protect myself. Now, I had to protect us both from a path that I wasn't sure was good for either of us.

"What are you saying?" Her voice was barely a whisper.

"Things are moving too fast. This morning was proof of that. We should take some time, let the dust settle for a while, and figure out what we really want here."

"Is this about Reilly?"

I shrugged. "Maybe."

"I don't know what he said—"

"Falling for you is ripping my fucking life apart, Vanessa. I'm risking things I'd never risk."

She swallowed hard and straightened before me. "Your timing is impeccable, Darren." The strength in her voice wavered, as if she were close to tears even if her expression didn't show it.

I opened my mouth to speak, to somehow justify how I could have sex with her and then say the words I'd just said. But before I could, she pushed past me.

"Vanessa."

I was calling her back and I'd barely let her go. Sickness twisted inside me.

"Vanessa!"

She was out of sight, and I rushed out the door. Down the hall after her and a second later, I was standing outside the station, watching her get into a cab and disappear down the street.

She was gone.

And I'd let her go.

VANESSA

Once the tears started, I couldn't stop them. The cab driver was eyeballing me in the rearview mirror. I didn't care.

Darren had ripped my heart out tonight, and I had seen it coming a million miles away. I'd known it weeks ago. Falling in love with Darren had been a mistake. Maybe I hadn't said the words, but I'd said it in my heart. I loved him. I'd let him inside me in all the ways that mattered.

Despite his promises, despite the passion between us, I'd known full well that I was flirting with disaster. A raging fire, so beautiful and seductive that I couldn't resist—I'd walked right into it, knowing full well the risks.

Some people couldn't change. They weren't meant to. Deep down I knew this. I'd grown up knowing it.

I scolded myself over and over, but the truth was that Darren was temptation personified.

Now I had to pick myself up from the ashes.

I walked into the apartment and dropped my things onto my chair. I paused at the threshold into the living room.

Eli was sitting cross-legged on the couch, a full glass of wine in his hand. "You okay?"

I shook my head, and the tears started again. "No, I am not okay," I muttered. I'd just been screwed and disposed of by the man I loved.

"What's wrong?" He jumped up and came toward me.

The closer he came, the less control I had over the sobs that racked my chest.

"Come here, hon."

His arms came around me, and we crumbled into a heap on the floor. He, hushing me as I cried, and I, purging the last of Darren Bridge, swearing to everything holy that I'd never let him hurt me again.

DARREN

I felt her slipping away every second she was gone. She was upset, and rightly so. I'd fucked her and told her to get out of my sight. Something I was used to, but the fact that I'd done it to the woman I loved was making me sick.

Something had snapped. Reilly's words clanging in my head. The feel of his face too fresh on my knuckles. I balled my hand into a fist, ready to find the guy and punch him into next week, even knowing it would solve nothing.

What I needed was a stiff drink, but the punching bag at the station gym was calling my name. I walked in, and Ian was doing pull-ups nearby. He said something as I passed that I didn't hear. I went right to the heavy bag and hit it hard without breaking stride.

"Whoa, buddy. You all right?"

"Stay away from me." I hit the bag again hard. This wasn't exercise. This was violence.

"Darren. Buddy. Slow down. You're going to break your hand." Ian was beside me now but giving me a wide berth.

"Don't fucking care." I hit again and again. Slowing down only every few rounds.

"You're going to care when you're out on disability getting fat. What's going on?"

I kept hitting it. How many times it would take before I could get her out of my head? Never had a woman do this to me. Never. Why now? Why her?

Bang. Bang. Bang. My hand was starting to ache, but I

welcomed the pain. Had to feel it, until I couldn't feel anything at all.

"Is it Vanessa?"

I paused. Ian had never used her name before. She was always the redhead, the chick who had me pussy whipped, the broad. I narrowed my gaze at him.

"So she's a person to you now?"

"She's your girlfriend."

Bang. "Not anymore."

He hesitated, eyeing me cautiously. "What happened?"

I stopped to catch my breath.

"I broke her boss's nose, and when she came to talk to me about it tonight, I fucked her and told her to leave."

"Wha— Okay." He shook his head. "Tell me about the boss."

"He came onto her when they were out of town. They got off the plane and I punched him. She freaked out and told me to leave. Yeah, that was about thirty seconds after I told her I loved her. Not sure. She could be fucking him."

"Jesus Christ, I do not envy you."

Deep down I knew she wasn't. But like her, I was becoming prone to believing the worst.

I continued throttling the bag and abusing my knuckles. I spoke through my clenched teeth. "Doesn't matter now. I'm sure I'll be back on the plan shortly. Go to a bar, get a few drinks, fuck a girl I don't care about."

An old tape, one that had lost its glimmer a long time ago. I could go out after work and find anyone to get Vanessa out of my system, but I knew it wouldn't fucking work.

Meanwhile, she could do the same damn thing. Let Reilly finally take what he wanted from her. The scene played out in my head, and white rage cut through me.

I hit the bag as hard I could and stifled a groan when I felt a snap. Pain speared through my hand and ricocheted up my arm. Gritting my teeth, I slowly accepted what I'd done.

Stupid. You're a stupid piece of shit.

I closed my eyes and let my head rest against the cool leather of the bag. I'd broken my hand. What was worse, I was destroying the only thing in my life that had ever really mattered. I was losing her. I might have already lost her.

VANESSA

I mumbled the lyrics from a sad old song that played from my speakers. My throat was froggy, and my eyes stung from all the tears I'd cried.

After about a half hour of bitching and crying, I convinced Eli I'd be fine even when I knew it was an outright lie.

I'd put on one of my mom's old Bonnie Raitt albums, grabbed Beau, and stared at the ceiling.

Darren Bridge had campaigned for my heart, and then he'd thrown it away. He was an amazing lay and a total bastard.

I squeezed my eyes closed, willing away a fresh wave of tears.

I could still feel him inside me. My muscles already ached from being pounded against a desk. I'd feel him for days...

The memory was imprinted on my skin. Literally. I was still wearing marks from the incredible sex we'd had. Maybe that's what he'd wanted all along. Worse, the memory was imprinted on my heart. I could only hope it would fade like the marks.

The phone rang, distracting me from my misery. My heart

pounded unevenly when I thought Darren might call. Not that I'd answer.

It was an unknown number. I picked it up.

"Hello?"

"Vanessa?"

"Who is this?"

"It's me, Michael."

I hesitated a second. "Oh." I'd completely forgotten about his call last week.

He cleared his throat. "Did you get my message?"

"Yes, I did. I'm sorry. I've been really busy."

"No problem. I understand. I've been in town for a couple of days. I was hoping we could catch up."

"Now's not really a good time." The inopportune timing of Michael's reintroduction into my world compounded with the devastation I now felt, knowing my relationship with Darren was definitely over.

"Are you crying?"

I swallowed over the painful knot in my throat. "It's been one of those days."

"That sucks. I'm sorry."

I sighed. "Me too."

"Listen, I'm free after one tomorrow. Can I take you out? Buy you a drink or something?"

I shook my head, knowing he couldn't see me. This really wasn't a good time. But what could I say? If my mother found out I'd avoided him on his trip, she'd never let me hear the end of it.

"Sure, that sounds good. I have to run a couple of errands, but I can text you in the morning and we can coordinate something."

"Great. I wish I could see you tonight. You sound like you could use a drink."

I laughed weakly. "I definitely could, but I'm afraid that's impossible." I was in no position to be seen in public. I didn't want to think about the wreckage that was my post-cocktail, post-fucked, post-breakup state. "I'll text you tomorrow."

"Sounds perfect. I can't wait to see you."

"See you then."

I hung up quickly and tossed the phone onto the bed. Bonnie's bluesy voice faded back into the speakers. I closed my eyes, letting the familiar sound soothe the ache of today.

I pushed thoughts of Darren away, making room for the broken faded memories of Michael. I hadn't seen him in years. We'd cared for each other, once upon a time. We'd grown apart, making the betrayals a little less painful. I'd never held a grudge because he'd never sliced me open the way Darren had tonight.

Suddenly, the prospect of seeing Michael didn't seem so terrible.

CHAPTER EIGHTEEN

DARREN

I'd never felt this kind of agony before. Trying to accept that I'd ended things with Vanessa was like a physical ache all through my body.

But...as miserable as watching her walk away from me was, maybe it was the best thing. After all, hadn't we been doomed from the start? Maya had me pegged. Cameron knew I was bad news. Now Vanessa knew better than anyone.

I'd been so determined to make it work, to prove them all wrong. Why the hell had I pushed? I'd been chasing women half my life, and I'd never wanted a relationship. I'd never wanted to stake my claim over a woman so damn bad.

Having the right to meant I had to change.

I wanted to change, and I had. Even if I survived the torture of letting her go, I'd never be the same. There'd never be another Vanessa, and my heart wouldn't take back its old shape. She was forever there.

The sad fucking truth was, I'd ache for her until I got her back. If she'd ever take me back. I'd given her no reason to. I'd been heartless and cruel.

After moping around my apartment most of the day, I headed for the gym. Maybe the familiarity there would give me a shred of solace.

Once there, I went through the motions. I couldn't really challenge myself with my busted hand. Another painful reminder.

I cursed inwardly and headed back to the office to talk to Cam.

He was dressed in his workout gear. He looked up from the computer and then down at my hand. "What happened to your hand?"

I lifted it casually. "Messed it up at work. It's nothing."

He lifted an eyebrow and nodded slowly.

I sat down in the chair across from the small metal desk that filled most of the small office.

"What's new? Anything I can help with?"

He shrugged. "I've just been trying to dot my i's and cross my t's for this proposal. The investor is ready to write the check for the expansion."

"That's great."

"It's only great if all the math is right."

"You've pulled it off before. You'll do it again."

"Sure. Except this time I've got a gym to run and a thousand other things coming at me." He blew out a breath.

For the first time, I actually felt sorry for him. I'd always been happy enough letting Cameron take the risks. I'd always have his back, but being a business owner wasn't my thing. I had other priorities. A bunch of nothing filling up my life that now had been turned upside down by the most incredible woman I'd ever met.

"Cam, I'm sorry. I've been so caught up in my own shit I haven't been helping as much as I should."

He frowned. "No, it's fine. It's my job."

Not like I'd given him any other choice. He'd had the balls

to take the reins, and I'd let him. Now he was going to be a father. And what was I doing? I was part-time and probably causing more problems than I was solving.

I cleared my throat and traced the line of the bandage wrapped around my hand. "What do you think about letting me be an investor, a partner?"

He cast me a tentative look.

"You can't keep doing it all on your own, Cam. You've got Maya now, and a baby on the way. If this all goes through like I'm sure it will, you'll have two gyms to manage."

"Maya's been helping. I couldn't have done all this without her." He flipped through the hefty stack of paperwork.

"I'm glad, but her life's about to change in a big way too."

"That's true. But where is this coming from? You've never mentioned it before."

"I'm comfortable," I admitted. "Too comfortable. I have everything I need, but I've never looked any further. Mom and Dad were always so focused on having and buying and keeping up with the neighbors. I never wanted a life like that. I know this is different. It's a livelihood, but it's also your dream. I've shared it, but I've shared from the sidelines."

He drummed his fingers on the edge of the desk. "Is this about Vanessa?"

I worked my jaw. I hadn't seriously thought about investing in the gym until about five minutes ago, but without a doubt, the thought of taking on a role that would make me worthy again in her eyes was there, under all of this.

"That's probably part of it." No point in lying.

"How are things going with her?"

I gnawed at the inside of my lip and avoided his stare. "Not very well."

"And you think me giving you stake in the business is going to be a Band-Aid for whatever is going haywire now?"

"No. Maybe." Yes. I was grasping at straws.

He sighed heavily and put his elbows on the desk. "Listen, I'm up to my eyeballs with this right now so we can break ground on the new gym on schedule. Why don't we talk about it more when things settle down? For me, and for you."

He might as well have said no, but I wasn't giving up so fast.

"Cameron, I've got all the money from the trust fund they set up. I never touched it. I'll put it all in. Run the numbers and figure out how much stake it's worth. I trust you. You know this gym is like a home to me. I'll do whatever you need me to do. I want to be all in."

He rubbed the back of his neck and released a tired sigh. "I'll think it over, okay? And in the meantime, you should figure things out with Vanessa. You look like shit. What's going on anyway?"

"We're taking a break."

He rolled his eyes. "I thought you were in love with her. Now you're taking a break?"

"I *am* in love with her. I punched her boss, and that didn't go over real well."

He grimaced and shoved a hand through his hair. "Fuck, Darren. Is he pressing charges?"

"No. He knows Dad, so he squeezed him for a mil to invest in his stupid hedge fund."

"Typical."

"Seriously." I rested my elbows on my knees and let my head fall into my hands. "I've spent my whole life trying to carve out my own life. This is where I landed. I can't give her the private jets and the wealth and the status. I hated that life, but I can't help but feel like she deserves all of that. She grew up poor. She doesn't see the world the way I've seen it."

His expression was thoughtful. "Is that what she wants? The money and status?"

I shrugged. "I don't know what she wants. She's got this incredible voice, but she never uses it outside of a karaoke night here or there. She's talented and smart, but she works long hours for a guy who treats her like crap and is pulling out all the stops to get in her pants. Why would she do it if it wasn't about the money?"

"Have you talked to her about it?"

"A little. But...shit happened."

I'd tried to call her a dozen times and abandoned my courage every time. I was too mixed up. I didn't know what I'd say, or if any of it would matter now.

"I'm so fucked up over this, Cam. I'm sorry I wasn't more supportive when you were having trouble with Maya. Now I know what it was like for you."

Cam's eyes took on a faraway look. "We went through a lot, but we made it."

My jaw tightened, and emotion twisted inside of me. "I'm glad. I really am."

"It's not too late. If you love her... If you really want this to work, Darren, you have to fight for her."

"She deserves better than me." That was the truth.

"Maybe she does, but my gut tells me you're the only one she wants."

VANESSA

I'd arranged to meet Michael at a little Thai restaurant in Brooklyn that had amazing takeout. I was camped out at a table in the front of the restaurant when he walked in. Like most things in Callaway, Michael Browning hadn't changed at all, from his even tan to his neatly trimmed blond hair tucked under his university baseball cap. He wore a polo shirt and blue jeans.

I rose when he saw me. He gave me a long hug that could have made me uneasy but didn't.

"It's good to see you," I said, surprised at how much I meant it. I pulled away.

Michael was a friendly face, and the hatchet had been buried long ago. I wasn't sure suddenly why I'd dreaded this moment so much.

"Good to see you too. Damn, you look great."

His slight accent brought back old memories. I'd really been living in a different world, and Michael was a very long way from home.

We settled at the table and ordered drinks.

"What's good here?" he asked.

"Basically everything. But you can't go wrong with pad thai." I studied the menu, hopping between my go-to favorites.

"You sounded pretty rough last night. I was worried I wouldn't get to see you. Everything good now?"

"Yeah," I lied, plastering on a smile. "Everything's good. So tell me about Callaway. What's new? I haven't been back in ages."

"I'm running for mayor. If you can believe that."

I laughed. "Mom told me. That's crazy. She says you're

going to win. I know you'll get her vote."

"She's a sweetheart. Always was. She talks about you every time I see her."

The mention of my mom made my heart twist a little. "I miss her. I can't get her up here very often."

"That's too bad. The city's great. Never been until now, but I can see what drew you here."

The waiter came then, breaking what was about to be a potentially awkward moment.

New York had been our breaking point. He was never going to leave Florida, and I was never going to stay. We'd loved each other, but our dreams were too different, our paths too far apart.

We talked for a long time. I talked about work like I was living the dream, because I couldn't give him the satisfaction of knowing I'd sacrificed our future for a life I didn't love. He gave me the latest gossip on everyone back home. Girls who'd been bitches to me getting embroiled in local scandal. His old football buddies who were still his buddies. The weather, which I admittedly missed.

After an hour, the conversation wound down. I was tired. I had enjoyed seeing Michael, but deep down I really wanted to be with someone else. If I couldn't be with that person, I'd settle for Eli, stuffed Beau, and a bottle of wine. We packed up our leftovers and walked out together.

Michael turned to me, looking at me in a way that I remembered used to make me warm all over.

"Thanks for meeting up with me, Vanessa. This was really great."

I swung my bag back and forth a little, anxious for goodbye. "Thank you for coming all the way to Brooklyn and saving me a trip."

"My pleasure." He took my hand and rubbed this thumb across my knuckles. "I'd be lying if I said I didn't want to bring you back with me though."

Maybe I should have been happy to have the company of someone who wanted me in the wake of what I'd been through with Darren. Once upon a time, I might have jumped on that invitation and justified a one-night reunion with a man I'd once loved. Memories and warmth glittered in Michael's eyes, but it wasn't enough. He could never be Darren. Michael's touch and his presence only made me want Darren's more.

"Michael, I've been seeing someone. I'm sorry."

He nodded and released my hand after a moment. "I understand."

"Thank you."

He put his hands in his pockets and rocked back on his heels. "Do you ever think about us?"

I laughed softly. "My mom is still holding out hope that I move back to Callaway and become Mrs. Michael Browning. So yeah, can't help but think about us sometimes."

He laughed. "We had a good time."

"Most of it was really good, yeah."

His smile faded, and he scuffed his shoe on the sidewalk. "I lost you."

"We lost each other, Michael. I think that happens when two people who aren't supposed to be together try too hard."

My heart hurt when I said the words, because I could have said the same thing about Darren and me. Were we trying too hard?

Michael exhaled heavily and stared up at the night. "God, maybe you're right. Seems like all I remember is the good stuff.

240

It was always easy with you."

Easy and comfortable. That's what had made it stifling too. He was everything I should have wanted, but I knew I couldn't have been happy spending forever with Michael. Here or there.

Michael was sweet and charming, and his heart was in the right place. But he'd never sock someone in the nose for me. My mom would probably think that was a good thing, but deep down I wanted a man who'd lie in the street to protect me. Someone who'd fight for me, even if his passion got a little bit ahead of him at times.

Because being in love with the wrong person was like experiencing life without one of my senses—the one nameless sense that makes all the others more intense. Michael was a good guy, but he didn't set my heart on fire the way Darren did. I'd risk getting burned again to feel that way. To feel that kind of love with all my senses.

We hugged good-bye, and I knew it would be a long time before I saw Michael again. I wished him well and went home, my heart no lighter.

DARREN

I stopped dead in my tracks. Ian was already several feet ahead by the time he realized he was walking alone.

"Dude. We're not there yet. Let's go." He started to circle back.

But I couldn't move. Across the street, Vanessa was standing under a restaurant canopy. She wasn't alone.

"Vanessa." Her name left my lips in a murmur, but I wanted to shout it.

Ian squinted and then looked back to me. "Okay. No big deal. Let's keep moving."

He slapped my shoulder, but instead of following Ian to our destination, I started moving in her direction.

"Whoa, whoa. What do you think you're doing?" Ian put his hand on my chest to halt my journey into the street.

"I'm going to talk to her."

"I don't think so. You look like you're out for blood."

He might have been right. I was already half in the bag. I'd convinced Ian to switch bars with the hope that maybe I'd see her at the place where we'd reunited weeks ago. I'd called her a few times, but every time the call went to voice mail. She was done with me. I knew it.

Ian slung his arm over my shoulder. If I was half in the bag, he was at least three-quarters.

"I'm telling you this as a friend. Not because I fundamentally disagree with your decision to date. But you're going to get your ass in a world of trouble if you walk across the street right now. Because she"—he pointed to where she stood talking with the man I didn't recognize—"does not want to see you right now. That I can guarantee you."

"I want her back." I swallowed hard, unable to tear my gaze from her. "I can get her back. I know I can."

Ian sighed beside me. "Come on, man. You can win her back another night. Let's go have some fun."

Ian might have been drunk, but there was a measure of wisdom in his words. I'd gotten myself into this mess by being impulsive and reckless, and already I was entertaining visions of leveling anyone who was a threat.

My legs started moving under me as Ian led me toward our next stop.

"We'll get some shots, find some pretty girls to keep us company, see if we can find someone to ease the pain, buddy. All will be well. I promise you." He patted my chest.

I didn't want anyone else. I wanted Vanessa. And if I couldn't have her, I didn't want to spend the night envisioning her with someone else. Who the fuck was that guy? How could someone have slipped into her world so quickly?

I glanced back. The way she smiled at him reminded me of the happiness we'd had together. When we weren't tearing each other apart. When he took her by the hand, a fierce jealousy took over. I could barely harness it.

With clenched fists, I turned away. I had to before I did something I'd regret in the morning. I followed Ian into the loud bar. But no amount of hard liquor could dull the pain that lanced through me. She was my girl, and that smile was meant for me...

CHAPTER NINETEEN

VANESSA

Monday came fast, and the days weren't getting any easier. Despite being emotionally exhausted, I hadn't slept well. The places where Darren's mouth had marked me hadn't faded much. I reached for anger, but tears and regret flooded me. If only I could do it all differently...maybe Darren wouldn't have felt the need to push me out of his life.

He'd called a few times, but I couldn't bring myself to hear his voice yet. Time wasn't mending the wounds very well, but maybe he was right. Maybe we needed a break.

I kept remembering the angry way he talked about my relationship with Reilly. Frustration and jealousy seethed beneath the surface of our heated words to each other. He couldn't really think that I was after anything more with Reilly. He had to know me better.

All day my thoughts ran on the same hamster wheel of questioning, doubts, and regret. One day, all of this wouldn't hurt so damn bad.

Reilly barked at me for coffee so I brought him some, and on my way back, I noticed a fat manila folder on Adriana's desk labeled *NYC Youth Arts Initiative.*

"Is Bill involved with them too?"

Adriana looked to where my hand rested on the folder.

"Oh, yes. He's been a patron for several years. The nonprofit has become an accredited investor in the fund though. Should be a great opportunity to help their endowments grow."

I nodded. "Do you mind if I take a look through? I'm still trying to catch up on all these structures."

"Sure. I'll need it later this afternoon to take care of some of the paperwork. But go for it."

"Thanks."

I took the folder back to my desk and sifted through it. Reilly Donovan Capital was taking a healthy chunk of their investment—in excess of thirty percent, which didn't match up with what we'd been selling at the investor cocktail. Why would he charge a nonprofit so much more...especially one he'd devoted so much time to?

I returned the file and went back to work, but I couldn't stop thinking about it.

I opened our shared file storage and did a search for the initiative. They hadn't been set up as a client yet, but I found a folder with their name under Reilly's protected account, one that I had access to as his admin.

I clicked through, looking for anything that might look out of the ordinary. Several invoices had been logged from another company, TriCorp, billing the initiative for an enormous list of services. Everything from consulting to accounting, all being billed at six hundred dollars an hour. The invoices went back at least eight years, and there were too many to count.

I'd never heard of TriCorp, but a quick search pulled it up. TriCorp was a New York corporation with two shareholders: David Reilly and Kevin Dermott. An older version of the incorporation documents listed only Kevin Dermott.

A sinking feeling crept over me. Something felt very

wrong about this.

I opened my drawer. Jia's card sat at the top of the stack that I'd collected from the investor party.

Reilly and Bill emerged from their offices. I slammed the drawer shut.

Reilly frowned. "We're headed out to lunch."

"Me too," I said quickly. "I'll see you when you get back. Call me if you need anything."

He didn't respond as he passed me by. As soon as he left, I picked up my phone and called Jia. She picked up after the first ring.

"Jia, this is Vanessa Hawkins with David Reilly's office."

"Vanessa. Good to hear from you."

"I was wondering if you wanted to chat. About that thing we talked about," I hedged. I glanced up to Adriana who seemed distracted with her own work. I didn't suspect she was listening, but already I sensed that I was digging too deep and should proceed with caution.

"I'd love to. You free for lunch?"

"I am. Where do you want to meet?"

She cleared her throat. "How about someplace private?"

I thought for a moment. "Delaney's on Pearl."

"I've never heard of it."

"Look it up. I'll meet you there in fifteen."

When she hung up, I grabbed my purse and headed downstairs.

★ ★ ★

Delaney's was as dark and dingy as I remembered. I'd met up with Maya here a few times for lunch when she needed to get away, far away, from the office. If Jia wanted privacy, this was the place. I sat at a small table in the back. A thick varnish covered the tabletop, but despite the half inch of protection, the surface was still scratched.

At the bar, an older woman with long gray hair sat beside a younger guy who seemed like he was already lit. He was hanging half off his stool and talking her ear off. Maybe Delaney's didn't host a very lively crowd during the lunch hour, but by Maya's accounts, things could get rowdy at night.

The door to the bar opened, light pouring in behind the silhouette of a woman. As soon as the door closed, I recognized Jia's face as she came toward me.

She situated herself across from me. The less than luxurious wood chair squeaked a bit as she sat. "You picked quite the place."

"You said you wanted private."

Before she could respond, the bartender arrived at the table with two paper menus. "Ladies, can I get ya anything to drink?"

"Perrier, please," she said.

The man scrunched up his face slightly. "Eh, we've got beer, liquor, and tap water."

"Tap water would be fine, thank you." Jia held her tight flawless smile.

"Same, thanks," I said. "And a hamburger."

"Coming right up." He scooped the menus and left us alone, returning less than a minute later with our waters.

"So what brings us to this fine establishment?" She shrugged off her blazer and leaned back in the chair.

"You said that if I ever wanted to know more about my boss, that we should talk."

"So what do you want talk about?"

You tell me. But I didn't guess it would be that easy. I'd invited her here, and we were dancing around a potentially dangerous subject. I sensed that she held a grudge against both Dermott and Reilly. But I couldn't get her to reveal anything damaging without making myself vulnerable too.

"I found some things. Can I speak to you in confidence? If I'm completely wrong about any of this, I don't want to lose my job."

"Reilly isn't with the firm anymore, and between us, I have no loyalty to Dermott anymore. So the answer is yes. You can speak to me in confidence." She rested her forearms on the table and leaned in.

"I want to know more about the Youth Arts Initiative. I'd only heard about it in passing since I've been with Reilly, but now the organization is investing with the hedge fund. I started looking closer, and Reilly's financial involvement with them has been significant."

"He's a major donor and a member of the board. David and Cheryl Reilly have been dumping money into the organization for years and bringing all their friends with them."

"Right, but the money is going the other way. A huge amount of money has been funneled into a third-party company that's been charging them for all kinds of things. The paperwork goes back years. Reilly's a shareholder, but the corporation was only in Dermott's name until this year."

"Good eye." She grinned, and her eyes took on a satisfied glimmer.

"I'm not sure if it's relevant, but I'm pretty sure he's trying to get Cheryl off the board too. I overheard some conversations with other board members. He was campaigning pretty hard to get rid of her."

She arched an eyebrow as if that part was news. "Cheryl's whole life is that organization. She took it over and turned it into what it is. Reilly put in the money, but she made it happen."

The bartender swung by with my hamburger, not bothering to ask me if I needed anything. Didn't matter, I was starting to lose my appetite the more we talked about Reilly.

"Would he kick her off just out of spite? I thought they had parted amicably."

Jia took a sip of her water and set the glass down. "Maybe he has something to hide. Or something to gain."

I waited, but she didn't continue. I sensed that she knew more than she was telling me.

"If something shady is going on, I need your help to know what to look for."

"The question is, what do you want, Vanessa? This only works if we both get what we're after."

I stared at my hamburger and took a nibble on a fry. What *did* I want? I'd started digging with no idea what the consequences could be.

"I've dedicated my life to Reilly and to this job for two years. Every day, with very few exceptions. If he's doing what I think he's doing, I don't want to be a part of it anymore. I mean, this is really wrong. Not to mention illegal."

She stared at me a moment without saying a word. "About a week after Reilly's divorce was final, Dermott transferred a large sum of money out of TriCorp into an offshore bank account."

"How much money?"

She pursed her lips. "The transfer was in the amount of twenty million dollars."

My jaw fell. I hadn't had the time to look through all the invoices, but... "Oh my God. If what you're saying is true, half the money that passed through TriCorp is technically Cheryl's."

"I can guarantee it wasn't on the table in the divorce. So, yes, technically, it's hers, or the organization's. However you want to look at it, it's in the wrong hands. Cheryl never knew about it because she's always been on the ground floor of the organization's operations. He's been managing the finances at the top, setting up kickbacks for Dermott and Donovan and anyone else who he didn't want talking about the millions he was skimming off. So while Cheryl's tapping all her friends to keep donating to the cause, he's skimming as much off as he can into an account that Dermott managed up until a couple of months ago. They've both been using the initiative as a tax shelter for years. The CFO at the initiative is in completely over his head. It's a gold mine for everyone else."

"This is horrible."

I swallowed over the huge knot that had formed in my throat. Reilly was a monster, and suddenly I felt like the biggest fool for ever doubting my instincts.

"How do you know all this?"

Jia shrugged and stole a fry from my plate. "Dermott talks too much."

"You haven't known him very long."

"I think I know him better than his wife does at this point."

She winked, and even though I found her casual attitude toward his implied infidelity unsettling, it did explain why Dermott would confide all of this to her. It would also explain why she was so angry to have been passed over after Dermott's promotion. She was indeed a woman scorned.

"So what do we do? I mean, this needs to stop. It's fraud. So many people are getting ripped off."

"Like you, I have a ton of paperwork showing money passed between him and the initiative. It looks shady and would cause a scandal, but at the end of the day, these are smart finance guys. Even if no one's been paying attention, they probably aren't going to cook the books to the point where they can't loosely justify the expenses in a court of law. That's not the smoking gun we'd need to really take them out of the game."

"What is?"

"I can prove that Dermott wired the funds. But it doesn't matter unless you can find where the money went."

"And what if I find it?"

Her lips pursed slightly, and I could see the calculating in her eyes. "If you can find me that account's records, Dermott and Reilly are both finished. I'd take it to the top of the firm, and I'd have Dermott's job within a week."

"You want revenge," I said simply.

"I like to think of it as my own personal brand of justice."

"What if you're wrong? What if all of it's legitimate? I lose my job over nothing." Not that I wanted to keep it, in light of all of this.

"Go to Cheryl. If she thinks your heart is in the right place, she'll never tell Reilly. Life goes on. And if I'm right, she's got ten million reasons to believe you."

"I'll get blacklisted if Reilly knows I'm behind it."

"Maybe. Maybe not. I could probably get you a highly paid administrative position back at the firm. I could hire you directly under me, if you'd like."

I appreciated that Jia was trying to sweeten the deal, since the future was looking bleak regardless of the outcome. But I couldn't think of anything worse.

"No offense to you, but I don't want to run around after overworked execs anymore. If I leave Reilly, I need to start over."

"I'm not sure how I could help you there."

I thought it over. The possibility of starting over had featured more prominently in my thoughts lately. Still, I wasn't sure what my next steps would be. I had a couple years of solid work experience to add to my résumé and some savings to get me by for a while. "I'll figure out a way to land on my feet."

"Whatever you decide, just don't let Reilly catch you snooping around. If he gets wind of any of this, he'll move the money and start covering his tracks. Sounds like he may already be trying to do that by getting Cheryl off the board."

"The meeting is at the end of the month."

"Clock is ticking." She slipped her blazer back on. "I'll courier the wire transfer statement and anything else I can find to your apartment later tonight. That way you'll have everything you need when the time comes."

"Will this come back to you?" I looked up as she rose.

"The only way this comes back to me is through you. Take the information to Cheryl. When everything blows up, I'll make my move."

Jia was the only one who was really going to win. I cared more about justice than vengeance. And if everything she said was true, there was a lot of justice to be served to David Reilly.

She was about to leave but stopped mid-turn.

"How's Maya doing anyway? Someone told me she got married."

"She did. They're expecting a baby boy in the fall."

Her expression softened. "I'm happy for her."

"Me too."

"Do me a favor, and send her my best."

I nodded. "I will."

"Good luck."

"You too."

★ ★ ★

I replayed my conversation with Jia in my head at least a hundred times. I was still in shock. All of this information had fallen heavy on my shoulders. If what she said was true, and if I could find that smoking gun, I'd be responsible for exposing something bigger than I could really fathom. I was a personal assistant. I was not cut out for this.

Reilly strolled into the reception area, breaking my focus from the computer screen and my tumbling thoughts. The sky outside had grown dark and the office was empty. I was only doing time until he left.

He slowed at my desk. "I'm heading out. Do you have any plans tonight?"

I shrugged. "Probably not."

"How are things going with Darren?"

I could tell him the truth, but I didn't want to give him the satisfaction of knowing that we weren't together. No doubt, he'd had a hand in Darren's decision to push me away so suddenly.

"It's complicated," I said finally.

Satisfaction glittered in his eyes. "We had an interesting chat."

"So I heard."

He canted his head. I hoped he couldn't see how broken I was inside.

"We'd make a great team, Vanessa. I hope you've thought about that."

I looked down, doodling circles on my notepad. "I'll be here a bit longer. Call if you need anything." *Please leave.*

"I'll be across the street grabbing a quick drink before I head home. Come down if you need a break."

I nodded, trying my best to ignore him and end this conversation. But he didn't leave. He circled the desk slowly and leaned in behind me. I cringed when he rested his hand on my shoulder, squeezing me.

"David..." I tensed, shifting away from him as much as my desk would allow.

"I pushed you too fast, I know. After waiting for you this long, I can accept a slower pace. But we need a place to start."

I swallowed hard, searching for a way out of this situation that could easily spiral out of control. Adriana and Bill were long gone already. Reilly wasn't drunk this time, but that circumstance didn't make me feel any safer being alone with him.

"Vanessa... When you ask me what I need, the answer is always you."

I closed my eyes. "I'm going through a lot right now. Let me think about it, okay?" I hoped he couldn't hear the tremor in my voice.

He kissed my neck, and bile rose in my throat.

"Good," he whispered. He straightened and walked out of the office.

Once alone, I willed myself not to cry. Not to break down.

I couldn't make excuses for him anymore. This had to end.

CHAPTER TWENTY

DARREN

I'd been nursing my hangover for hours, and my head was still throbbing. But no amount of shots last night could have gotten me to go home with another woman. Catching a glimpse of Vanessa with that guy had been an unlucky circumstance that had only made me drink harder and longer, well into the night. I couldn't stop thinking about who he was and if they'd left together.

She couldn't have moved on that quickly.

I sure as hell wasn't able to.

I was ready to call her again, because not knowing was killing me. Then the tones went off. The other guys on Ladder 9 went for their truck. I followed suit and went through the motions. A routine I'd done a thousand times, thank God, because my mind was all over the place. Pining over a woman I'd pushed away like a goddamn fool.

The dispatcher's voice scratched through the radio at my hip. "Four-alarm fire at East Ninety-Second and Clarkson. Reports of flames from the windows and occupants inside."

I grabbed my gear and started to dress quickly, forcing my aching brain to think about the task at hand. We loaded up, hit the sirens, and pulled out toward our destination. Ian was at the wheel, dominating the road and cussing the whole way as we maneuvered around traffic.

Hundreds of calls and dozens of fires had trained my body to stay calm in the worst situations, but already I could anticipate the adrenaline rush coming. Someone with nerves of steel couldn't stay unaffected when he was running into a building that everyone else was running out of. All my life, I'd wanted nothing more than to do that very thing.

In the distance, a string of black smoke billowed up into the sky, dissipating high above the tops of the buildings.

The radio continued. "Engines 2 and 7 are en route. Occupants on the first and third floors."

Ian's eyes were dead on the road. In the back, one of the new guys was looking a bit green as we pulled up in front of the three-story building. The engine trucks pulled up quickly behind, and their crew started working the hydrant.

"All right guys. Let's roll," Ian said.

On the sidewalk, a woman was crying hysterically. I went to her. "What's wrong? Who's still inside?"

The woman started speaking Spanish quickly, too quickly for my weak command of the language. I kept making out a name though. Leo.

Ian came up beside me and listened for a moment.

"Who's Leo?" I asked him.

"Her little boy. He was playing hide-and-seek, and they couldn't find him. He's inside on the third floor. Let's go."

"Move!" I shouted at the crew, moving away from the woman who had every right to be hysterical.

Two cop cars pulled up, and an officer immediately went to her, pulling her away to a safe distance.

Usually Ian and I partnered up, but since we were looking

for someone, we decided to split into two teams. I took Travis, the new guy, whose complexion wasn't looking any better. Ian went with Ray, a veteran firefighter who felt breathing masks should be optional and had been known to smoke cigars inside an active fire.

He was old school, funny as hell, and more times than not, a dangerous person to have by my side at a time like this. Between the two, I felt better having Travis with me. At least he wasn't going to go rogue once we got in there.

We neared the building, and I turned to Travis. "We're taking the third floor. Follow the right-hand wall. Stay with me. And when I say go, we get the fuck out of there, no matter what. Got it?"

"Got it."

"Good. Use your head."

He was probably shitting himself already, but there wasn't time for any of that. Sink or swim. Keep your wits about you, or put yourself and possibly others in danger.

We made it through the moderate haze to the third floor before the smoke got too thick. I put on my mask and hit the air, gesturing for Travis to do the same. The steady whoosh of my breath—in and out, in and out—triggered an almost meditative calm. Whenever I heard that sound, my life was on the line. So were others'. When others succumbed to panic and anxiety, I found resolve. Clarity, even in the pitch black of the fire we were at war with.

I led the way. Travis trailed a few feet behind me. My hand followed the wall as we turned several corners. Carefully we checked each room and found no signs of the child. Then we reached a closet. Inside on the floor was a small body. The boy couldn't have been more than two or three years old. I turned behind me and yelled to Travis.

"I have him!"

We'd have to move quickly now, retracing our steps back, all the way down until the boy was safe. I scooped him up into my arms and moved back toward Travis. The boy coughed and twisted in my arms. Relief flooded me. He'd be okay. We just needed to get him out. Fast.

Travis led the way quickly.

As we neared the entrance, I yelled to him, "I'm going to find Ian and Ray. You take the boy out! Go!" I urged him ahead of me.

He hesitated only a moment before rushing out, the boy's body tight against his gear.

Someone might still be trapped in the first floor unit, but I had no idea who it might be. The fire licking up the back of building had spread quickly, and smoke was thick all around.

I moved down the empty hallway. My air alarm started going off. I still had time. I'd find Ian, and we could move out. I felt around and found a door. I pushed at it and then shoved against it.

When it gave, I stepped into nothing. A free fall, broken by something hard and uneven.

The next few seconds were a blur, a black blur.

I cursed and thrashed around. I tried to get my bearings, but I was tangled up in something. Boxes and a bunch of crap.

My heart was beating loud in my ears. The reassuring whoosh of my air had been replaced by the alarm. I reached for calm, but panic was winning. And I was sucking down too much air.

I swallowed through the pain radiating down my side. After a moment, I realized I was in a basement. A basement with no goddamn stairs into it. Black water dripped down the stone walls around me and seeped through the wood floors that glowed with heat above.

I twisted to bring myself upright, and pain lanced through my side. My ribs felt like they were cutting into my lungs, making it even harder to breathe. All the while, my bell kept dinging, reminding me that I was running low.

Short panicked breaths. Slicing pain.

I tried to push up from my side. A different kind of throbbing shot down my right arm, which was almost of no use to me now. I'd really fucked myself up good. I had to get out of here. Only problem was there was no way out of this godforsaken hole in the earth. No wonder the goddamn door didn't want to budge. This place was a death trap.

"Mayday. Mayday. Mayday. This is Bridge," I rasped into my mask. "I'm in the basement. No fucking steps."

No response.

My alarm got louder, dinging faster. A reminder that time was running out.

The orange glow on the other side of the basement was the only indicator of an alternate exit route. Fire.

I went toward it, hoping to find stairs that would take me back to the main floor, but there was nothing. Nothing but thick black smoke. The immense heat pushed me to the ground. I could feel it through my gear.

I heard a voice that sounded like Ian's yell down. "Bridge! There's a stepladder propped against the wall. Can you get back to it?"

I traced the wall back, trying to pull myself back up to standing as I got farther away from the heat of the fire. I tripped over something, landing myself right back on my side.

I groaned in pain. My whole right side was fucking useless.

On my hands and knees, I felt my way through the garbage on the floor. I needed to get back to where I'd started. Fast. If they didn't get the fire under control, the building could compromise. And I was stuck under it all.

Then, in an instant, I ran out of air.

The mask suctioned to my face.

Fuck.

I ripped it off. I inhaled my first gulp of choking smoke and crumbled back down onto the floor to find the cleanest air I could. I had to get out of here.

I thought of Vanessa, my family. Everyone who needed me...people I refused to live without.

"We need to get him out of here. Now!" Ian's voice was loud with panic.

I tried to crawl toward his voice, but all the adrenaline couldn't take me there fast enough. I coughed, toxic smoke filling my lungs. I had to be close. I struggled over more unknown obstacles as I crawled as quickly as my body would go.

I couldn't die here. Not like this.

VANESSA

With very little effort, I'd been able to track down the account that Jia had mentioned. Working late in the office and being so intricately involved in all of Reilly's affairs, I had access to nearly everything he touched. He trusted me, and I was a few clicks away from breaking that trust and every confidentiality agreement I'd signed over the past two years.

The account resided in Grand Cayman. Ironically, the

place where he'd hidden money from his wife was the same place I'd fallen hopelessly in love with another man.

I'd made digital duplicates of all the files anyone could ever need to expose what Reilly and his cronies had been doing. Statements, wire transfers, incorporation documents, and a few cryptic e-mails between him and Dermott that came up with a search for the account number.

They'd both go down, without a doubt.

I had my finger on the trigger. All I had to do was pull.

But who was I? An unimportant cog in an operation that Reilly had been running smoothly for years. Despite everything that Jia had confessed to me, I still doubted whether I was capable of bringing it all to an end. The prospect terrified me. What if somehow it all came crashing down on me?

Even if it didn't, I'd still lose my job. The pressure of working under Reilly day after day would be replaced with the very real pressure of finding gainful employment elsewhere. I didn't have Darren's security blanket, and I couldn't survive in the city without an income.

Anxious and edgy, I stared outside the conference room window as Bill and Reilly rattled on about prospects. Outside, the city I'd grown to love sprawled as far as I could see. Building after glassy building, dim and gray under an overcast sky. I was about to be out of a job, and I'd just lost the only relationship that had made me really feel alive. Life was nothing more than a dull gray without the promise of Darren lighting it up, even if he'd broken me beyond hope.

I had no business trying to reform a man like Darren, but I still wanted to.

"Vanessa. Did you get that?"

I jolted back to reality, but I'd completely missed whatever Reilly had said that was so important.

"I'm sorry. What was that?"

"I've got it. No worries." Adriana shot me a tight smile.

My phone vibrated on silent, providing a fresh distraction. Seeing Maya's number, I sent the call to voice mail and forced my attention to the meeting agenda. She called twice more, and I finally texted her.

I'm in a meeting.

Darren was in a fire. We're headed to the hospital.

I reread the text. Terrible possibilities flashed through my mind and heat rushed to palms. I typed out a reply, my heart racing in my chest.

Is he okay?

We don't know very much yet. Call me when you can. New York Methodist. Room 204.

I held the phone with trembling hands. "Oh my God."

"Is everything okay?" Adriana's eyes filled with concern.

"I have to go."

Reilly shot me an annoyed look. "We're in the middle of something here."

"I'm sorry. It's an emergency. I have to go. I'll be back as soon as I can."

I gathered up my things and left the room.

"Vanessa!" Reilly followed me out.

I didn't care. I had to see Darren.

I stopped at my desk and grabbed my purse. "Darren's hurt. He was in a fire last night. He's at the hospital. I have to go see him."

"I thought you were finished with that loser?"

I glared at him, so ready to unleash my hatred onto this horrible man. "You have *no* right to judge him."

Little did he know how he was about to be judged. His whole world was about to come crumbling down. All his self-importance and wealth and pomp.

I slung my purse over my shoulder and moved around Reilly. He caught my arm, holding me tightly. I had a flashback to the airport when he'd done the same thing in front of Darren. The results had been disastrous.

I stared into his cold gray eyes. "Let. Me. Go."

His jaw was set tight. "Leave, and you can forget you ever had this job."

I was already done with it. I wrenched my arm out of his grasp.

"You're a bad person, David. You're hateful and cold and disillusioned. You hate what you can't have. And you will *never* have me."

I stopped at the door when he called after me.

"You're making a mistake, Vanessa"

I turned. One last look.

"Wasting another minute of my life here with you would be a mistake. Good-bye, David."

DARREN

My whole goddamn body hurt, but the cold air burning in my lungs was a welcome reminder that I was alive. Hurt, but alive. Pieces of the previous night came back in flashes. The black of the fire. The bright white of the hospital. The terrifying prospect of dying in that hole and then Ian hauling me out on his shoulder. I'd gotten closer to the door I'd fallen through than I realized. Close enough for him to get me out before it was too late. He'd cussed at me every step of the way as I choked on the toxic air all around us.

I'd put my life and my brothers' in danger. And I owed Ian my life.

I shouldn't have gone back in alone. Whatever pain I was feeling now was nothing compared to the agony of knowing that someone else could be hurt because of me.

Slowly I emerged from the memories that played like a bad dream behind my tired eyes.

"You're awake." Olivia was by my side. She put her hand in mine.

"Liv." My voice croaked, and the sound seemed to scrape down the flesh of my throat.

She hushed me and brought a glass of water to my mouth. I tightened my lips around the pink bendy straw and sucked up the lukewarm water.

Relieved, I rested my head against the pillow with a sigh.

"How do you feel? Do you want the nurse?"

I shook my head. "No."

"Cam and Maya were just here. I can get them. They went to go call Mom and Dad. They didn't want to talk to them until they knew how you were doing."

I squeezed Olivia's hand, grateful she was here. We'd never been really close, but I couldn't imagine my life without her. And I could never shake the worry that she needed me and Cam. Mom and Dad would try to shape her future, but we'd always be there to keep her safe.

"I'm glad you're here."

Her eyes misted with tears. "Needless to say, we're glad you're here too. We got the call, and I thought the worst. I was so scared."

I hushed her, brushing away a tear that streamed down her face. "Going to take more than a little tumble and some smoke to take me out, okay?"

The door to the room swung open, and my heart nearly stopped. All my relief and regret walked in the door with Vanessa. Her face was streaked with tears. She'd been crying. She came closer, and the door swung closed behind her.

"Darren. Oh my God." She brought a shaky hand to her mouth.

Liv stood, wiping away her own tears as she did. "He's going to be fine, Vanessa. He dislocated a few ribs. He broke his arm and his hand, but everything will heal in time."

"My hand was already broken."

Liv turned to me with a frown.

I shook my head. "Don't worry about it." Every word was scratchy and uncomfortable.

She glanced between Vanessa and me, and with a sad smile, she let my hand go. "I'll leave you two alone. I'm going to go check in with Cam. Just ring the nurse if you need anything, okay?"

"Thanks," I said.

When we were alone, she came to my side. I turned my

palm up, asking for her touch. She answered, taking my hand. I closed my eyes, suddenly overwhelmed with that smallest connection.

"You came."

"Of course I came. I headed straight over as soon as Maya called me. I didn't even think about whether you'd want me here."

I opened my eyes, acutely aware of the pain I'd caused her and how it had plagued me too. "I always want you with me."

She chewed on her lip, fresh tears glistening in her eyes. "I thought you wanted to take a break."

I shook my head. "I was wrong."

I coughed. Excruciating pain shot out from my ribs and radiated down my side. I inhaled a careful breath and rested back on the pillow. Vanessa came closer, settling on the edge of the bed beside me. Her beautiful features were pinched, and her eyes betrayed her worry.

Then suddenly I remembered the last time I'd seen her. On someone else's arm. Smiling at a man who wasn't me.

"Vanessa, I don't know who that guy is." I swallowed over the sting in my throat. "But I'm going to fight for you. I'm fighting for us. Being away from you is killing me."

Her brow wrinkled. "What guy? What are you talking about?"

"I saw you the other night with someone. Blond hair. You were laughing and smiling with him. I wanted to kill him."

She smiled and touched my cheek. "You're crazy."

"Who was he? And where does he live?"

She laughed and shook her head. "That was Michael, and he lives in Florida, so you've got a journey ahead of you. Also, it's a pointless journey because he's a relic. So far in my past, you don't have anything to worry about."

"An ex?"

She nodded.

"Do you love him?" I braced myself for an answer that could break me more badly than my fall had.

"I used to. A long time ago. We were really young."

I wanted her to love me. I'd felt it. I'd been so sure of it at times. But goddamn, I needed those words. After everything we'd been through, I craved them more than I could explain.

She leaned in, pressing a soft kiss to my lips. Her kind eyes captured me, held me in her tenderness.

"You're the only one who has my heart, Darren."

"How can you give me your heart me after what I did to you?"

She winced, and emotion flickered behind her pale green eyes. I'd live through another fire to take away that day and the hurt I'd put her through.

"I can give you my heart, because you keep fighting for it. And because I love you. More than you can possibly know. When I thought something had happened to you..." Her breath caught and her eyes misted with unshed tears.

"Shh," I hushed her and squeezed her hand. "I'm good. A little banged up, but I'm good."

"What if..."

"You got me out of there, Vanessa. Shit was not looking good, but I kept thinking about you. I knew I had to get out of there to get to you. To make things right with us. To win you back."

Tears fell down her cheeks, and I wished I could kiss them all away. Hold her and love her. I hoped she'd give me that chance again.

"I'm never letting you go again," I whispered.

Vanessa stood up when the nurse came in to check my vitals.

"I'm afraid we're only allowing family visits right now, dear. He's had a rough night. He needs to rest."

"She is family," I said.

Vanessa's lips fell apart and then snapped shut again. The nurse looked to me with a raised eyebrow.

"She's my wife."

"Oh. My apologies, Mrs. Bridge." She jotted something down on my chart and put it back at the foot of the bed. "Very well. I'll be back in to check on you in an hour or so. Press the button if you need anything." She rested her hand on my leg, one part of me that didn't hurt a bit. "Thank you for all you do, son." She winked at Vanessa. "He'll be good as new in no time."

The nurse left, and Vanessa didn't waste a second coming back to me. I shifted to the side, wanting to make more room for her.

I hissed at the pain that lanced down my side.

"Darren. Stop it. You're hurting yourself."

"I'm fine." I patted the empty sliver of bed.

She crawled up beside me, careful not to lean into me. She rested against the pillow we shared with a soft exhale. "You're not afraid of anything, are you?"

"Only thing I'm afraid of is losing you again."

"Then don't let me go."

I shook my head. "I don't plan to. Ever."

She leaned in to meet my lips, sealing the promise.

CHAPTER TWENTY-ONE

VANESSA

Darren's apartment was silent save the quiet murmur of the television in his room. I crept in quietly. He was asleep, shirtless. A light blue sheet bunched at his waist. His body curved carefully on the uninjured side, and his chest moved with steady breaths—a simple motion that I knew had caused him a great deal of pain the past couple of weeks as he healed.

I moved through the room, picking up a few articles of clothing that had been thrown about and putting them in a hamper. The second I switched off the television though, he stirred.

His raspy moan was swiftly followed by a sharp intake of breath. He winced, pausing a second before moving flat onto his back.

"Baby." He smiled when his tired gaze locked on mine.

"Go back to bed. I was just tidying up."

"You don't have to pick up after me."

"I know that. But as long as you're laid up this way, I'm going to take care of you. Like it or not." I moved to his bedside table and began to gather up a couple of half-empty glasses.

He reached out with his uninjured arm, trying to draw me closer to him. "Stop that and come here."

"You should rest."

"I've been resting for weeks. You're here now, and I want to spend some time with you."

Resigned, I put down the glasses and settled beside him on the bed.

He hummed, taking his warm hand up and down my bare thigh. "You're a sight for sore eyes, red. I never get tired of being with you."

I glanced down at my simple outfit. A pale pink T-shirt and white shorts. My new "unemployed" uniform now that the days were getting warmer. Like summer vacation with no end in sight, at least until I found a new gig or cool weather came. Eli was helping out more with the rent, and my mom had sent me some money to help me get by while I was on the job hunt.

"Why won't you stay over here for a while? I like waking up to you."

"You need your rest, and I can't sit still. I'm not used to having this much downtime. I need to keep busy, which is obviously why I'm here fussing over you when I should be letting you rest."

"I can keep you busy," he murmured suggestively.

I did a poor job of hiding a smile. I knew he could keep me very busy, all night every night, but he needed to heal before we did anything.

Still, I couldn't help but drink him in. If I was a sight, he was a wonder. I looked him over, from his messy bedhead to the faint laugh lines that his dazzling smile had always rendered invisible to me. His chest was bare perfection. Weeks away from the gym were barely noticeable, and even resting, he was impressive and toned.

"See anything you like?" He shot me a grin.

"I love everything I see. You know that."

He dragged his touch up the inside of my thigh, leading me toward a dangerous surge of sensations.

I stilled his hand before he could go any further, but he coaxed me toward him. I leaned in the rest of the way, careful not to put any pressure against his chest. My lips met his, soft and warm. I tangled my fingers through his hair and traced the strong line of his jaw over the rough hairs that had grown in. He was rugged and gorgeous, and I'd never loved him more.

"I think I have something else you might like." He reached into a drawer in the bedside table and withdrew a small narrow box.

"What's this?"

He placed it in my hands. "It's for you."

"You didn't go out, did you?" I couldn't help the concern lacing my tone. He was the type who'd push himself when he should be healing.

"No. Thanks to modern technology, I'm able to make romantic gestures from the convenience of home. Now open it."

I smiled, a bubble of anticipation growing inside me. I untied the silver bow and opened the box. Inside laid a fine rose gold chain. Hanging from it was a pendant molded into the shape of a five-petal flower—a plumeria, like the one that tinted the air with its sweet scent every day we were on the island together. In the center, a diamond shone brightly.

He lifted the delicate necklace from the box, and even with his bandaged hand managed to fasten it around my neck. The flower fell cool against my chest.

I was speechless, in awe of the gesture and the memories it brought back. Those days on the island had been precious—so precious I couldn't believe we could possibly bring such paradise home. But somehow we had.

"It's so beautiful. Thank you."

"Beautiful, just like you."

"I love it."

"Do you know what it means?" He traced the pendant with the tip of his finger.

"The plumeria?"

"Means new beginnings. The minute you came back into my world, everything started over for me. You're the beginning of the rest of my life, Vanessa."

I caught his hand against my heart and squeezed it tightly. "And you're mine."

"I'm sorry for everything I put you through. I can't tell you how much. The man I was before I met you—that wasn't the real me. I was trying to protect myself from the hurt I'd watched my parents inflict on each other for years. I'd completely lost faith in what love could be with the right person. I never believed I could have something like this."

My heart ached when I thought about a younger Darren becoming so guarded with his heart over the years. I recognized a shade of that in my own journey, though, too.

"I understand. It took me a long time to know what I really wanted too. But I found it, with you."

"I love you, Vanessa." His eyes were dark with emotion.

"I love you too."

"Come here," he whispered, pulling me close.

He kissed me, long and deep sweeps of his tongue. He caressed me, over my face, down my arms, and back down to my thigh. His touch on my skin lit up like a trail of fire. A little voice in my head reminded me that we couldn't keep going, as much as I might want to...

"We can't. Not until you're completely healed."

"I can't go without you that long. I have a feeling you can't wait that long either."

"Sure, I can," I lied. My resolve withered with every passing second. "I don't want to hurt you."

"I don't care how broken I am. Every minute inside you is pure pleasure. And that's all I'm going to feel. I can guarantee that."

"But the doctor..."

"The doctor says I'm clean as a whistle." His touch slipped past the edge of my panties, grazing the sensitive skin there. "I want you bare, Vanessa."

My breathing sped up along with my heartbeat. I wanted that too...

He'd never asked before, but the question had lingered unanswered between us. Darren's past was plentiful, and I couldn't take anything for granted, no matter how much I loved him. But knowing we were safe to take this next step and the thought of removing that barrier between us was intoxicating. Intimate on a whole new level.

"Come on, red. Live a little." He palmed my breast and gave my nipple a gentle squeeze through my shirt.

The doctor wouldn't approve of what we were about to do, but Darren didn't give a damn. He was bad and impulsive, and I loved that about him.

Fueled with the crazy passion only he could ignite in me, I rose off the bed. "Don't make me regret this."

"I can promise you won't."

He caught his lip between his teeth as I undressed, slowly, drawing out every precious second. I pushed my panties over my hips, and they fell to the floor, leaving me naked except for his beautiful gift. My skin felt hot under his hungry gaze.

Under the sheet, he was already hard. I went to him and straddled his legs. I kissed his chest, licking lightly over the dark disks of his nipples. Then I went lower, and the sheet slipped away, revealing his beautiful thick cock.

I'd never thought the male anatomy was especially beautiful, but the prize between Darren's legs matched the rest of his physique. Hard flesh beneath velvety soft skin, jutting out confidently from his groin. I trailed a finger down his length and softly cupped his balls. One quick glance up revealed just how wound up he already was. His eyes were dark. His jaw was set tight, and his chest heaved under shallow breaths.

I held his cock in my hand and guided the tip to my lips. There I taunted him with tiny, lazy licks around the sensitive tip, all the way down to the base and back up where I took more of him.

His eyelids fell, and a low sound rumbled from his chest.

I shifted over him, trying to take as much of his length as I could. I licked and sucked, punctuating each stroke with the blunt pressure of the back of my throat. We moaned in unison, and I reveled in his pleasure. I wanted to give him all the pleasure he'd given me so many times.

I was already wet, aching for the feel of him thick inside me. My thoughts circled around how he'd feel bare. The simple act of our bodies joining had brought me toe-curling ecstasy time and again. No one else had made love to me as he had, arresting my heart and mind as he claimed my body.

"Enough," he rasped. "Come here."

I let him slip from my lips and crawled up his body, praying that this was more pleasure than pain for him. He rested his wounded hand on my hip and used the other to guide his cock to my pussy. He notched there and squeezed my hip tight before pulling me down.

"Slow and deep, baby. I want to feel every beautiful inch of you coming down on me. All the way down."

Anticipation hummed through me. I wanted to drop down and take all of him inside me. But, like him, I also wanted to treasure this new experience between us. Make it last as long as we could.

His hooded gaze was riveted where our bodies joined, his lips apart as we became one. I sheathed him completely, stretched and tight around him. His cock buried in the deepest part of me.

He licked his thumb, wetting it before bringing it to my clit and stroking gently over the taut bundle of nerves. I inhaled sharply as the sensation shot through me. I could have come right then. I pulsed around him, craving friction and release.

He gazed up at me, heat and hunger raw in those beautiful brown depths. And in that fiery warmth, I saw love. Adoration. Wonder. All the things that kindled in my heart when I was with him.

His dark olive skin tightened over his muscles, like a thin veil of control over the mass of man before me who was capable of so much strength, so much passion... Sifting his fingers through my hair, he brought me to him. Our lips melted together, soft and then rough. He nipped at my lower lip and slid his tongue over the sting. I fluttered around him, craving more of him. More sensation. More heat.

"This"—he thrust his hips up gently—"is the way it was always supposed to be. And this is how it'll always be."

I closed my eyes, feeling light and heavy at once.

"Now ride me, sweetheart."

I was almost too overwhelmed in that moment to follow through on his demand, but the promise of the pleasure launched me into action. I found the edge of the headboard behind him. Using it for leverage, I rose and dropped down.

He groaned against my lips. "Fuck."

Whether that was a compliment or an order, I had no plans to stop. I rode him, taking him deeper, over and over. Breathless, I climbed to that place where we could fall apart together.

A fever slid over my skin, radiating from my heart as it beat a wild tempo in my chest. I was slick around him, taking him to the root with ease.

His fingertips dug into my flesh, marking me with the pressure of his touch. I welcomed it. I wanted memories of this moment.

"Now hard, Vanessa."

The reality of his injuries sobered me a moment. "I don't want to hurt you."

A grin curved his lips. "I promise you that in this moment I can feel no pain. Now ride me hard until I tell you to come."

That quickly I was back in the moment, ready to fuck him breathless. My muscles trembled, but I chased the pleasure. I did what he wanted, taking him fast and hard until I was so close to the edge I could scream.

"You feel so good," I whimpered.

His jaw was tight, an agonizing strain on his features. "Going to feel so good to come inside you, baby. But I need you first. Come for me, Vanessa. Let me feel you let go."

His thumb came back to my clit. My head fell back with a cry. I gripped him and the friction took me over. The world went white. Shards of pleasure shot through me like flashes of lightning.

In a single moment, Darren, our pleasure, and this love overwhelmed every one of my senses. I soared, flying into a thousand pieces. He followed me, a rough cry echoing off the bedroom walls as he came.

VANESSA

I thought I'd be meeting Cheryl at her penthouse, but her assistant assured me that most days she could be found at one of the charity's offices making her rounds.

The sun was out and warmed my skin as Maya walked beside me. After I explained the whole Reilly money-laundering debacle, she'd insisted on coming with me for moral support.

"I was reading up about this place online," she said. "Seems like it's a pretty big operation."

"It's been doing well. I guess despite all the things Reilly was doing wrong, between him and Cheryl, they must have done something right."

"Hopefully it can survive when all this news comes to light."

I had worried about the same thing. With Reilly at the wheel, the charity would survive as long as he needed a front for his creative money management. When all his wrongdoing was out in the open, the damage could be irreparable. Regardless, I had no choice. Reilly was stealing from Cheryl and the charity he touted as his most cherished cause. It had to stop.

Maya caressed the little bump that showed through her T-shirt. Suddenly she stopped short, her hand on her belly.

"Oh, wow," she said. Her big brown eyes were wide as

saucers.

I stopped. "Is everything okay?"

She nodded quickly. "I think the baby kicked."

"Oh my God!" I squealed and might have danced in place a little.

She grabbed my hand and pressed it firmly to her belly. We stood there in the middle of the sidewalk, waiting for what felt like several minutes. We didn't say a word. We just breathed. Then finally, the tiniest little movement fluttered under my fingers. I sucked in a breath.

Maya beamed. "Did you feel it?"

Tears welled in my eyes, and I nodded. I had listened to Maya's pregnancy milestones and complaints these past several weeks with no small amount of envy. There was no denying it—I wanted babies one day. Maybe my biological clock was ticking. Maybe I'd finally met someone who I could see forever with, and suddenly I was eager to see that future realized with a family.

Darren and I were a long way from having that conversation, but he was the one I wanted to take that journey with. I'd almost lost him. I wasn't letting him go again. I could only hope the next chapter of my life away from Reilly would give us the space to even consider it.

"That was amazing," I whispered.

"It's a good sign." She smiled broadly.

Suddenly I was too excited about Maya's little miracle kick to worry about what the next few hours would bring. Life was too short, too precious to waste it the way I had been.

Reilly had made a mess of his career and mine, but I was so blessed to be able to move on. Even if things were about to get messy.

The Brooklyn office of the NYC Youth Arts Initiative resided in an old storefront, a commercial space in a neighborhood that was on the cusp of being revitalized. We walked into the office's open floor plan. Student artwork covered every available wall space. Charcoal faces, bright-colored abstracts, and three-dimensional pieces that came off the wall and into the room.

A young girl sat at a desk near the entrance. "Can I help you?"

"Is Cheryl here?"

She pointed to an area in the back where several children were gathered around a table. I spotted Cheryl talking to another young girl who looked like a student volunteer.

"Thanks."

I walked over, and Cheryl waved when she noticed me. She said something to the volunteer and came my way, meeting me and Maya as we approached.

"Vanessa. What brings you in? Does David need something?"

"No, but I was hoping we could talk if you had some time."

"Sure." She gazed over to Maya.

"This is my friend Maya Jacobs."

"Bridge," Maya corrected with a small smile. "I'm Maya Bridge."

Cheryl shook her hand. "Any relation to Frank and Diane Bridge?"

"They're my in-laws actually. You know them?"

"We have some mutual friends, yes. Small world. Are you interested in the initiative?"

Maya lifted a shoulder and looked around the big room. "Maybe. I've been seeing events advertised in the neighborhood. You have some great things going here."

"Maya's a writer," I added.

Maya's cheeks turned pink, but she didn't deny it. Not long after she'd left Wall Street, she had opened up to me about wanting to get into writing more. She'd been writing poetry for years but never took it seriously until Cameron started pushing her to do something more with her creativity.

"That's wonderful!" Cheryl smiled. "As you can see, we have some great visual arts programs, but we have a poetry program that we started this past fall also. We work with local high schoolers who put together poetry pieces, usually free verse. Then we organize monthly slam competitions. It gives the kids a chance to perform, but it also attracts new participants."

Maya's eyes lit up. "That sounds incredible. I would love to know more."

Cheryl pointed toward the reception desks that we'd passed. "You passed Casey on your way in. She can tell you all about it."

"Perfect. I'll go explore and let you two chat."

Maya walked off, and I was left alone with Cheryl.

"Do you want to chat in the courtyard? It's a beautiful day."

"Sure." I followed Cheryl through a door in the back that led to a large courtyard. Several older students were gathered around different tables and benches. Some talking, some working in notebooks by themselves.

Cheryl and I settled at a wrought iron table.

"I'm sorry for showing up out of the blue, Cheryl, but I had to talk to you about something that's kind of time sensitive."

But the words were lodged in my throat, unwilling to

come out. This was going to sound awful. All of it.

"I'm sorry. I don't know where to start."

"I don't know what David's told you about me, but I'm not the wicked ex-wife he probably makes me out to be. Whatever it is, just tell me."

I inhaled a deep breath, exhaled slowly, and began. "David has been using the nonprofit to funnel money to himself and his friends. Long story, but I found a trail of paperwork that implicates him and a lot of others around him."

"How much money are we talking about?"

"Over twenty million dollars. Half of that should have been yours, or the charity's really, since you'd both agreed to put that much into it over the course of your marriage."

"You have proof of all this?"

"I have all of it. Invoices, the LLC he set up to feed money into, and statements for an offshore account that the bulk of the money was transferred to."

To her credit, she didn't show an inkling of emotion. She could have been made of stone for the lack of a reaction. She looked away, over to the group of school-age children that were sitting in a circle around their leader.

She took a deep breath and returned her focus to me. "Why would you bring this to me? You work for him. Your loyalty should be to him."

"Well...I..." I struggled for the best answer. In the end, though, the answer was simple. "It was the right thing to do."

"Even with your job on the line?"

"Let's just say that David's given me a lot of reasons to question my loyalty to him. And for the record, I hated my job. You had his nights, so you know how it was. I had his days."

"Fair enough."

"He wants to try to get you off the board. Probably so he can keep you far removed from what he's been doing."

"I knew about the board. The monthly meeting was last week, but for some reason he didn't bring it up. Maybe because I've been doing my own campaigning to keep my place, but of course, the one with the gold makes the rules. I did well in the divorce, but I can't keep the organization going by myself. He's had the upper hand."

"If all this comes to light..."

Her emotionless mask seemed to come down. She rubbed at the frown between her brows. "I can't begin to think of the repercussions of all of this. It's a lot to take in."

I slid the thumb drive across the table. "It's all here. You can do with it what you wish, but I'd be grateful if you didn't tell him that I gave it to you. I don't expect to have a job in finance after this, but I don't want to be in the middle of the storm if I can help it."

She sighed. "I can relate. I've weathered the storm with him for many months now. I want justice too, but I'm not looking forward to facing off with him again. We do what we must, though."

I was sorry she'd have to deal with him a little bit longer. Unlike me, however, she could console herself with more money than I could really wrap my head around possessing.

I stood, satisfied with having completed my mission. I was ready to move on. So ready. To what, I had no idea, but it wasn't with Reilly. I had Darren by my side, which made the vast unknown ahead of me seem a little less frightening.

"Good luck with everything, Cheryl."

I stood to leave when she said my name.

"Is this something you could see yourself being a part of?"

She motioned around the courtyard. "Helping the initiative?"

"Like, to volunteer?"

"No, at a higher level."

I shrugged. "I'm not sure how qualified I'd be to help. All I've been doing—"

"You've kept his life in order for two years, which is no small task. I'd say you're highly qualified." She held me in a thoughtful stare. "I have no idea what will come to pass when the truth comes out about what he's done, Vanessa. I don't need an occupation, but I want one. This place has been a home to me at some of my most difficult times. If I'm able to stay, I could use help from good people like you who see its value and can honor our vision."

I was flattered and overwhelmed at the proposition. I'd had no idea where I could go from here. I'd never have a life on Wall Street again.

Cheryl looked down at the thumb drive and back up to me. "Think about it."

I nodded with a sigh of relief. "I will."

EPILOGUE

DARREN

"Well, aren't you quite the catch?"

Vanessa's mom stood at least a head below me, and at least a few inches below her daughter. Her hair was coarse, a sharper shade of red than Vanessa's. It had definitely been dyed.

Happiness lit up her smile, like I'd been the one she'd been searching for all along. I hoped like hell I was.

"He is, Mom." Vanessa blushed a little.

Melody looked to her daughter and shook her head. "Isn't she amazing?"

I followed her warm gaze to the woman who'd stolen my heart. "One in a million."

"I can't wait to hear you sing, sweetheart," she said.

I couldn't either. I'd been looking forward to this day since Vanessa had told me about the concert. She'd taken a spot at the Youth Arts Initiative not long after the news about Reilly's shady business dealings became public. Even with an investigation under way, the organization had to go on, and Vanessa had found a place.

Today was their first open-air concert where Vanessa and her students would be performing. I couldn't think of a better way for her to channel her love of music and make a difference in the lives of others.

An older man with a guitar in hand walked up to us. His wavy gray hair hit his shoulders, and he was dressed casually in blue jeans and a Hawaiian shirt.

"Dad!" Vanessa brightened and went to him.

He held her in a long tight hug that I guessed was long overdue. She hadn't seen him in a year. I had a feeling today was going to be one of the most meaningful visits they'd share.

When they broke apart, he looked to Vanessa's mother.

"Heaven, I think I missed you, Melody."

Her cheeks turned pink. "Oh, stop."

"Honest to God, I think I did."

Their gazes settled over each other. I wish I'd ever seen my parents look at each other that way. Even if it meant knowing they weren't together anymore.

The group singing *a capella* on the stage wound down, and applause filled the air.

"Okay, they're about to start. You ready, Dad?"

"Always, darling." He grasped the handle of the guitar in one hand and slid the strap over his shoulder.

A teenage girl wearing a T-shirt that associated her with the organization hopped up on the stage. She tapped the microphone. "Thank you, everyone, for coming out to our debut Youth Arts Initiative summer concert. And now to wrap things up this afternoon, our program director, Vanessa Hawkins, will perform with her father, singer and songwriter Beau Lehane."

The audience clapped and hollered, and a few people shouted Vanessa's name in support. Together they went up onto the stage. Vanessa sat on a stool. Beau was beside her, guitar poised in his arms just so. She smiled to the audience and then to him before looking down to the ground, the same way she'd done that first night doing karaoke at the bar.

Up there, she looked gorgeous and natural as she always did. But also happy and relaxed. The tension had left her in a way I couldn't name. She was free of an old life, a chapter past, and reaching for a dream she'd never really accepted as her own before.

This is where she was supposed to be, using her talents and her mind, sharing the goodness inside of her that others had taken for granted. The sentiment lingered right next to the other one that struck me daily and often—that I loved her. That she'd defined love, personified it for me. She'd transformed before my eyes, changing from a set of physical features that had lured me in to becoming my reason for living.

Beau spoke into the microphone. "Thanks, y'all, for coming out. We're going to sing a little song for you. Hope you like it." He glanced over at Vanessa and then out into the crowd with a crooked grin. "I wrote this song a long time ago for a beautiful woman who I had the pleasure of performing with for many years. She went on to bigger and better things, but I'll never forget the good times we had. This one's for you, Melody."

Beau strummed his guitar. The opening notes of a song that I didn't recognize rang out over the park through the speakers on either side of the stage. He sang the first verse, and then Vanessa's voice took over the next. Goose bumps raced over my flesh, and my heart sped up.

The song was about love, a love so wild and passionate that it made you take chances, do crazy things you'd never do.

Vanessa's voice rang out, strong and true, mingling with her father's, fading back and taking over in a beautiful harmony.

She was singing her heart out, and I wondered if I'd ever loved her more.

As the song faded out, I released a breath I didn't realize I'd been holding.

She and Beau took a bow, and the clapping went on and on. She was loved here, appreciated in a way she hadn't been before. She left the stage, and the crowd started to move now that the show was over.

When she reached me, she seemed tentative. But as soon as she was close enough, I went for her, hauling her into my arms and lifting her off the ground. She squealed and laughed when I held her tight.

"Did you like it?"

"I loved it," I said. "You were amazing. I have no words."

I lowered her down, but kept her close, tight against my chest. My heart raced. Adrenaline thrummed. Like I was about to do something crazy, launch myself into a situation that someone else would run away from. I gazed down into her eyes, at a face I wanted to cherish for the rest of my life.

"Marry me."

She blinked once, scanning my features. Her jaw fell a fraction. "What?"

"Marry me. Be my wife. I want forever with you, Vanessa. Every single day. I love you so much, and if I don't do something about it right now, thirty years are going to go by and I'm going to look at you the way your dad just looked at your mom. And I'll know that I wasted a lifetime not loving you the way I should have."

"You're serious."

I kissed her softly. "You know I am. Now say you'll marry me. You know I love you."

She smiled. "You make me do crazy things."

I waited, breathless, like I was at the edge of the cliff.

"Vanessa..."

"I'll marry you," she whispered.

BONUS SCENE

From Cameron & Maya

CAMERON

Maya Jacobs was my life. My whole world. And in a matter of hours, she'd be my wife.

I'd carried her with me everywhere...for years. Through war. Through painful separations. By some miracle, I'd found her again. Now we were together and so close to taking the next step in our relationship.

But something wasn't right. I could feel it.

I was supposed to stay with Darren tonight. Go out with the guys and throw some back. But nothing could keep me from her. Darren didn't even try to argue. I knew something was wrong, and I was determined to unearth it before we said our vows tomorrow.

I knocked on the door to our penthouse room.

After a few seconds with no answer, I opened the door. Ocean air wafted over me, and the curtains at the balcony billowed with the wind. I shut the door and crossed the room. The sky was a midnight blue. Only a sliver of moonlight reflected over the ocean waves.

Through the tall arched doors, I found Maya curled up on a wicker couch with a light shawl around her shoulders. She looked up at me, wide-eyed. Her blond hair whispered in the wind.

"Cam. What are you doing here?"

"I wanted to see you."

"But we're not supposed to see each other until tomorrow."

"I know. I guess I don't care." Probably sounded crazy that I couldn't spend a single night without her.

"I don't really either," she said softly. "I'm glad you're here. I've missed you."

I sat beside her and took her hand in mine. We hadn't spent a night apart since I'd proposed to her months ago. I hoped we'd never have another reason to. Why start now?

We sat in silence for a while. She leaned against me, and together we listened to the soothing sounds of the ocean.

"How are you feeling about tomorrow?"

She looked down at our fingers now entwined. "I'm ready. A little nervous, I guess, because of all your family being around. But if all goes to plan, I think tomorrow will be wonderful."

I traced the contours of her hand, tightening my grasp in hers.

"Maya..."

She looked up at me with her thoughtful brown eyes. "What?"

"I know you, Maya, and something feels off. It's like a stone in my stomach, and I can't shake the feeling. I want tomorrow to be perfect for you, but I can't do that if you don't tell me what's bothering you. Is it your mom?"

She stared silently a moment before looking out to the horizon. "No. I mean, I miss her, of course. I wish she could be here more than anything. But every time I think about it, I think about how grateful I am that I have you and our friends who've become my family."

"Then what is it?"

She sighed, and all my instincts told me I'd been right. The stone only grew in size as the seconds passed.

"Baby, tell me. Whatever it is, we can handle it. That's what I promised you, right? We can get through anything together."

I grazed her cheek with my hand, guiding her gaze to mine. Her eyes were glassy but not sad. She captured my hand and brought it down until it rested over her lower abdomen.

My heart started a rapid uneven beat in my chest. Our gazes locked, and I couldn't breathe for a minute.

"Maya." I exhaled her name like a prayer.

Her jaw was tight, her eyes wide, as if she were waiting for my reaction.

"Are you pregnant?"

She nodded, and her throat moved with a swallow. "Please don't be angry."

Ten thousand trumpets could have sounded in the distance. I couldn't hold back a smile so big it hurt. I lifted her from her seat and brought her over me and into my arms.

I tucked her tight against me, smelling her sweet scent, reveling in her warmth. "I'm not angry. I'm so happy I can barely breathe. This is amazing."

"I was worried I would ruin everything," she whispered, her breath soft at my ear.

I caught her cheek, tilting her back so I could see her face. "This is without a doubt the best wedding present you could possibly give me."

She smiled sweetly, and in that moment, my love for her took residence in every cell of my body. I wanted her happiness more than I wanted my own. I lived for that smile and for the tears of joy that glistened at the edges of her eyes.

I'd sworn I would make her happy every day of her life.

"We're going to have a baby." I said the words out loud because I still couldn't believe it.

She kissed me softly, a tender touch that matched this beautiful moment. I brought my hand down to her belly. My heart swelled with all the emotions consuming me in this moment. The thought that our child was growing there overwhelmed me—a rush unlike any other.

"Half you and half me," I whispered against her lips.

"Half you and half me," she whispered back.

Full of an energy that felt too big for my body, I took her lips and kissed her deeply. She folded her arms around me, holding me close to her. I held her, caressed her, cherished her. My beautiful Maya.

When we broke away, we were both breathless.

"I don't want to leave," I finally said.

She sifted her fingers through my hair. "Then don't."

In the distance, we heard a loud whoop. I glanced down over the balcony to the beach below. I could make out Darren's figure. He was walking bare-assed into the ocean. A minute later, Vanessa followed him out in nothing more than her underwear.

I couldn't stifle the laugh that broke free. "I don't think I have much choice. Looks like Darren's room might be occupied tonight."

Maya followed my gaze. "I hope that doesn't backfire."

I trailed my fingers along her jaw, turning her back to me. "Maybe love is in the air, and we shouldn't worry about them so much."

Her shoulders softened with a sigh. "Maybe you're right. I should probably give him the benefit of the doubt. He is going to be my brother-in-law after all."

"He can also be a real jerk, so I don't blame you if you don't."

She toyed with my hair and canted her head. "Do you think he deserves her?"

"Probably not. But something feels different when he talks about her. Call me crazy, but they might have a chance."

"I hope so."

She brushed her mouth over mine, teasing her tongue against my lips. All thoughts of my crazy brother and his beautiful conquest vanished. Maya was warm under my touch, responding when I ran my hands up her thighs and over her soft skin.

"We have a big day tomorrow," she murmured.

"Should I go?"

Even as I said the words, I knew I couldn't leave her tonight. I had to have her. Tonight, and tomorrow, and every day after that.

She shook her head. "No. Don't ever go."

Continue reading in:

Over The Edge
The Bridge Series
November 22nd, 2016

ACKNOWLEDGEMENTS

Penning Darren and Vanessa's story was a challenge. Every book I write is. My biggest thanks goes to my characters, for their patience, for letting me ignore them and neglect them while life pulled me in a hundred other directions. Thank you for never abandoning me.

I haven't conquered a significant writing project to date without the support of my husband. Thank you, Jonathan, for your tough love and for attempting to hide books from me that were taking me too far away from the task at hand. Thank you for reading, for lending your unique firefighter knowledge to Darren's world, and for being the first fan of anything I do.

Many thanks to the Waterhouse staff, Shayla, Kurt, Yvonne, and David. Without your daily efforts, this book would not exist. There simply weren't near enough spare minutes in the day to both write a novel and pull off everything that we've accomplished as a company these past several months—further proof that as a team of individually passionate people, we can do amazing things! Special thanks to David Grishman for your story insights and for helping me connect the dots of Vanessa's seedy financial underworld.

As always, thanks to my editor, Helen Hardt, for balancing your valued work as an editor with your dreams as a truly talented author. I'm so thrilled to be a part of both!

Big thanks to the ladies in my Skype sprint group for motivating me and keeping me company during critical writing pushes!

Many thanks to my awesome beta readers for your critical feedback and to my amazing Team Wild ladies for giving me the motivation and drive to keep writing.

Thank you, Mom, for helping me cut through the chaos and the noise.

Last, but never least, thank you to one of my best friends. Mia, I can't help but feel like you're on the sidelines ready to cheer me on whenever I need a push or a hug. That unfailing support gives me more comfort than you can possibly know. You have such a special place in my crazy world! I love you, through and through.

ABOUT THE AUTHOR

Meredith Wild is a #1 *New York Times, USA Today,* and international bestselling author of romance. Living on Florida's Gulf Coast with her husband and three children, she refers to herself as a techie, whiskey-appreciator, and hopeless romantic. When she isn't living in the fantasy world of her characters, she can usually be found at www.facebook.com/meredithwild.

You can find out more about her writing projects at www.meredithwild.com

Over the Edge

THE BRIDGE SERIES: BOOK THREE

Coming November 22nd, 2016

Olivia Bridge has always been a good girl—good grades, good friends, and a good job that her wealthy parents handed her. Desperate to carve out a life that is truly hers, Liv walks away from it all and takes on the challenge of helping her brothers open a chain of fitness centers in New York City. Just as she's beginning to find her footing in a new place, she's caught between two men who couldn't be more determined to turn all her goodness inside out.

Will Donovan has the capital to make the Bridge brothers' entrepreneurial dreams a reality. Taking their uptight sister to bed seems a reasonable perk for the risk. Liv is the smartest, sexiest prude Will's ever met, and he can't wait to break her down.

Life is too short for Ian Savo to play by anyone's rules. Sharing women with his friend isn't anything new, so when Will introduces him to Liv, he can't wait to get a taste. But falling for the same girl, or falling at all, was never in the plans...

Visit MeredithWild.com for more information!

Mount Laurel Library
100 Walt Whitman Avenue
Mount Laurel, NJ 08054-9539
856-234-7319
www.mtlaurel.lib.nj.us